ECONOMIC IMPACT OF THE INTERNET PLUS ERA

A Case Study of Shanghai

ECONOMIC IMPACT OF THE INTERNET PLUS ERA

A Case Study of Shanghai

Li Youmei • Yin Feng • Nie Yongyou

Shanghai University, China

社会科学文献出版社
SOCIAL SCIENCES ACADEMIC PRESS (CHINA)

World Scientific

Published by

World Scientific Publishing Co. Pte. Ltd.

5 Toh Tuck Link, Singapore 596224

USA office: 27 Warren Street, Suite 401-402, Hackensack, NJ 07601

UK office: 57 Shelton Street, Covent Garden, London WC2H 9HE

Library of Congress Cataloging-in-Publication Data
Names: Li, Youmei, 1956– author. | Yin, Feng, author. | Nie, Yongyou, author.
Title: Economic impact of the Internet plus era : a case study of Shanghai / Li Youmei, Yin Feng, Nie Yongyou.
Description: New Jersey : World Scientific, [2019]
Identifiers: LCCN 2018039249 | ISBN 9789813272514 (hc : alk. paper)
Subjects: LCSH: Internet--Economic aspects--China--Shanghai. | Information technology--Economic aspects--China--Shanghai. | Economic development--China--Shanghai. | Shanghai (China)--Economic conditions.
Classification: LCC HC428.S47 L464 2019 | DDC 330.951/132--dc23
LC record available at https://lccn.loc.gov/2018039249

British Library Cataloguing-in-Publication Data
A catalogue record for this book is available from the British Library.

Ms. Chen Yongjuan, Beijing Chinese-Foreign Translation & Information Service Co., Ltd.

For any available supplementary material, please visit
https://www.worldscientific.com/worldscibooks/10.1142/11049#t=suppl

Desk Editors: Herbert Moses/Lum Pui Yee

Typeset by Stallion Press
Email: enquiries@stallionpress.com

Preface

In recent times, human society has stepped into a new stage of Information Revolution, characterized by mobile Internet and artificial intelligence. While steam engine represented the first Industrial Revolution and electric power epitomized the second one (also known as the Technological Revolution), the computer blazed a trail, and was seen as the symbol of the Information Revolution later on. However, with the advent of the Internet, there is an intense interconnection within a city and among cities, where information is efficiently pooled, processed, and transmitted. Internet innovation has led to a number of important applications in economic and social fields, helping traditional industries upgrade and organizations gain new core competencies, thereby engendering new business models and new industries. This is what we call the "Internet Plus".

Technological progress is a key factor that drives the social development and economic growth. The Internet is a product of the times, and thus, rapidly extends its reach to various social and economic fields thanks to its advantages of convenience, flatness, scale, agglomeration, and inclusiveness. Only by diving into the futurity can one yield twice the result with half the effort. The "Internet Plus" action plan was first introduced by Premier Li Keqiang in his *Government Work Report* at the Third Session of 12th National People's Congress on March 5, 2015. In this "New Normal" economy, "Internet Plus" has become a new engine driving economic growth.

Once the term "Internet Plus" got its way around, it is likely that people would just "Internet" everything, which means that they would assume anything would've been transformed and upgraded as long as the Internet was even slightly involved. In fact, "Internet Plus traditional industries" is more just lumping things together. Instead, the Internet can stay relevant only through an in-depth integration with traditional industries and it can only extend its reach by application of artificial intelligence and other technologies. Here is how the "Internet Plus" transforms and influences traditional economy:

First, it creates a deep interconnection within traditional organizations. In the context of transformation, China's industrialization and informatization are intertwined, and many organizations are still undergoing the process. With the help of mobile Internet-based standardized systems, traditional organizations can not only achieve interconnection at lower cost, but also broaden their creative horizon by extending the value chain.

Second, it enables information pooling and intelligentization in the inter-organizational network. Among every highly interconnected organization, there will be information nodes of varying significance, and the structuralized dynamic information will become the Big Data. Software and hardware can be embedded in the network as required, producing a complex with intelligent decision-making capabilities. By providing the interconnected terminals with a collaboration platform, the "Internet Plus" does more than just motivating organizations and cities to join the club — it makes sure that every individual that's already in the club actually has a say.

Third, it allows high intelligentization and fast iteration of systems. With the platform's organization and coordination capabilities, the "Internet Plus" unifies individuals' fragmented time and information silos into a target, accelerating the development of global intelligence. Thanks to fast iteration of systems, cities, organizations, and individuals can have opportunities to catch up from behind; however, they may be eliminated if they remain stagnant and conservative. Disruptive innovation has become a common phenomenon.

Fourth, it facilitates the systematic upgrade of the economic growth model. The "Internet Plus"smartly improves quality of economic factors, enhances workers' learning and innovation capabilities, and accelerates accumulation of human capital. It also improves technological features of physical capital and increases its production and allocation efficiency. Furthermore, the "Internet Plus" strengthens agglomeration of factors in the urban space, especially in large core cities, provides a platform for integration of the Internet into industries and their development, boosts growth of new-generation information industries symbolized by core technologies such as Cloud Computing, Big Data, and the Internet of Things, and engenders cross-field, integrative emerging industries. The "Internet Plus" enables upgrade of the entire industry system, leading to prominent positive externalities that greatly improve convenience of free resource sharing, and raise quality and quantity of public economy and public services, thereby enhancing well-being of residents.

In addition to impacting technological and economic aspects of industries, the "Internet Plus" is extending its reach to people's daily lives, creating more profound social implications. Like any industrial revolution in the history of mankind, the "Internet Plus" embodies structural and systematic social changes, encompassing innovative changes in a comprehensive system of knowledge, ideas, structures, and ways of organization. In the "Internet Plus" era, traditional industrial society's ways of organization and rules of logic are challenged, and multiple legitimacies of power may be superimposed, while non-traditional public risks lead to more complex social uncertainties. Thus, social reorganization is particularly urgent and critical. Differing from traditional industrial society, the new "Internet Plus"-based society is organized in a more open, flat, decentralized, digitized, and virtual manner that overcomes restrictions of traditional top-down formal authority and bureaucracy, and stresses individual freedom and autonomy.

In the "Internet Plus" era, no organization or individual can ignore the power of new technologies, as well as significant changes and effects brought about by new business models and new ways of social organization. Since the reform and opening up, China's rapid social and economic development has laid a solid foundation for further technological innovation and social progress. Scholars from Shanghai University have taken the lead in carrying out this research to serve the national strategy, which includes building Shanghai's "Four Centers" and a globally influential center for scientific and technological innovation in the "Internet Plus" era. They reviewed conceptualization and background of the "Internet Plus", analyzed the Internet's influence on a city's function and economic impact, studied trends of integration of the Internet into traditional industries and their development, and analyzed problems and risks in the process of promoting the "Internet Plus". They also studied inherent logic of the "Internet Plus" and industrial transformation and upgrade, identified the new environment and new situation Shanghai faces in building "Four Centers" during the "13th Five-Year Plan" period, as well as advantages and disadvantages of the same endeavor made in the "Internet Plus" era. Along with this, they put forward construction measures and suggestions for Shanghai to promote development of the "Internet Plus", enhance the city's economic impact and service level as a core city, and plan the direction and priorities for the new round of construction of the "Four Centers".

The publication of this book is a preliminary achievement of this research, and also an important manifestation of Shanghai University's endeavor to serve the national strategy and development of Shanghai, and play the vital role of a university think tank. This intensive study aims to make a modest contribution to Shanghai in building "Four Centers" and a globally influential center for scientific and technological innovation. This book represents just the first step in this subject's research. Experts and readers are welcome to give comments on omissions and deficiencies found in this book.

Prof. Li Youmei
Shanghai University
September 6, 2018

About the Authors

Li Youmei earned a Ph.D. in sociology from Paris Institute of Political Studies (Sciences Po). She is professor at Shanghai University, and serves as president of Chinese Sociological Association, first vice president of Shanghai Academy, vice president of Shanghai Federation of Social Science Associations, chief editor of *Sociology*, head of the editorial board of *Chinese Journal of Sociology*, director of Research Center for Local Governance, one of the first University Think Tanks in Shanghai. Her research focuses on the changes of human cooperation mechanism in modern society, the practice of Chinese social governance transformation, and theoretical paradigm of the sociology of transition in China.

Yin Feng holds a Ph.D. in economics from Nankai University. In 2008, she was a visiting scholar at Universite Paul Cezanne — AIX-Marseille III, France, and conducted the Hermes Postdoctoral Program. She was a senior visiting scholar at Oxford University and the London School of Economics and Political Science in 2013. Her main research areas include open economy and service economy. She has served as researcher for projects funded by the National Natural Science Foundation, National Social Science Fund of China, The Ministry of Education, etc. Currently she is professor and doctoral supervisor at the School of Economics,

Shanghai University. She has been named a ShuGuang Scholar and Pujiang Talents of Shanghai.

Nie Yongyou received his Bachelor's degree in economics from Fudan University, Master's degree in management from Shanghai University of Finance and Economics, and Ph.D. in management from Zhongshan University. He was a senior visiting scholar at Tokyo University and Ryukoku University. His main research areas include industrial economics and economics of environment and resources. Currently he is an executive president and doctoral supervisor at the School of Economics, Shanghai University. He also serves as the deputy chair of Shanghai Commercial Economics Society.

Acknowledgment

The authors would like to thank all those who contributed to the writing of each chapter.

Contents

Preface v

About the Authors ix

Acknowledgment xi

Chapter 1 Technological Base for Urban Development in the "Internet Plus" Era 1

I. Understanding the "Internet Plus" Era 2

II. Macroscopic Background to the Rise of the "Internet Plus" Era 4

III. Technological Base of Urban Development in the "Internet Plus" Era 14

Chapter 2 Social Reorganization in the "Internet Plus" Era 31

I. Understanding the "Internet Plus" Era Beyond the Technological Dimension 32

II. Challenges to Traditional Social Life Order in the "Internet Plus" Era 33

III. Network Society and Its Organization Method in the "Internet Plus" Era 40

IV. Information and Power Issues in the "Internet Plus" Era 48
References 51

Chapter 3 Study About the Economic Impact of Core Cities on Surrounding Areas 53
I. The Economic Impact of Core Cities on Surrounding Areas: Size and Reach 53
II. Changes in Core Cities' Functions 73
III. Evolution of Urban Morphology in Core Cities 87
References 96

Chapter 4 Shanghai's Industrial Transformation and Upgrade Path 97
I. From Manufacturing to Intelligent Manufacturing: Value Realization Model for Manufacturing in the "Internet Plus Industry" 98
II. Intelligent Manufacturing Capability and Equilibrium Effect of a Core City's Manufacturing Industry Under International Industrial Division of Labor 106
III. "Industry 4.0" and "Made in China 2025": Current Situation of and Challenges to Shanghai's Manufacturing Industry 122
IV. Transformation and Upgrade Path and Policy Suggestions for Manufacturing Industries in Core Cities Under "Internet Plus Industry" 127
References 129

Chapter 5 National Strategy to Build Shanghai into an International Financial Center 131
I. Shanghai Financial Center Function and National Strategy 131
II. Establishing Shanghai as a Commodity Pricing Center 147

III. Financial Agglomeration and Economic Impact of China (Shanghai) Pilot Free Trade Zone 154
References 172

Chapter 6 Building Shanghai into an International Trade Center — A Global Trading Network Hub 173
I. Internet and Trade 173
II. Innovation in "Internet Plus Trade" Development Model 183
III. Construction of an International Trade Center in Shanghai in the "Internet Plus" Era 191

Chapter 7 Construction of Shanghai International Shipping Center to Enhance Industrial Value Chain 217
I. Basic Status of the Construction of Shanghai International Shipping Center 218
II. Economic Impact of Shanghai International Shipping Center's Functions 229
III. Core Measures Taken to Enhance Shanghai International Shipping Center's Agglomeration and Economic Impact 239
References 244

Chapter 8 Legal Protection and Public Security in a Core City in the "Internet Plus" Era 247
I. New Challenges Faced by a Core City's Traditional Public Security Management in the "Internet Plus" Era 249
II. Theoretical Mechanism Assumptions 251
III. Measurement Modeling, Data Source and Research Method 258
IV. Testing of Assumptions 261
V. Conclusions and Policy Suggestions 268
References 271

Index 273

Chapter 1

Technological Base for Urban Development in the "Internet Plus" Era

In keeping with the continuous development of science and technology, modern information technologies represented by the Internet have been changing people's mode of production and way of life. From efforts to synthesize modern information technologies with traditional industries emerges the "Internet Plus". Capitalizing on the Internet's capabilities of optimization and integration in the allocation of social resources, the "Internet Plus" is a new economic model that helps the entire society become more innovative and productive by finding practical applications for the results of innovative developments of the Internet in a wide range of social and economic fields. Over the past several years, the "Internet Plus" has extended its reach to almost all aspects of our lives, leaving profound, revolutionizing impact on many industries and sectors. Its rapid development has engendered the emergence of a range of new fields, such as Internet finance, e-commerce, intelligent transportation, smart healthcare and online education. The recently concluded Fifth Plenary Session of the 18th CPC Central Committee has helped turn the spotlight on the implementation of the "Internet Plus" Initiative and China's Big Data strategy. The "Internet Plus" era is here.

I. Understanding the "Internet Plus" Era

With the advent of the "Internet Plus" era, modern information technologies represented by the Internet have been shaping and changing how people work and live in almost every aspect. The concept of the "Internet Plus" was first introduced by Premier Li Keqiang in his *Government Work Report*, along with a specific action plan. People who had long been working on the exploratory frontline of the Internet industry welcomed this with great excitement. For many others, this meant a new path for innovation and a new direction for development. Everybody wants to know just what this new thing called "Internet Plus" is or does.

A good place to start would be to understand what the "Internet" is. China National Committee for Terms in Sciences and Technologies defines the "Internet" as a network of interconnected computer networks that make indiscriminate use of all and any currently available protocols and technologies. This relatively narrow definition captures only the technical dimension of the Internet[1] and is by no means the only way to understand the phenomenon. But there is no space here for a fuller discussion of the definitional matter. As the Internet continues to grow, its conceptualization has also evolved. A more or less comprehensive theoretical interpretation is already in place of the main features of the Internet. According to this interpretation, the Internet has four fundamental properties: it is open, convenient, user inclusive, and free of charge to all users. It also has a unique operational model. Firstly, to maximize its own appeal to potential customers and form positive user flow, it must make available an abundance of high-quality resources and services free of charge. Once a user base of reasonable size has been established, revenue can be generated through advertising or other value-added services, thereby achieving profitability. At its core, the Internet amounts to a new business model that lets the real needs of Internet users dictate all aspects of its operations, from product design to marketing. The fundamental principle guiding the Internet is to put customer at the front and experience at the center. Increasingly, the Internet is not only transforming people's lifestyle but also helping people adapt to the changes.

---

[1] Chinese terms in Communication Science and Technology, *China Terminology*, 2007 (1).

In recent years, not only has the Internet itself seen rapid development, it has also driven or otherwise helped facilitate the growth of other industries. The large number of Internet users in China means massive business opportunities. The combination of the Internet with traditional industries points in a new and promising direction for future development, and the Internet can even lead to transformation of the business model of every industry. Such was the circumstances under which the concept of "Internet Plus" emerged.

What, then, is the "Internet Pl"? How it is understood depends very much on the perspective of the person attempting the definition. For the country and the economy, the "Internet Plus" represents a new form of economic activities in which the Internet plays a critical role in optimizing and integrating the allocation of productive factors and Internet-based innovations areas widely applied in as many fields as possible. This helps enhance the creativity and productivity of the real economy and foster a wider range of new forms of economic development using the Internet as an infrastructure and implementation instrument.[2] From the technological point of view, the Internet Plus "refers to the process in which a complete package of Internet-based information technologies (including Mobile Internet, Cloud Computing, Big Data technologies, and so forth) is diffused and applied in a variety of economic and social sectors."[3]

"Plus" in the "Internet Plus" does not refer to a kind of "physical reaction" in which the Internet and traditional industries are mechanically joined together. Instead, here the concept of "plus" refers to a type of "chemical reaction" in which the addition of the Internet as a new ingredient triggers changes in the production mode, economic model and industrial structure of traditional industries. "Plus" here goes beyond incorporating what can be done on the Internet in marketing and business management in traditional industries. It also involves the collection, analysis, integration, mining and intelligent sensing of Big Data via a

---

[2] Abbreviation annotations for the *Government Work Report* in 2015, The Chinese Central Government's Official Web Portal, March 11, 2015. Available at: http://www.gov.cn/xinwen/2015-03/11/content_2832629.htm.

[3] AliResearch: *Research Report on "Internet Plus" — New Engine for China's Economy*, March 24, 2015. Available at: http://www.aliresearch.com/blog/article/detail/id/20324.html.

mobile communication network, from which new business models and operational systems emerge. The most important thing about the "Internet Plus" is its ability to transform people's vision and thinking, and change technologies and business models. If it could not realize such transformation and was only used to add the Internet on to traditional industries as a form of superficial attachment, then not only would the "Internet Plus" fail to lead industrial development, it could also risk passing up opportunities and even being eliminated.

The essential purpose of the "Internet Plus" is to help traditional industries become data-driven and web enabled via a transformation by the Internet. Such transformation is only possible when the necessary Internet infrastructure is widely in place. The infrastructure on which the "Internet Plus" functionally depends has three main components, namely, Cloud (Cloud Computing and Big Data infrastructure), Network (the Internet and the Internet of Things), and Device (equipment that directly serves individuals). These three components will, if well integrated, help realize the connection between human and things, among people, between human and the environment, and between services and the future, and it is on them the efficiency and depth of the "Internet Plus"-induced transformation and upgrade of traditional industries will depend.

II. Macroscopic Background to the Rise of the "Internet Plus" Era

1. *Upgraded Industrial Revolution as the Trend of the Times*

Industrial Revolution refers to the phenomenon in which major breakthroughs in science and technology bring about significant changes in the industrial structure of the national economy and open up new possibilities for economic and social development.

The Age of Discovery and overseas expansion dating back to the late 15th century created the basic conditions for economic globalization. In the mid-tolate-18th century, the first Industrial Revolution began in Great Britain. Symbolized by the improvement of the steam engine, the

Industrial Revolution turned Great Britain from an agricultural country to an industrial country, replacing manpower, animal power, and hydro power with power machinery. The Industrial Revolution that was driven by the steam engine and centered on the textile industry gradually spread to other advanced countries in Europe and the United States, enabling these countries to produce more products than were needed to meet domestic demands. This led members of the capitalist class in these countries to look for markets overseas. Large quantities of surplus and cheap industrial products became available around the world, outside their place of production, which contributed to the formation of the international division of labor and the world market as well as the development of economic globalization.

The second Industrial Revolution, which occurred in the second half of the 19th century, started with the transformation of heavy industry. It was marked by the application of electric power. At that time, the progress of science and technology was mainly reflected in three areas, namely, the widespread use of electricity, the invention of new means of communication, and the invention of the internal combustion engine, and new means of transportation this enabled. The second Industrial Revolution concluded with profound changes in the industrial structure.[4]

The world entered the era of science and technology in the second half of the 20th century. With the advent of cloning and aerospace technologies, European countries and the United States predicted that systems biology and synthetic biology would spark the third Industrial Revolution, one centered on Biotechnology, in the 21st century. Symbolized by the invention and application of electronic computers, the third Industrial Revolution has not only brought us information technology, new energy technology, biotechnology, space technology, and marine technology, but also given birth to the Internet. These inventions have engendered significant social, economic, political, and cultural changes, and had profound

---

[4] Pang Li, Machinery development history of the world, *Time Education: Education and Teaching Version*, 2011 (9).

impact on how people live and think, thereby facilitating of the modernization process.[5]

In essence, an industrial revolution is any comprehensive and fundamental transformation of a society's production method and equipment and industrial structure within a certain period. Professor Qian Xuesen was expressing the same idea when he noted that an industrial revolution consists in changes in the organizational structure and economic structure of the production system. The conventional identification, numbering and naming of different episodes of Industrial Revolution reflect the production equipment associated with emerging technologies, the speed of productivity growth, and fundamental changes in the existing industrial structure.

2. *The "Internet Plus" Era and Industrial Transformation of the Global Economy*

Economic globalization is the overarching theme of the 21st century. Propelled by industrial revolution and transformation, the process has picked up pace since the end of WWII. There have been many new developments in the globalization process over the past decade, including the constant emergence of new types of regional economic cooperation schemes. For example, the United States has proposed TPP, TTIP and the "New Silk Road Initiative", and China the "Silk Road Economic Belt" and the "21st Century Maritime Silk Road", among other major strategic initiatives meant to capitalize on the country's strengths in production capacity and to meet its present development needs. Economic globalization and these new types of regional cooperation schemes go hand in hand and will jointly push globalization to a new level.

In the process of economic globalization, the world economy is faced with great threats, though. As opposed to high-speed growth since the 1980s, the world economy has been fluctuating with slow growth after the

---

[5] Chen Lihong, Summary of research on the history of the third technological revolution, *History Teaching in Middle Schools*, 2002 (10).

2008 global financial crisis because of no major innovations in science and technology for a long time. The development of productive forces had to rely on overseas expansion as the original technological base on which it depended had seen no major breakthroughs for a long time. After the outbreak of the financial crisis, the United States and other developed countries began to realize that finance-based virtual economy could not underpin the economic development of a country, so they shifted their attention back to the development of domestic manufacturing industries. In addition, as a result of increasing manufacturing costs in developing countries, foreign manufacturing industries returned to their local countries at an accelerated pace, causing considerable impact on developing countries around the world. The inability of productive forces to expand overseas in developed countries and the subsequent impact on traditional manufacturing industries in developing countries forced the world economy to transform and upgrade.

The large-scale diffusion and use of existing scientific and technological achievements has become saturated, and the world economy is experiencing comprehensive transformation and adjustment in the technological revolution, international division of labor, industrial structure, and world economic regulation mechanism. From the perspective of resources, the reality shows that extensive manufacturing production has led to increasingly severe resource waste and environmental pollution. This urges developing countries to explore new paths to industrial development as they can neither totally follow the old practice of "treatment after pollution" nor completely transfer manufacturing industries to underdeveloped regions using the gradient transfer theory like developed countries. The more intensive use of resources is an inevitable choice. From the perspective of industries, like in the manufacturing industry, gradient transfer in the service industry is constantly strengthened, and international service trade is expected to see new space for development. Thanks to new advents in science and technology, large-scale production and industrialization will be less dependent on the development of heavy and chemical industries, which directly promotes the independent development of the service industry. The importance of heavy and chemical industries will also be weakened in the process of "intelligent" production. For instance, inventing a new kind of 3D printing material may be more important due to a higher profit margin than building a steel mill.[6]

The emergence of new ways of thinking encourages innovation, which plays an important role in economic transformation. The rise of the Internet in recent years has brought the world valuable opportunities for economic transformation, and helped boost economic growth. For example, by helping manufacturers and consumers reduce the amount of time they spend on searches, the Internet can slash transaction costs. According to the theory of market equilibrium, the relative parity in the bargaining powers of consumers and manufacturers and the greater attainability of an equilibrium state can in part be attributed to the development of the Internet. Consumers are also likely to be in a higher position than manufacturers in trade negotiations and gain dominance, thus greatly enhancing the role of consumers in production and management and forming the theory of consumer sovereignty.[7]

3. *The "Internet Plus" Era and Innovation-driven Development of China's Economy*

3.1 *Development of China's Economy and Information Technology*

Since its invention in the 20th century, computers have led to profound changes in the way people live in all aspects. In the 1970s, the rise of the Internet reduced the costs of inter-regional communications, allowing information to travel much faster and communication much easier. Today, Internet-based information technologies have been fully embraced by society and will even bring about bigger changes in people's lives.

For over a decade, China's economy has made gainful strides, and China's GDP reached second in the world in 2010. Despite high-speed

---

[6]Xu Mingqi, Trend of transformation and adjustment of world economy and China's response strategy, *Guangming Daily*, August 7, 2013, p. 11.

[7]Li Haijian, Tian Yuexin and Li Wenjie, Internet thinking and traditional enterprise reengineering, *China Industrial Economics*, 2014 (10).

economic development, China's economy still has such problems as an inadequate development model, high energy consumption for industrial development, strong dependence on resources, and lack of sustainability. Confronted with severe challenges such as decelerated growth, overproduction and sluggish foreign demands, China's economy is now in a critical period of transformation and upgrade of economic structure, so changing the economic development model is an urgent priority. Under the background of modern economic development, China called for sustainable and healthy economic development in line with the New Normal in 2014. The New Normal stressed that the economic structure, economic growth model, and economic development drive should be thoroughly changed. The economic structure should be constantly transformed and upgraded; the economic growth model should change from traditional high-speed growth to medium- and high-speed growth; the economic development drive should shift from resource-driven development (mainly driven by traditional factors and investment) to innovation-driven development. Innovation-driven development has become the new engine for China's economy.

3.2 *Innovation-driven Development in the Context of the "Internet Plus"*

In the current era of Internet-based information technology, innovation no longer involves production technology alone, but the mode and concept of production as well. With the development of the modern economy, network technologies play a key role in all kinds of innovation based on new thoughts and new modes. The "Internet Plus" refers to the combination of the Internet with traditional industries. In the past, the Internet was mainly used in the tertiary industry. Now, in the era of rapid development of global information technologies, the application of the Internet is no longer limited to the tertiary industry. It can also be integrated with the primary and the secondary industries by driving the transformation of development models in these industries, thereby propelling industrial development. Modern Internet technologies are applied in a more diversified fashion than traditional Internet technologies, shifting from information technologies to the mode of production. Recently, the emergence of new network technologies represented by Big Data, Cloud Computing, and the Internet of Things has boosted the innovation and upgrade of the manufacturing and service industries. For example, flourishing e-commerce allows traditional industries to open online shops, which saves a large amount of investment costs and makes it easier to start a business with lower cost risks. The traditional mode of production involves too many links between production and consumption, such as wholesale, retail, distribution, etc., slowing market transactions. In the "Internet Plus" era, process links can be reduced, and manufacturers can deal directly with consumers, thus realizing individualized production and promoting innovation of the mode of production. Moreover, the accelerated process of market transactions facilitates information flow and further expands market demands, thus inspiring huge market potentials, improving the production, and boosting the rapid development of economy.

At present, China has 668 million Internet users and 594 million mobile Internet users, with figures still rising. The Internet will further influence people's way of life, including access to information and use of public services such as education, health care, transportation, and more. In recent years, Alibaba has become the leader in the field of e-commerce. Driven by such new information technologies as Big Data, Cloud Computing, and the Internet of Things, all kinds of innovation based on the "Internet Plus" will push forward the transformation and upgrade of China's industry, agriculture and service sectors, in order to adapt to the New Normal and realize the sustainable development of China's economy.

4. *"Internet Plus" Era and Evolution of City's Main Functions*

There is a close relationship between technological revolution and urban development. The technological revolution can boost the formation and development of a city, and a city's development can in turn lead to a new revolution in science and technology.

Before the first Industrial Revolution, a city's economic activities were mainly concentrated in the handicraft industry and featured by relatively simple functions. These activities were basically intended for living as the primary function, and involved handicraft production with a small amount of business activities as auxiliary functions.

From the late 18th century to the mid-19th century, advanced countries in Europe and the United States, shepherded by Great Britain, launched the first Industrial Revolution driven by the steam engine and centered on textiles. The great machine industry quickly replaced the workshop handicraft industry, leading to hundred-fold increase in production capacity. A city's main function was accordingly transformed to industrial production. In the era of the traditional industrial economy, the rise of economic core cities mainly relied on the manufacturing industry as the core industry. People improved the means of transport in order to overcome transport-related obstacles, while putting more efforts into the manufacturing industry, particularly production and processing derived from industrial activities.

On the basis of the great machine industry, the technological revolution accelerated the process of economic globalization. From the second half of the 19th century to the beginning of the 20th century, mankind stepped from the age of steam to that of electricity, peaking at the midst of the information revolution. A city shifted its focus from a light industrial revolution centered on textiles to a heavy industrial revolution represented by iron and steel, petrochemical engineering, electrical appliances, machinery, and automobiles. Productive forces exhibited grand new developments.

During the first two Industrial Revolutions, traditional industries played a leading role in a city's development. However, as a result of major breakthroughs in and the extensive application of information technology, biological engineering, new energy, and new material technology, there emerges the service economy that involves communications, consulting, finance, and logistics and has become a dominant source of a city's economic growth. The service economy is an inevitable trend of social development. Human beings pursued material satisfaction (which could be accomplished by traditional industries) in the first two Industrial Revolutions, but now people are paying more attention to spiritual satisfaction than material satisfaction. Therefore, the service economy plays a markedly enhanced role in a city's development. As a service center, a city performs important management and coordination functions in a region and even a country. The functions of a city are fully reflected by how it serves and coordinates in and for society and the economy.

The 21st century witnesses the emergence of a new knowledge revolution marked by the rapid development of information technology and knowledge industry. At its core, the knowledge revolution amounts to the invention and innovation of information technologies that drive industrial spatial organizations to go global. As a joint result of knowledge-based development and globalization, cities, which act as cluster centers of economy, society, science and technology, and cultural activities, play a crucial role in the era of globalization and development of knowledge economy. Particularly, global metropolises, being in a milestone position with global strategic significance, should be home to the increasing number of global professional economic activities and serve as centers that control global key technologies. Therefore, under the context of knowledge-based development and globalization, cities are no longer just economic centers, but function as vital scientific and technological innovation centers.

Today, smart city has been a modern economic topic which was proposed in response to the development needs of the times. Due to the rapid development of information technologies overseas, developed countries such as the United States, Britain, Japan, and South Korea began to study how to use the new-generation information technologies to take a new look at the essence of cities, positioning of urban development goals, cultivation of urban functions, adjustment of urban structures, urban images and characteristics, and other key issues related to modern urban development. As to how to increase the innovative use of information technologies in urban management, service and operation, developed countries put forward the strategic initiative of development of a "smart city". Building a "smart city" is an important means to enhance the competitiveness of cities. In this way, the new model of intelligent urban development started to take shape. But for China, the situation is completely different. The urban population does not grow in pace of the population carrying capacity, increasing ecological pressure on resources and environment. The contradiction between the government public administration and public demands leads to poor collaboration on urban management and low work efficiency. The industrial structure is ill-adapted to economic development, making it difficult to continue the use of traditional production technologies and management methods. In addition, the booming development of the Internet of Things, Cloud Computing, new-generation mobile communication technology, and Big Data in China brings opportunities for the new development of cities. With the construction of new-type urbanization in China, and in profound consideration of the conundrum whether the GDP growth should be realized at the expense of the environment, all sectors of society started to explore such solutions as e-city, digital city, intelligent city, and smart city. For example, the old Shanghai was a small town depending on fishery and a cotton textile handicraft industry. In the 19th century, Shanghai began to stand out by virtue of its excellent port location. Today, Shanghai has become China's foremost center for science and technology, trade, finance and information, and served as a platform for the exchange and integration of international cultures. None of the above explorations or attempts can succeed without the development and innovation of science and technology. The Internet plays a connecting role in this process. According to Ma Huateng, President of Tencent, the Internet is not omnipotent, but it "connects everything". The Internet should not be deified, but it will become a new ecology in the future. In the "Internet Plus" era, economy is intended in the service of life, and efforts are made to develop a high-end, smart economy, improve the intricacies of smart city administration, establish integrated smart government affairs, and create a smart life with universal benefits.

Following industrialization, the "Internet Plus" concept can effectively expand a city's size, improve a city's quality, and drive a city's development. It promotes the integration and innovation of new-generation information technologies represented by Cloud Computing, the Internet of Things, and Big Data with the modern manufacturing industry and productive service industry. Together they will develop emerging industries, and create new industrial growth points in a bid to provide an environment for entrepreneurship and innovation and support for intelligence-based industrial development, enhance new driving forces for economic development, and improve the quality and efficiency of national economy.

III. Technological Base of Urban Development in the "Internet Plus" Era

1. *Infrastructure Upgrade in the "Internet Plus" Era*

In essence, the "Internet Plus" enables traditional industries to operate through an online and data-based model. Data go "live" only when they get "online", and their value can be maximized as long as they flow. Therefore, the "Internet Plus" is established based on the basic premise of widespread popularity of the Internet which serves as a kind of infrastructure. Accordingly, upgrading the existing Internet infrastructure is an inevitable action.

(1) Implementing fiber-based transformation of broadband networks, improving the service ability of mobile communication networks, promoting network interconnection, increasing network access speeds, and reducing network charges are necessary efforts to be made to build the Internet into the infrastructure for ubiquitous interconnection among people, machines, and things.

(2) The global service ability of BeiDou Satellite is enhanced, and a three-dimensional space inter-network is built.

As a global satellite navigation system that was independently developed and operated by China, BeiDou Navigation Satellite System is committed to providing global users with positioning, navigation, and timing services. Since 2012, users in most areas of the Asia-Pacific region have enjoyed these services. China also plans to complete construction of a global system by 2020.

The combination of BeiDou Navigation Satellite System with ground networks will greatly facilitate the integrative development of aviation, marine, transportation, electronic information, geographic information, the Internet of Things, and smart city, resulting in huge industrial demands. According to the prediction of GNSS & LBS Association of China, by 2015, the output value is expected to exceed RMB 225 billion Yuan and the total number of navigation and positioning terminals held in society is expected to reach around 500 million; by 2020, the output value will arrive at RMB 400 billion Yuan and the total number of navigation and positioning terminals will exceed 1 billion. Some experts predict that BeiDou Navigation Satellite System will represent an 80% share in the domestic market and a 20% share in the international market by 2020.

(3) The address management, identification management, and analysis of IPv6 are strengthened, and a future network platform will be built.

IPv6, abbreviation for "Internet Protocol version 6", is the most recent version of the Internet Protocol (IP). It is a network layer protocol that is intended for packet switching of interconnected networks. The previous IPv4 enables the man–machine dialogue alone, while IPv6 is extended to the dialogue between any things. IPv6 is intended to serve not only humans, but a great many of hardware devices as well, such as household appliances, sensors, remote cameras, cars, and more. It is a real broadband network that is seen in every corner of society anytime and anywhere. IPv6 can bring about enormous economic benefits. In the "Internet Plus" era, all objects can be connected to the Internet. Applications provided by the Internet, such as terminal instant messaging, video, games, music, location-based services, and mobile advertising, will grow dramatically. The Internet using the IPv6 protocol as the core technology is characterized by faster network transmission speed, larger network size, securer network, and a wider range of network applications, all of which are intended to satisfy the growth needs in the "Internet Plus" era.[8]

2. *Construction of Basic Information Service in the "Internet Plus" Era*

In the informatization process that lasted for nearly half a century, the extraordinary-speed development of information technologies led to the explosive growth of information (data) volume and processing capacity. Thus, information (data) becomes an independent production factor, and human's economy and society usher in the "Era of Big Data". The

[8] *Guiding Opinions of the State Council on Actively Propel the "Internet Plus" Action Plan*, Xinhuanet, July 5, 2015. Available at: http://news.xinhuanet.com/zgjx/2015-07/05/c_134382951.htm.

accelerated transformation of the economic form from "industrial economy" to "information economy" has resulted in dramatic changes in its infrastructure. Information, knowledge and intelligence, serving as the infrastructure of the "information economy", play a dominant role in the "information economy", where the "Internet Plus" is a new transformative force. To get inexhaustible power and exert the power in the "information economy", it is necessary to improve the new information infrastructure.

Big Data comes from all walks of life. Large amounts of data are produced in daily shopping transactions, industrial manufacturing, social networking and media, online videos and images, enterprise information management systems, and e-government affairs. In recent years, with the rapid development of the Internet of Things and Cloud Computing, the value of Big Data is getting more evident. In the era of the Internet of Things, billions of network sensors are embedded in all kinds of real-life devices used to sense, create and exchange data. These data turn into an equally important production factor as physical capital and manpower resource. Additionally, the mass data generated by the Internet of Things are stored in the memory space provided by Cloud Computing and makes it possible to perform real-time online processing. Furthermore, Cloud Computing does not provide the cloud storage service alone, and its core and key service is the intelligent processing of Big Data.

2.1 *Big Data*

Gartner, a well-known research institute in the United States, defined "Big Data" as that "Big Data" is high-volume, high-velocity, and high-variety information assets that demand innovative forms of information processing that enable enhanced insight, decision making, and process optimization.[9] Big Data analysis is often associated with Cloud Computing. The strategic significance of the Big Data technology lies in the specialized processing of meaningful data, rather than just in the grasp of data information. In other words, Big Data means improving the data processing ability to realize added value of data.

---

[9] Jin Yi, Development trend of advertising and marketing strategy under big data, *Science & Technology for China's Mass Media*, 2013 (7).

Big Data are derived from various status and behavior records of objects, individuals, businesses, and governments. Big Data are often characterized by "Vs." Volume: Big Data are measured in a unit ranging from TB to PB and even EB, showing the sharp increase in the data volume. Variety: Big Data cover web logs, videos, pictures, geographic locations and others, representing a variety of data types. Velocity: High value information can be obtained quickly from various types of data, indicating fast processing velocity. Value: The correct and accurate analysis of data leads to considerable returns, suggesting the high density of data value.

Data are necessary components (such as financial transaction data, e-commerce transaction data) that drive business. The development of data products opens up a new source for raking in data wealth. For example, the extension of data use creates new values, such as online targeted advertising. In economic fields, the accumulation, exchange, analysis and application of mass data lead to significant improvements in production efficiency and full exploration of the value of data elements.

The processing of Big Data generally includes four major steps, namely, data preparation, data storage and management, computing and processing, and data analysis. Data preparation: Before storage and processing, data need to be cleaned and sorted, which is known as the ETL process in the traditional data processing system. Data storage and management: The storage system of Big Data should satisfy two requirements. On the one hand, the system needs to store mass data at an extremely low cost, and on the other hand, it should allow the expandability in data format so as to adapt to diversified needs of management of unstructured data. Computing and processing: The traditional standalone or parallel computing technology is difficult to compute and analyze Big Data due to inadequate computing speed, expandability and cost. As a result, divide-and-conquer distributed computing becomes the mainstream computing architecture for Big Data. However, there are some deficiencies, such as the real-time performance that needs to be significantly improved in some particular scenarios. Data analysis: It seeks to discover laws from large amounts of complicated data and extract new knowledge, which is the key to value exploration of Big Data.

2.2 *Internet of Things*

The ITU Internet Reports launched by the International Telecommunication Union (ITU) defined the Internet of Things as follows: Everything in the world from houses to tissues and tires to toothbrushes can be connected to the Internet as per agreed protocols through information sensing equipment, such as QR code reading device, radio-frequency identification device (RFID), infrared sensor, global positioning system (GPS), and laser scanner, for the purpose of active information exchange and communication. Being in a position to carry information of the Internet and the traditional telecommunication network, the Internet of Things enables all ordinary objects that can perform independent functions to be interconnected.[10] A real object that is connected to the Internet of Things via an e-tag can be specifically located on the Internet of Things. The Internet of Things, similar to an automation control system, allows not only centralized management and control of machines, equipment and personnel through a central computer, but also remote control of household appliances and cars as well as location search and prevention of burglary. The development of the Internet of Things expands data sources in the "Internet Plus" era and enriches the interface of "Internet Plus" services. With the Internet of Things, the real world is networked, informatized, and digitized. The Internet of Things has been applied to a wide range of fields, mainly covering transportation and logistics, health care, intelligent environment (home, office, and factory), and individuals and society. In the "Internet Plus" era, the Internet of Things pools and digitizes decentralized information. With the help of "Cloud Computing" and "Big Data", instrumented devices are endowed with "intelligence" that enables them to store, process and analyze data.

The connection of these "intelligent" devices enhances the interconnection and sharing of data, information and control. It provides better services for users, eventually allowing people to live a convenient, simple and intelligent life (Figure 1.1).

---

[10] Internet of Things, Baidu Baike, Available at: http://baike.baidu.com/link?url=bmAUDZ_fA5vNfUJxpP1xEhuwBUObWNgeTTFBOl240MYLab0o6NkR3j-bWHSkidBNLIgMx3fzb7rISg0xKPDmPa.

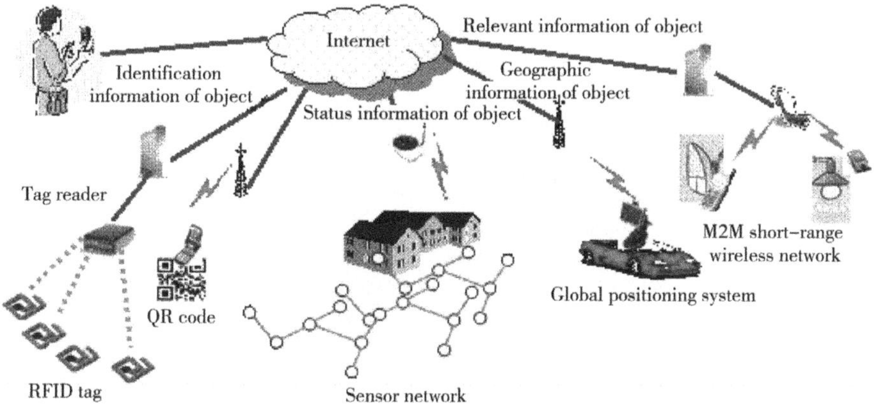

Figure 1.1 Schematic Diagram of the Internet of Things

Four technical forms of the Internet of Things[11]:

RFID: RFID is an "enabling" technology that allows ordinary "objects" to be instrumented (IBM "3I") and connected to the Internet of Things. Relevant EPC/UID and PNL/ONS technologies can serve as reference technologies of "unified identification" for the whole system of the Internet of Things.

Sensor Network: Such technologies as WSN, OSN, and BSN are terminal nervous systems of the Internet of Things and intended to solve the problem of the "last 100 meters" connection. The terminal of the sensor network is generally a micro-sensing system like Mote which is smaller than a M2M terminal.

M2M: It focuses more on the interconnection and centralized control management of mobile terminals, and is mainly used in a telecommunication operator's business of the Internet of Things. Its business model

[11] *Ten Basic Functions and Four Technical Forms of the Internet of Things*, ChinaIRN.COM, September 16, 2013. Available at: http://www.chinairn.com/news/20130916/162006115.html.

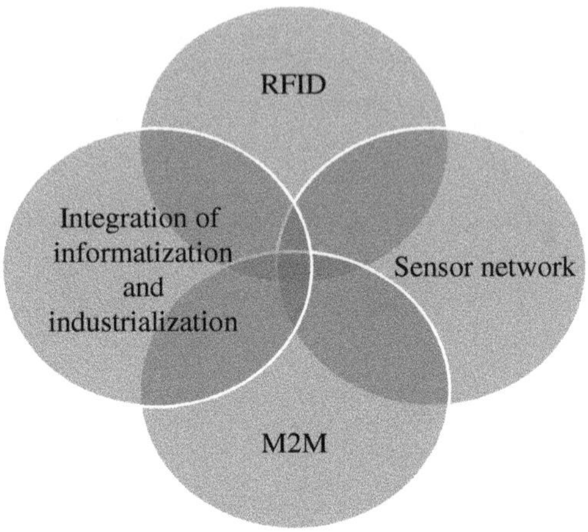

Figure 1.2 Four Technical Forms of the Internet of Things[12]

includes MVNO (Mobile Virtual Network Operator) and MMO (M2M Mobile Operator).

Integration of Informatization and Industrialization: It refers to information-based upgrade of industrial automation and control systems. Enterprises in the industrial control and building control industries are main driving forces for the integration of informatization and industrialization. The integration also covers smart power grids and other industrial applications (Figure 1.2).

2.3 *Cloud Computing*

As the Internet's reach continues to expand in the "Internet Plus" era, computing, storage, data, and application resources are converging at an increasing pace. The Internet is changing from a traditional communication platform to a ubiquitous, intelligent platform for computing. Cloud Computing is a new form of Internet-based model that allows addition, usage, and delivery of IT services. In short, it is a form of Internet-based

[12] *What Features Does the Internet of Things Have*? Available at: http://www.rdbuy.cn/article-228.html.

computing that enables the Internet to provide dynamic, extensible, and usually virtual resources. There are numerous definitions of Cloud Computing, and the most widely accepted one is provided by the National Institute of Standards and Technology (NIST): Cloud Computing is a model for enabling ubiquitous, convenient, on-demand network access to a shared pool of configurable computing resources (e.g. networks, servers, storage, applications, and services) that can be rapidly provisioned and released with minimal management effort or service provider interaction.[13]

Companies can provide their customers with a variety of Internet services by leveraging superior computing power and unlimited storage space of a cloud computing platform, without a lot of upfront investment in equipment. They are neither hindered by infrastructure requirements and specific expertise associated with the "Cloud" when using Cloud Computing, nor do they need to manage it directly by themselves, as the cloud computing platform's staff are responsible for maintaining the infrastructure and platform, to ensure normal operation of services. In addition, as long as customers have access to the Internet, they can enjoy services provided by the companies.[14] Cloud Computing is able to realize economies of scale through resource sharing, which is similar to some infrastructure services (such as power grids).

Cloud Computing has changed not only the traditional model for using IT resources by end users, but also the business management model within the IT industry, creating a huge impact on IT decision-makers. Some IT decision-makers believe they will be marginalized in enterprise management if they don't quickly migrate to the Cloud. Their concern comes from the fact that Cloud Computing brings reforms not only to the way that IT resources are used, but also to internal and external service models.[15] For example, if a hotel group comprehensively places its IT

---

[13] Cloud Computing, Baidu Baike. Available at: http://baike.baidu.com/link?url=JvmNGPuMV8jJG0YkUrRQTfGQG-nCF7Y21rvIvpkPT7P9voqm59T69LEA-3_h74ivQrLWANuedfJfftj3AJhTAq#reference-[3]-1316082-wrap.

[14] AliResearch: *Research Report on the "Internet Plus" — New Engine for China's Economy*, March 24, 2015, Available at: http://www.aliresearch.com/blog/article/detail/id/20324.html.

[15] Wang Bai, Xu Liutong: Cloud Computing (3), *ZTE Technology Journal*, 2010 (3).

resources on the Cloud, it can help accelerate the launch process for its new branches, while reducing each branch's staffing and other management costs. A steel company can strengthen coordination among its different business divisions, and make the whole progress of each order available to end users, by storing all of its data in the Cloud.[16]

3. *Access to the Internet in the "Internet Plus" Era*

Internet access can be divided into "soft" and "hard" access. "Hard" access refers to all hardware, such as PCs, mobile terminals, in-home terminals, and a variety of devices connected through the Internet of Things, whereas "soft" access refers to websites and APPs. Internet access' development has undergone four stages, classified by the way that Internet users access services:

3.1 *First Stage: Access to Information*

Lack of information was the biggest pain point for people before the birth of the Internet. Once the Internet emerged, it quickly became a resource pool into which a large amount of information flooded from all aspects of society. A platform that can rapidly put together huge amounts of information in a structured manner will naturally be favored by users. This is the root cause behind the rise of web portals such as Sina and Sohu.

3.2 *Second Stage: Access to Accurate Information*

Mass information pooled together through the Internet solved the lack of information; however, how to quickly find the correct information was a problem to be solved in the second stage. Thus, search engines, navigation sites, and classification sites such as Baidu and Google came to the fore.

[16] Meng Xiaofeng, Ci Xiang, Big data management: Concepts, technologies, and challenges, *Computer Research and Development*, 2013 (1).

3.3 *Third Stage: Access to Social Networking*

The Internet has greatly expanded people's social space and reach. Social networking websites, forums, software, and APPs such as Weibo and WeChat, have been flourishing to fulfill people's needs for social communication. Social networking websites (tools) bring together groups of people having similar interests through the "Follow" function. Information can be disseminated more accurately and faster among such groups of users, whose needs for interaction are satisfied as well. Each person acts as both consumer and producer of information, and this has once again led to explosive information growth.

3.4 *Fourth Stage: Access to Services*

Users hope that the Internet can not only fulfill their needs for information and social networking, but also improve their quality of life. For example, Baidu Maps, DiDi, and other websites or APPs providing various kinds of daily life and government services are such Internet-based services users want. Users can easily find goods and services they need through these portals, including physical and virtual goods, as well as services related to education, health, entertainment, housekeeping, catering, tourism, and many other aspects. These goods and services are supported by a lot of relevant information such as product information, reviews, and usage methods. Portals such as those mentioned above are equipped with convenient payment tools that allow users to complete transactions online, without the need for traditional cash payments. Furthermore, users can even interact with friends within their "circles" through these portals, fulfilling their social networking needs. In addition, service providers can improve users' service experience, and enhance user engagement and stickiness, using data mining and artificial intelligence technology.

4. *Network Security in the "Internet Plus" Era*

The Internet, which connects people and people as well as people and information via social networking tools and search engines, is quickly changing into one that aims to connect people and devices as well as people and services. However, this change poses security risks at every link of the connection, and exposes people's daily lives to danger all the time. In September 2014, a group of Chinese white hat hackers — KeenTeam, hacked a Tesla smart car through a laptop, remotely controlling its brake and gas pedal. This drew the industry's attention to smart device security issues.

Network security problems have become increasingly prominent in the "Internet Plus" era, wherein data and user information are more likely to leak through new technologies and applications such as the Internet of Things, Cloud Computing, and Big Data. The main security risks of the Internet Plus are displayed in Figure 1.3.

At present, we need to pay attention to the following major security problems:

(1) Threat of denial-of-service attacks continues to escalate, affecting the underlying network's stable operation.

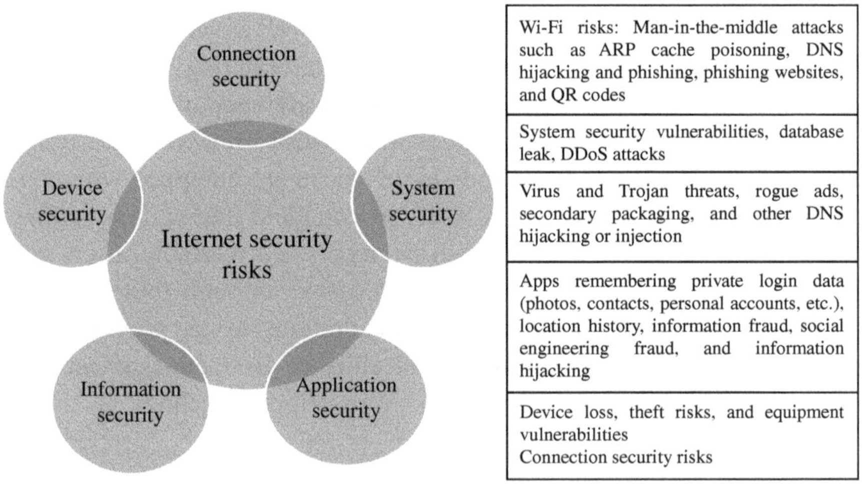

Figure 1.3 Security Risks of the Internet Plus[17]

[17] Ma Huateng *et al.*, (authors), Zhang Xiaofeng and Du Jun (editors). *Roadmap for National Internet Plus Strategic Action*. Beijing: CITIC Press Group, 2015.

(2) Malicious mobile apps countersecurity testing by means of "reinforcement" more frequently, and counterfeit applications are more rampantly used to implement phishing scams.
(3) The popularity of cloud platforms increases risks of Big Data leakage and network attack, necessitating improving protective measures and management mechanisms.
(4) More targeted attacks take place to discover vulnerabilities in basic applications, general hardware and software as well as domestic hardware and software, giving rise to challenges against coping mechanisms and disclosure management.
(5) Smart terminals provide new entry points for attacks, leading to security challenges against the Internet of Things.
(6) Intelligent manufacturing is exposed to prominent threat of network attacks and the development of the industry-based Internet is challenged.

The increasingly striking Internet security problems have brought new challenges to a country's political, economic, cultural, and national defense security. Additionally, national economic and social development has led to growing demands for enhanced Internet security.

Network security technologies refer to technological means intended to address how to exercise effective intervention control and ensure secure data transmission, including physical security analysis technology, network structure security analysis technology, system security analysis technology, management security analysis technology, and other security services and security mechanism strategies.[18] They cover message authentication technology, digital signature technology, access control technology, data encryption technology, key management technology, secure transmission media technology, network monitoring, tracking, and isolation technology, routing control and traffic analysis control technology, network management technology, network firewall technology, and so on.

[18]Liu Zhongping. Study of computer network security technologies. *Electronic Technology & Software Engineering*, 2015 (8).

5. *Smart City Construction in Shanghai in the "Internet Plus" Era*

Smart city is a new model meant to strengthen urban planning, construction, administration and operation, by comprehensively using modern science and technology, integrating information resources, and coordinating business application systems. It is a vision to build, serve, manage and sustainably develop a city smartly. Governments at all levels are dedicated to building and pushing forward continuous development of smart cities, resulting in a range of sub-programs such as smart education, smart livelihood, smart transportation, smart government services, smart healthcare, and smart security.

Shanghai has been at the forefront in promoting smart city construction in China. It released the first-round of a three-year action plan for smart city construction in September 2011, and completed all objectives and tasks in the plan by the end of 2013. Shanghai's comprehensive index in China's assessment of informatization development level was 111.02, ranking first in China, along with its two secondary indices, namely, information and communication technology (ICT) application, and network readiness.

In future, Shanghai's smart city construction will focus on improving people's livelihood, industrial innovation, administrative transparency, and other deep-seated areas, which can be placed into five specific application actions[19]:

(1) Build resident-friendly cities where people lead smart lives with universal benefits. Programs include smart education, smart meteorology, smart tourism, smart health, smart employment, smart old-age care, smart transportation, and smart culture.
(2) Promote industrial innovation and develop a high-end, smart economy. Programs include smart enterprises, smart shipping, Internet finance, intelligent manufacturing, and smart commerce.

[19] *Shanghai Releases Smart City Construction Plan*. Xinhuanet. September 10, 2014. Available at: http://news.xinhuanet.com/2014-09/10/c_1112427161.htm.

(3) Improve intricacies of smart city administration to ensure reliable urban operation. Programs include public safety informatization, intelligent urban lifeline, comprehensive city administration informatization, environmental protection informatization, and food safety management informatization.
(4) Exercise transparent and efficient administration and establish integrated smart government services. Programs include public credit information service platform, integrated e-government services, optimized public service channels, government-public data open service, and upgraded e-government network service level.
(5) Implement regional pilot application and create "new landmarks" for the smart city. Programs include smart new towns, smart industrial parks, smart communities, smart business districts, and smart villages.

According to the Action Plan of Shanghai for Promoting Smart City Construction (2014–2016), a series of specific targets have been formulated, with focus on building a convenient and efficient information perception, and smart application system. The end of 2016 will basically see a completed smart city system framework underpinned by a next-generation, high-speed, ubiquitous city information infrastructure system, a new-generation, high-end, green information technology industry system, as well as an independent and reliable network security system. Smart city construction will become a strong support and important foundation for Shanghai to enhance its international competitiveness and soft power. Shanghai will continue to maintain a leading position in China in terms of its overall informatization level, and take the lead in joining international advanced ranks.

5.1 *Improved Level and Benefit of Informatization Application*

Smart life will begin to take shape as informatization application effectively promotes information consumption. Smart education, healthcare, old-age care, transportation and other network-based public services will be available to all citizens. Smart economy will develop rapidly, and information technology will drive development of new types of business, industries, technologies, and models (hereinafter referred to as "Four New Developments"). The integration index between industrialization and informatization is expected to reach 86.5, and e-commerce will achieve RMB 2 trillion gross merchandise value (GMV). Smart city administration will be continuously deepened with a comprehensive grid-based city administration platform covering the city's administrative areas. Informatization will play an increasingly prominent role in helping governmental reform and innovation, leading to tremendous breakthroughs in smart government services, and remarkable progress in e-government service construction and management model. The smart city will have a significant regional demonstration effect, engendering a number of demonstrative smart new towns, smart villages, smart parks, smart communities, and smart business districts.

5.2 *Improved Level of Urban Information-related Infrastructure Services in the Next Generation*

A true broadband city will be realized in all aspects; fiber-optic broadband networks will basically cover the city's administrative areas, and up to 60% of the city's households will have Fiber to the Home (FTTH) installations. Home fiber-based network users will have an average network transmission speed of 40 megabits per second, and 6 million households in urbanized areas will use Next-Generation Broadcasting network (NGB). A wireless city will be built comprehensively, with 3G and 4G network users accounting for 70% of total mobile phone users, and there will be strong 4G network coverage across the city's administrative areas. There will be more than 200,000 wireless network access points, further optimizing WLAN setup in public places. The city's Internet data center will have 50,000 racks, further improving functional capacities. Inter-network switching capacity between international network exports and local networks will be significantly enhanced, and the network readiness index will be improved.

5.3 *Improved Innovation and Development Capacities of New-generation Information and Technology Industries*

Integrated circuit, high-end software and other areas will see significant improvement in independent innovation capabilities. A number of new models and new types of enterprises will be incubated in industries such as Big Data, Cloud Computing, the Internet of Things, and mobile Internet and so on. Shanghai will become home to leading innovations and industrial clusters of new-generation information technologies, and will become a strategic location in China for developing information service industries. New-generation information technology industries are expected to achieve a total scale of RMB 1 trillion, accounting for more than 70% of information industries, and are expected to employ more than 800,000 people. The added value from the information service industries will account for more than 7% of the city's GDP.

5.4 *Improved Comprehensive Abilities to Ensure Network Environment Security*

Shanghai's capabilities in security supervision in key areas, metropolitan area network (MAN) monitoring and early warning, network security emergency response, and comprehensive cyberspace management will be significantly enhanced. Network security protection levels will be effectively improved in key areas and key organizations. Citizens will be more aware of network security. Network security technology industries will exhibit healthy and orderly development, and smart city network security will be even more dependable, reliable and controllable.[20]

---

[20] Shanghai Releases Smart City Construction Plan. Xinhuanet. September 10, 2014. Available at: http://news.xinhuanet.com/2014-09/10/c_1112427161.htm.

Chapter 2

Social Reorganization in the "Internet Plus" Era

We have entered the "Internet Plus" era full of innovations, especially "disruptive innovations." Big Data, for example, has pervaded all aspects of our life, disrupting the knowledge theory that has been in existence for 10,000 years in human society regarding information acquisition, memory and storage.[1] In the new wave of global scientific and technological revolution and industrial transformation, the Internet's application in various fields has become an irresistible trend, presenting broad prospects and unlimited potential, with an overall strategic impact on economic and social development of countries all over the world.[2] Today, network

[1] "Disruptive innovation" was first coined by famous economist Joseph Schumpeter in 1912, who argued that innovation constantly initiates changes in internal economic structure. In other words, disruptive innovation constantly disrupts old structures and creates new ones. "Innovation, by its nature, means taking a big step and making a big change... In fact, the best 'way to do things' before innovation, is no longer the best way after innovation." Professor Clayton Christensen (2013), an American scholar, articulated disruptive innovation in 1997, making up for and improving Schumpeter's theory of innovation.

[2] *Guiding Opinions of the State Council concerning Vigorously Moving forward the "Internet Plus" Action Plan*, GF 2015, (40).

information technologies enable the construction of a complex network system for full information exchange, connecting the online, physical and social world. Information sharing and collaboration worldwide has further driven globalization, and information and communications technologies have been extensively applied in various aspects of society, changing their operating states and structures.

Global economy has begun to operate through production, identification, and utilization of information. An Internet-based global platform endows individuals with a sense of power and high social autonomy, enabling the possibility of large-scale and even worldwide social cooperation. A network society has become an ideal place for people to apply new rules and new mechanisms. However, due to its strong impact on social organizations, people are still unable to totally adapt to it. They are confronted with more difficulties and obstacles to reach a consensus in the real world. In the new "Internet Plus" era, China needs to ponder and explore issues focused on social reorganization, such as how to comprehend and establish "rules" for living in a network society; how to comprehend and apply social mobilizations and organizational mechanisms that have sufficient autonomy, but are independent of traditional dominating institutions and organizations' networking logic; and how to lead the wave of innovation-driven development in the global community.

I. Understanding the "Internet Plus" Era Beyond the Technological Dimension

As an emerging trend of the times, the "Internet Plus" has extended its reach to all aspects of people's daily lives, while sparking creative changes in traditional industrial manufacturing, organization and management. At present, the "Internet Plus" cannot be understood simply from the perspective of technological change, but must be deeply analyzed in terms of its possible social implications and consequences from a social, systematic perspective that goes beyond the technological dimension. Like any industrial revolution in history, the "Internet Plus" primarily embodies systematic and structural, economic and social changes. Any transformation of technology is accompanied by innovative changes in knowledge, ideas, structures, and organization methods.

History bears proof that any industrial revolution in human history means transformation and innovation of technology in the narrow sense, but it more embodies systematic and structural, economic and social changes. Any transformation of technology is accompanied by innovative changes in knowledge, ideas, structures, and organization methods. The invention and improvement of the steam engine and the development of electric power technology sparked the first and second Industrial Revolutions, leading to profound changes in industrial production, life-style, cognitive concepts, and even political systems in the entire western capitalist society, when compared to the pre-industrial era. The introduction of large-scale production technology changed organizational models of factories, as well as social connections and ties among people in western capitalist countries. Entire society is organized based on the logic of division of labor, which works like an industrial production line, as observed by Durkheim. Rational industrial and administrative organizations have become the main representatives of industrial society. Thus, it is more appropriate to say that qualitative leaps in production technology have produced outcomes that are far beyond the technology itself, making the production technology an important source and component of social change, rather than saying that technological changes alone bring about productivity improvement. Similarly, the rapid development of Internet technologies and the "Internet Plus" in recent years cannot be simply understood from a technological dimension. Modern information technologies and the "Internet Plus" need to be thoroughly analyzed and understood from the perspective of changes in social systems. Empirically, people have been able to clearly identify or foresee the advent of a higher-level networked era that is vastly different from industrial society.

II. Challenges to Traditional Social Life Order in the "Internet Plus" Era

As a change agent, the Internet has changed how people connect, work and live; it has changed people's ideas about contemplating and observing the world, through in-depth integration of modern Internet technologies with industries, social governance, public services, and many other areas. The "Internet Plus" era has brought new challenges and changes to our lives. A more far-reaching question is how will all these changes interact and influence each other? The focus should be put on three aspects. The first is abrupt changes in rules and logic for coordinating social relations, when compared to traditional society. The second is the superposition of multiple power legitimacies, and the fragmentation of social identities in network society. The third is the impact of non-traditional social risks on network society.

Changes in social life or social transformations brought about by technological changes have drawn the attention of many sociologists and futurists. Their concerns are more or less targeted at modern information technology's far-reaching influence and significance on society and people's life, such as Daniel Bell's view on post-industrial society underpinned by technology and knowledge, Alvin Toffler's forward-looking judgment on information society, John Naisbitt's insight into the Internet era and globalization, and Manuel's (2001) analysis of identity in the network era. People are facing or will face an era that sees society featuring unique ways of life and organization, completely contrary to pre-industrial society or industrial society. Bell described different stages of human society's development as follows: traditionalism lies at the core of pre-industrial society, which was dominated by landlords and soldiers, and where human beings competed with nature; economic growth lies at the core of industrial society, which was dominated by entrepreneurs, and where human beings worked on processing nature; knowledge lies at the core of post-industrial society, which is dominated by scientific and technological elites, and where human beings compete with each other (Guan, 2013). Following a similar logic, a keen observer may realize that through application of modern Internet technologies to industries, social governance, public services, and other areas, the "Internet Plus" era will bring about new challenges and changes to social life order that has already been established in human society.

1. *Abrupt Changes in Rules and Logic for Coordinating Social Relations*

In the "Internet Plus" era, rules and logic for coordinating social relations change abruptly, when compared to traditional society. To quote some

"Internet Plus" advocates, the "Internet Plus" itself represents a change in thinking. It is the application of Internet-based concepts and game rules to traditional industries that enable emergence of brand new forms of industries and unprecedented growth in wealth. People's emphasis on changing rules reflects their common understanding of the conceptualization and characteristics of the "Internet Plus". From a sociological point of view, people may soon encounter abrupt changes in rules and logic for coordinating social relations, and thus become disoriented over a period of time in the "Internet Plus" era. In the traditional agricultural era, due to limited technology, people mainly relied on fine weather and favorable geographical locations, to conduct economic production. They lived in spaces with clear scopes and boundaries, and were connected primarily by land, blood ties, family relationships, and so on, resulting in social relations that were mainly coordinated by tangible identity of authority and logic of reciprocity. In the industrial production era, machine-aided production lines replaced traditional manual production and expanded division of labor and market size, leading to spatial and temporal extension for interpersonal interactions. As a result, social coordination was more characterized by bureaucracy in the industrial era, with transaction and redistribution of benefits as the core of the entire social interaction. Currently, human society is in the process of transitioning from the industrial era to the "Internet Plus" era. Due to sudden changes in modern Internet technologies and their characteristics of openness, equality, convenience, as well as spatial and temporal characteristics, human society will see great changes in rules or logic for coordinating social relations. For example, with regard to social order construction and integration, coordination of social relations has started to go beyond production line hierarchical model of relations linked by material and interests, of the industrial era; social resource allocation has started to go beyond boundaries of markets and formal organizations, and society's core resources are shifting from traditional capital, land and technology, to information as well as capability to produce, process and analyze such information; society's organization structures have started to go beyond formal and informal differences, as well as top-down bureaucratic or hierarchical structures, moving toward flexible, resilient structures or organizational processes with no clear boundaries (Li and Zhang, 2014). Human society is unlikely to be organized through a single logic, due to changing rules for coordinating social relations in the "Internet Plus" era.

2. *Superposition of Multiple Power Legitimacies and Crisis of Fragmented Identities*

The "Internet Plus" era may bring forth superposition of multiple power legitimacies and crisis of fragmented identities. Any technological revolution poses a significant impact on our conceptual sense system, its source of legitimacy, and construction. People may see the following scenarios occurring in the "Internet Plus" era: CEOs of platform companies that have large databases and information networks, are discussing how to change consumption tastes and preferences of ordinary community residents, and how to make traditional monopolistic enterprises that lack capability to collect and process information and technology, become a less important part to help them achieve huge profits in production, by exercising the power to impose orders on these enterprises. In virtual production organizations, makers who have creative ideas and innovative resources may criticize and correct companies' managers. In metropolitan communities, individuals in virtual networks are engaged in heated debates on how to improve community environment and promote public service programs, raise funds through crowdfunding for these programs, and shepherd construction and provision of services for such programs. These scenarios show that legitimacy of traditional power is being constantly mitigated or even completely replaced in markets, enterprises, and communities in the "Internet Plus" era. In markets, the power no longer resides in investors with strong financial strengths, but in intermediary platforms having more information about markets, consumers, products, and so on. In enterprises, it is creative and innovative talents with unique personality that hold the power, instead of business owners, professional managers, or senior executives under the bureaucratic system. In communities, each individual has the power, and it is not necessarily held by community managers having traditional institutional identities. In this sense, there are significant challenges to legitimacy of power in the "Internet Plus" era, which possibly results in superposition of multiple power legitimacies.

Additionally, people quite often encounter crisis of fragmented identities in the "Internet Plus" era. Relatively speaking, no matter in the agricultural era or industrial society, people's self- and social-identities were built based on established relationships and boundaries among people, as well as on existing hierarchical structures and welfare dependence relationships. But the case is different in the "Internet Plus" era, where people's identities are shaped mainly by virtual online identities rather than citizens, residents, enterprise employees, and other tangible symbols. As individuals, people benefit vastly from the Internet (such as resource help, emotional exchange, and support), but in turn are stuck in a paradox of crisis. For example, people's high dependence on online networks and computers is likely to lead them into a self-identity crisis such as, "Who am I?" As argued by some researchers, the "Internet Plus" era brings to people a self-identity crisis in virtual society, which generally manifests as "fragmentation" and "illusion". On the one hand, work is becoming more mechanized with tasks getting simpler, and particularly, even knowledge-intensive work such as programming gets increasingly procedural, simplistic, and mechanized due to the use of machines; on the other hand, machine industry is exhibiting tremendous intelligence, making people concerned about their positions and roles in future. Online virtual society disintegrates and truly fragments group identities found in traditional society. To a certain extent, virtual and free networks have relieved people from realistic relations. It has introduced new identities and disrupted existing hierarchical relationships, enabling people to associate and establish relationships with each other freely. Most importantly, it has dispersed subjects, as they are no longer confined to original positions in time and space (Wang *et al.*, 2003).

3. *More Uncertainties and Many Non-traditional Public Risks*

Society may be faced with more uncertainties and non-traditional public risks in the "Internet Plus" era. The "Internet Plus" has its advantages as a force for boosting economic and social transformation and development. However, in the absence of effective regulatory systems and means, extensive and rapid expansion of the "Internet Plus" will bring about complex uncertainties and risks in society. For example, when Shanghai, as a megalopolis, promotes "Internet Plus" development and sets about building a globally influential center for scientific and technological innovation and a global city, all kinds of information, resources, and opportunities flow and are distributed rapidly via the open, equitable, and user inclusive Internet. It is possible for any person to use the "Internet Plus" as a tool to achieve his or her illegitimate goals by taking advantage of others' inadequate understanding of the same. In the absence of an effective credit system, unethical hackers or organizations may steal Internet users' private information or economic behavior data, to seek unjustified interests, seriously infringing upon Internet users' privacy. Another case in point could be that with the help of online networks, collective action, which is difficult to be mobilized and organized in the real world, may be launched clandestinely, based on the Internet's capacity for online and offline interactions and connections, triggering large-scale collective action or mass incidents. In recent years, frequent collective protests against PX projects have been organized all over China, by taking full advantage of fast speed, wide coverage, and large influence of Internet-based information exchange. This poses a serious challenge to traditional social management conducted by governments, to a certain extent. "Diversified sources drive rapid reorganization of social structure. The basis of social relations is changing significantly due to rise of new network society, as does the legitimacy of political authority. China must direct strategic attention to this situation" (Li, 2015).

Similar to growth of uncertainties in social life, the public may face more severe public security risks and resulting consequences, due to multiple aspects, including rapid application of the "Internet Plus" to economic and social life, as well as further acceleration of globalization and urbanization. Taking Internet finance as an example, as people gain access to new emerging financial management concepts, they will put more money and energy into the financial sector. Development of Internet financial platforms provides opportunities and space for people to participate in financial activities. However, as Internet platforms play the function of simplifying financial knowledge, and people have access to asymmetric information in the Internet financial sector, operating procedures and logics of Internet finance and resulting financial risks may go far beyond what ordinary people can comprehend and recognize. Due to China's limited regulation on Internet financial transactions, people, who are tempted by high returns on financial investment, are very likely to fall into the trap of irrational Internet financial speculation, and suffer huge financial risks, which may turn into a large-scale social crisis. In essence, private lending crises and illegal fund-raising activities that occurred in Wenzhou around 2012, may stage a comeback by means of Internet channels, creating financial risks and social crises that China and its people may find extremely difficult to cope with. Social risks associated with the "Internet Plus" era also include urban terrorist attacks and other public security risks that require attention. In the midst of turbulent political and economic situations in the world, globalization results in fierce collisions among different cultures, ethnic groups, religions, and other elements, possibly bringing about severe terrorist threats and public security issues to urban society. These issues may cause enormous social disasters as they are easily transmitted, mobilized, and organized through Internet channels, and are rarely discovered by regulatory authorities. Speaking of a typical case, it has been reported that ISIS (the Islamic State of Iraq and the Levant) which has an active presence in West Asia and the Middle East, infiltrates popular dating sites to recruit members, and disseminates information about terrorist attacks on specific cities, groups, and organizations via the Internet.[3]

In summary, as a new technological revolution, the "Internet Plus" adds a revitalizing force to changes in social structure. Free release of and non-hierarchical access to information changes the traditional pyramid-shaped, blocky, hierarchical structure, to a flat social structure. With emergence of new models and new business types featuring large-scale, social collaboration, created by shared economies, network collaboration and crowd sourcing, new types of organizations and new models of relationships between individuals and organizations will appear, changing and reshaping traditional social structures, which are undergoing a revolution of deconstruction and reconstruction. Society as a whole presents a

[3] IS Recruits Young Women through Dating Sites and Young Men through Games. *NetEase News*. October 26, 2014. Available at: http://news.163.com/14/1026/07/A9FECG8B00014Q4P.html.

multi-network structure maintained as an information network. As a result, society will show new characteristics in terms of interaction and communication, expressing public opinion, interest demand, values, lifestyles, etc., which differs from traditional society, making society more complex and uncertain (Tong, 2015). In the context of the "Internet Plus", the above crises and challenges confronting all aspects of social life, give rise to the need for an appropriate social reorganization model that enables re-connection of social ties, and effective realization of a sound social order. In this sense, rapid development of the "Internet Plus" brings a major problem of social reorganization to social administrators and researchers who need to deal with it through an innovative social governance model.

III. Network Society and Its Organization Method in the "Internet Plus" Era

Cutting-edge development of Internet technologies has promoted a leap in social communication efficiency and enabled all types of communication. Social transaction costs continue to decline and social interactions are getting flexible and complex. People have been given a tool to break through traditional organizational boundaries, and now have the ability to establish groups and act together outside organizations. Although this represents an improvement for today's society, it also poses an unprecedented challenge. In the "Internet Plus" era, the underlying "networking logic" behind "network society" is the key characteristic and basic structure of informational society (Zheng and He, 2004). Social organization methods are being continuously adjusted according to an organization's understanding of institutional and social environment changes.

1. *"Networking Logic" of Network Society and Characteristics of Social Self-organization*

Information technology revolution has greatly liberated individuals; the decentralized, flat, and self-organized Internet is deconstructing and reconstructing social structures. The Internet allows ordinary individuals to rise above professional barriers, authoritative evaluation, and path dependence that have been established for centuries, and obtain sufficient and equal display opportunities. Ties between individuals and traditional social organizations are getting weaker, and changes in transmission modes and social structures bring about changes in social power and domination patterns. Today's social structure manifests as a multi-dimensional, dynamic network development system, amounting to shared "network society", with new information technologies as the material basis in informational society. This social structure form exists independently like industrial society and agricultural society. Anthony Giddens pointed out that the information age, which is characterized by network society and driven by global economy, completely shakes existing forms of nation states or organizations based on fixed space. In a sense, the analysis of network society's "networking logic" and self-organization rules is no different from an exploration of futurology, because the knowledge on which our understanding is based, is in any case likely to become obsolete, as opposed to the expanding development of information and Internet technologies. However, it is possible for us to "discover" network society's new characteristics in terms of social mobilization, identity, and subject generation in the information era, by analyzing all changes that emerge in social structures and social lives in countries across the world, and focusing on elements of social autonomy such as social values, free association, community cooperation, and collective action involving social actors.

First, network society relies on new information technologies as the material basis that enables information to be transmitted beyond time and space barriers, thereby fostering a powerful social mobilization force. To begin with, network society's interpersonal relationships amount to a social relations network model featuring a "small world". In other words, it is not the majority of people who have hundreds of social relations that maintain the social relations network, but the minority who have tens of thousands of social relations. Social self-organization reflects mutually dependent prosperity, where individual autonomy has been greatly enhanced and everyone can participate in, share, and co-produce social products. Next, information communication technologies create an absolute possibility that minorities cannot be overlooked, and enormous visibility and search ability in social life enables like-minded people to find each other, to assemble and cooperate with one another, and to exist independent of social approval or disapproval (Clay, 2009: 127). Due to sophisticated means of communication and more flexible social structures, networking organizations are getting more resilient. When it is easy and convenient to form associations, forces that have been neglected are self-organized as an organic form of public organization and social self-organization. Some empirical facts show how the Internet has been successfully utilized for social mobilization. In September 2004, Japan proposed to become a permanent member of the UN Security Council. Some overseas associations launched online signature campaigns to protest against this, and received tens of thousands of signatures per hour until late March 2005. These signatures from various corners of the world were presented to relevant UN agencies and the Japanese government in different ways, reflecting the power of public opinion (Tang, 2007).

Second, collective action taken through Internet's online and offline intermediation and cooperation reveals a new logic for action. The seemingly loose online social organizations actually have the ability to mobilize people in case of critical emergency, while the Internet's potential for mobilization transcends and complements the traditional mobilization method (Wang, 2011). Real-time coordination is replacing planned arrangements, and group behaviors are being organized in an invisible fashion, producing instantaneous results. A case in point would be Zhejiang that was heavily struck by Typhoon Fitow in 2013. The worst-hit area was Yuyao in Ningbo, with over 70% of the city flooded, affecting 830,000 people. Volunteers across the country conducted massive non-governmental rescue operations with the help of information provided by many network platforms such as "Zhuo Ming Rescue Platform", "Typhoon Fitow Non-governmental Rescue Group" organized by Hao Nan, a dentist based in Beijing, and "Yuyao Middle School Alumni Group and Single People Group" organized by Shen Jili, a native of Yuyao, working in Shanghai. People running these platforms were thousands of miles away from Yuyao.[4] This new collective action model can be established through credible commitment, tools appropriate for the concerned action, and an

[4] Specific reference: CCTV big documentary: *The Internet Age*, Beijing United Publishing Co., Ltd., 2015.

agreement that is easy to accept. Commitment explains the problem "why" to participate in the action; tools explain the problem "how" to act and overcome coordination difficulties; and the agreement defines rules of collective action, clarifying what social actors can expect from the collective action, and what the group's expectations are (Clay, 2009).

Third, identity in network society no longer reflects how an individual is identified by society, but how the individual connected by the Internet evaluates, recognizes, and accepts society (Manuel, 2003). **The value of social networking is growing in the form of "power of organizing without organizations".** The so-called "power of organizing without organizations" refers to a situation where people can go beyond the limitations of bureaucratic organizations in network society. New social networking tools significantly reduce the costs of large-scale coordination, serious and complex work can be done without guidance from institutions, and collective action taken by loosely coordinated groups can yield results that are unattainable by any organization (Clay, 2009). People connect with one another as they do in daily life, and they are organized in a conversation-based, temporary, short-term fashion, and based on an immediate combination rather than a long-term contract. Organization forms stay closely related to social life, and organic organizations that emerge around topics and contents encompass enormous "power of organizing without organizations". Identity in network society is the most socialized social identity. In Castells' view, identity in the context of social life networking is different from individual identity, or identity defined in traditional sociology and individual psychology. Individuals connected via the Internet are no longer scattered and isolated, and constitute a new type of group connected by social identity in the network era, known as a network group. The network group has neither clear boundaries nor clear rules and systems. It is an open, dynamic, and extremely active intangible group formed through network communication, information exchange, and common value. Rapid and broad network communication allows the network group to expand quickly not only in the number of people and space it is present in, but also in communication efficiency and spread effect. Therefore, the social identity embodied by the network group is a strong social force or social power with unlimited potential (Liu, 2012).

2. *Social Organization in the "Internet Plus" Era*

According to the view of new institutionalism in the sociology of organization, changes in social organization models in essence result from adjustment of organizations in response to changing institutions and social environments. In the "Internet Plus" context, social life and order need to be reorganized. Compared to traditional industrial society, the social reorganization model in the "Internet Plus" era is reflected in three aspects: First, social mobilization and connection mechanisms, including sense system making and communication modes, increasingly transcend the traditional top-down model based on formal organizations and relationships (Li *et al.*, 2007). Second, information production and dissemination mechanisms typical to the "Internet Plus" era, differ from the linearized and centralized model specific to relatively enclosed space. Third, organizational forms and structures are no longer confined to clear boundaries, specific division of labor, and hierarchical structures, leading to the revolution in organizational structures and forms.

First, social reorganization in the "Internet Plus" era is an important manifestation of gradual transition in social mobilization and communication mechanisms from traditional, formal and structured, to diversified, open, informal, virtual, and digital. As modern Internet technologies like Big Data are extending their reach into daily lives, interpersonal communications and contacts are getting frequent, and even beyond the scope of specific time and space. People in any corner of the world can instantly establish connections for communication and knowledge transfer, as long as they have access to the Internet. Interpersonal communication and interaction is possible in society that is connected by the Internet and Big Data, without reliance on traditional, formal organizational structures, and channels. While opening up global markets, industries, trade activities, and financial transaction channels, the Internet is also shaping people's understanding of individuals, society, and the world. Therefore, in the "Internet Plus" era, all individuals can be extensively mobilized for specific issues or events, and assemble in cyberspace through information network channels. Such diversified, open, informal, digital, and virtual social mobilization goes beyond limitations of traditional, finite, local, and formal mobilization, saving mobilization and communication costs, and improving efficiency in organizing social mobilization.

Two aspects regarding the new social mobilization model in the "Internet Plus" era require attention. On the one hand, digital and virtual mobilization gives rise to important questions regarding the subject of mobilization, and how human cooperation or collective action can be achieved again. Several studies suggest that in the traditional industrial era, members of society were widely integrated into the modern industrial production process, and the state, government, market, business organizations, and economic, political and social elites initiated social mobilization, while ordinary people were mobilized and organized for shared values and interests. In the "Internet Plus" era, however, the identity of a subject or social mobilization initiator becomes more ambiguous and uncertain because of the Internet's strong ability and influence in transforming economic and social life, as well as its anonymity and virtuality. Individuals in cyberspace present symbolic features. They can either be the subject or the object of social mobilization. A considerable number of members of society participate in the mobilization process for causal and random reasons, and even through blind obedience. Therefore, social mobilization in the "Internet Plus" era is characterized by bottom-up mobilization, which goes beyond the traditional top-down mobilization, and submerges "authority" of those who initiated the mobilization. However, it must be clearly recognized that social mobilization typical to the "Internet Plus" era does not completely rule out the influence of "power" and "authority". Relatively speaking, organizations, platforms, and individuals that control Big Data and can process and analyze Big Data or information, have a bigger influence on social mobilization. For example, on China's financial repression and Internet financial relations, Alibaba's founder Ma Yun, ambitiously declared, "If banks do not change, we will change them," fully reflecting the subject's strong mobilization capacity, as an emerging Internet enterprise. On the other hand, social mobilization in the "Internet Plus" era needs to address the relationship between online mobilization and offline mobilization, which may affect people's sense system and change the logic of collective action. Most people are in two spaces at the same time in the "Internet Plus" era: the virtual space online and the physical space offline. Their real life is significantly influenced by cyberspace, which in particular gets more prominent in some cases of collective action. Many mass incidents have taken place in the past few years, where several issues and information were first discussed and disseminated online, which affected the process of collective action in the real world. The Internet is not just a trigger for broad mobilization of mass incidents in the "Internet Plus" era, but also an important tool to resolve mass incidents (Sheng, 2015).

Second, the information production and dissemination mechanism is decentralized and nonlinearized. Before the rise of information network, information production and dissemination in society were effected by certain factors, such as specific space and time, organization structure and power pattern, featuring centralization and linearization. Thus, information distribution was highly asymmetrical in market transactions and social interactions, while the release and delivery of non-residual information was monopolized and shared by some power subjects. To a certain extent, the nature of such information was also an important source of inequality in society. Information production and dissemination exhibit geometric growth in the "Internet Plus" era, as evidenced by faster speed and increasing bandwidth. The Internet's openness and equality allow each individual to produce, publish, and disseminate information. A case in point would be the popularity of Weibo and WeChat, where each Internet user has a channel to produce and transmit information, as well as the freedom to express his or her views and opinions on things. Comparatively speaking, this information production and dissemination mechanism breaks the traditional model featuring information asymmetry, centralization, and linearization. Information transmission in cyberspace does not simply involve a point-to-point relationship, but a point-to-network relationship. Such transmission and mobilization has vast coverage and goes beyond limitations of time and space. For example, when a mobile WeChat user posts a message in WeChat Moments, this message is forwarded through an uncontrollable path that is difficult to track. Thus, people may find that social communication networks such as WeChat Moments have become marketing channels as well as important platforms for government departments to publish information and refute rumors.

Third, in the "Internet Plus" era, social organization structures will change frequently as they become more flexible, flat, and mobile. Due to failure to effectively solve information asymmetry, transaction costs and other issues, structured organizations were needed to carry out economic and social activities, and regulate and allocate resources in the industrial era. Therefore, since the late 19th century and early 20th century, the rise of modern organizations, especially large enterprise organizations in the Western capitalist world, marked a milestone that influenced the development of society. These large enterprise organizations generally had bureaucratic structural systems, formal power hierarchies, top-down information transfer and relationship integration mechanisms, and clear inter-organizational boundaries. It is on this specific organization form that social structure was based. However, with rise of Internet technologies, the traditional, formal, and hierarchical organization form is quietly changing. For example, in the marketing field, large associated enterprise organizations have begun to abandon the traditional U-type structure and started using a flat and network-enabled departmental system. Two decades ago, it was hard to imagine a company dealing in clothing, shoes, and hats not requiring physical factories or stores, and operating simply by registering an account at Taobao, Tmall, or other new networking platforms. Government organizations are also geared to make changes with regard to governance. Traditional large and all-inclusive government departments are being cut down and changing. The Internet has made government processes more transparent, and has replaced manual operation of traditional administrative tasks with e-governance. At present, China's "Internet Plus Government" has made rapid progress. Smart management and smart service have been effectively popularized and applied, and new things such as P2P poverty alleviation, P2P charity, and P2P voluntary service have emerged (Liang, 2015). Organization forms in society are no longer limited to traditional families, enterprises or communities, and interpersonal associations have become more random and flexible. People's organization forms tend to show a combination of multiple networks.

IV. Information and Power Issues in the "Internet Plus" Era

The "Internet Plus" era has seen a huge and rapid leap in technological progress in many areas, ranging from the fixed-line Internet to the mobile Internet, and to the mobile Internet of Things, symbolizing that new technologies are changing rapidly and dominating manufacturing and society. The key factor differentiating countries in the "Internet Plus" era, is no longer developed countries and developing countries, but high-innovation countries and low-innovation countries. Countries that promote creativity and innovation are pioneering forces in this new era.

In the industrial era, material resources, monetary/financial capital, land, labor, science and technology, and institutional structure were the most important drivers of social wealth production and social progress. These factors constituted society's production function in a certain proportion or combination of parameters. They gave comparative and competitive advantages to countries or regions, enabling them to control resources and dominate power in this social system. In Western capitalist countries, monopolistic and oligopolistic enterprises held society's major wealth resources, whereas in countries with traditional planning systems, governments monopolized almost all important resources. Therefore, the combination of capital, land, and other key resources shaped various national and social institutions to a large extent, in the industrial era.

However, as opposed to the industrial era, the "Internet Plus" era has brought about great changes in the traditional model of resource and power domination, and even the most important sources of resources and power has been fundamentally replaced. According to traditional cybernetics point of view, information, material, and ability constitute the world's three basic resources (Huang, 2015). Information and people's ability to process and analyze information in the "Internet Plus" era, have replaced traditional capital and land as critical resources. Thanks to effective application of the Internet, Big Data, cloud computing, and other modern technologies, not only can people collect and access to large amounts of more complex information, but also they have the ability to process and analyze information as a whole, making it possible for people to promote economic and social innovation. For example, an e-commerce platform provider can comprehensively analyze demand in the consumer goods market, consumers' preferences and payment capacities, by processing and analyzing consumer behaviors and other information it has collected, thereby improving its business strategy and enhancing its business efficiency in a targeted manner. Many hold the view that data economy is at the core of the "Internet Plus" era's business models, making data industry a pillar industry. Data industry includes data collection, storage, analysis, application, and many other sub-sectors. Capitalizing on its core capabilities such as cloud computing, cloud storage, and Big Data, data industry comprehensively collects and mines business value of data, and provides support services for other industries based on the Internet and the Internet of Things.[5] Similar to marketing, the government can extract all kinds of requirement and demand information from grassroots communities by collecting massive information on the Internet, thus enhancing accuracy of public services in a targeted fashion. In this sense, those who have information and the ability to process information will have the upper hand in the "Internet Plus" era.

Furthermore, development of "Internet Plus" technologies provide possible spaces for individuals to engage in creative activities and innovations that are considered as important resources in the "Internet Plus" era. As Edmund Phelps described in *Mass Flourishing*, social development and prosperity since the Industrial Revolution were rooted in modern values such as the desire to participate in creating and exploring things, and in meeting challenges. Such values sparked grassroots economic vitality necessary to achieve a broad range of independent innovations. It is not just lonely dreamers like Henry Ford that enabled innovation, but millions of ordinary people, who had the freedom to conceive, develop and promote new products and processes, or improve current situations. It is this grassroots innovation that created prosperity for common people (Edmund, 2013). In the "Internet Plus" era, the Internet essentially encourages individuals to create beyond traditional constraints. Any new ideas, thoughts, methods, or products can be expressed, developed and promoted through the Internet, and become sources of value as long as they are identified

[5] Huang Jian, *The "Internet Plus" Will Trigger Deeper Social Changes in China. Dazhong Daily*. April 23, 2015. Available at: http://www.71.cn/2015/0423/811109.shtml.

and recognized by society or the market. Thus, it can be said that in the "Internet Plus" era, society's most-valued resources may not be traditional capital and other factors, but individual creativity and innovations generally known as "golden ideas".

From a more profound perspective, information, the ability to process information, and innovation are extremely critical resources in the "Internet Plus" era, but holding these resources does not necessarily entitle key power to social subjects, as the problem of power struggles in human cooperation remains. As a famous French sociologists said, "Power relations are critical in society, and power is obtained through decision-making abilities and strategic actions." (Michel *et al.*, 2007). Consumption and sharing no longer maintain a dominant position in post-industrial society embracing the "Internet Plus", in which participation, action, and development are valued. In this sense, effective collaboration depends on people's new strategic thinking and new collective ability in the social context of globalization and informatization.[6] For example, to obtain sufficient market access, an enterprise should not only strategically plan how to open itself up to the environment, but also tactically plan how to make the environment open up to itself (Li, 2008). In the "Internet Plus" era, people involved in social governance need to learn and develop cooperative decision-making abilities, in order to rationally coordinate and deal with conflicts among various stakeholders through dialogue, negotiation and consultation, thus achieving orderly social reorganization.

Since key resources and power sources have achieved major changes in the "Internet Plus" era, social administrators need to pay full attention to and discuss how to comprehensively control and use the above resources in the face of the "Internet Plus" wave. This task becomes more urgent especially in the backdrop of China's accelerated transformation of its economic development model, modernization of social governance capability, and realization of the Four-pronged Comprehensive Strategy. In recent years, for example, Shanghai has proposed several major development strategies such as "Establishing Four Centers", "Building a Global City with International Competitiveness and Influence", and

[6]In a sense, the ability of new strategic thinking and the ability to make collective, cooperative decisions are scarce high-end resources in the "Internet Plus" era.

"Accelerating Construction of a Globally Influential Center for Scientific and Technological Innovation." Shanghai has recognized the importance of the "Internet Plus" and key resources, in the course of achieving these goals. However, adapting to the "Internet Plus" era and making good use of information processing, innovation, creativity, and decision-making ability is a brand new area for everyone, particularly for urban administrators. Therefore, social administrators must not only respond to these changes promptly, but also increase their own intellectual input to improve self-innovation capability. Thus, we can promote sound development of the "Internet Plus" and provide strong intellectual support for sound social reorganization.

References

Clay Shirky. *Here Comes Everybody: The Power of Organizing Without Organizations.* (Hu Yong *et al.*, Trans.). China Renmin University Press, 2009.

Clayton Christensen. *The Innovator's Dilemma.* (Hu Jianqiao, Trans.). CITIC Press Group, 2013.

Edmund Phelps. *Mass Flourishing: How Grassroots Innovation Created Jobs, Challenge, and Change.* CITIC Press Group, 2013.

Guan Kai. The Internet and Cultural Transformation: Reconstructing the form of social change. *Journal of Sun Yat-Sen University (Social Sciences)*, 2013 (3).

Huang Huang. The "Internet Plus", National Governance and Public Policy. *E-government*, 2015 (7).

Li Youmei. *Focus on High-end Human Resources Factors from a Strategic Perspective. Jiefang Daily*, 2008.

Li Youmei. Social and cultural conditions for Shanghai to develop towards a global city. *Scientific Development*, 2015 (6).

Li Youmei and Zhang Huxiang. *Information Revolution and Social Reorganization — Analysis Based on Social Ties.* Draft for internal discussion, 2013.

Li Youmei *et al. Social Identity: Analysis from a Structural Perspective*, Shanghai People's Publishing House, 2007.

Li Youmei, Xiao Ying, and Huang Xiaochun. Publicity dilemma of contemporary China's social construction and how to overcome it. *Social Sciences in China*, 2012 (7).

Liang Haiyan. "*Internet Plus" Driven Innovation of Social Governance. Gansu Daily*. September 28, 2015. Available at http://gsrb.gansudaily.com.cn/system/2015/09/27/015719131.shtml.

Liu Shaojie. *Change of Power Structure in the Network Era. Sociology*, 2012 (1).

Manuel Castells. *The Rise of the Network Society*. (Xia Zhujiu, Wang Zhihong *et al.*, Trans.). Social Sciences Academic Press (China), 2001.

Manuel Castells. *The Power of Identity*. (Xia Zhujiu, Huang Liling *et al.*, Trans.). Social Sciences Academic Press (China), 2003.

Michel Crozier *et al. Actors and Systems*: *The Politics of Collective Action*. Shanghai People's Publishing House, 2007.

Sheng Zhiming. *Look into New Features of Current Mobilization of China's Mass Incidents from the Perspective of the Contradiction between Taxi Drivers and Drivers Providing Chauffeured Car Services*. Decision-Making Advisory Report of the Research Center for Local Governance of Shanghai University, 2015.

Tang Jie. A study of theimpact of internet development on social protest. *Social Science Journal*, 2007 (6).

Tong Liqiang. *The "Internet Plus" Brings about Social Changes. Guangming Online*. May 25, 2015. Available at http://theory.gmw.cn/2015-05/25/content_15766835.htm.

Wang Chengbing *et al*. Virtual society and contemporary identity crisis. *Journal of Beijing Normal University (Social Sciences)*, 2003 (5).

Wang Jianhua. Internet mobilization and OEM plant workers' collective protest. *Open Times*, 2011 (11).

Zheng Zhongyu and He Mingsheng. Analysis of conceptualization of the "Network Society". *Sociological Studies*, 2004 (2).

Chapter 3

Study About the Economic Impact of Core Cities on Surrounding Areas

I. The Economic Impact of Core Cities on Surrounding Areas: Size and Reach

1. *Literature Review*

1.1 *Economic Impact of Core Cities on Surrounding Areas in the "Internet Plus" Era: The Raising of a New Issue*

A core city emerges when economic and social development reaches a certain stage, and it is a very important node in a regional space system. Core cities play an important role in regional development. They often provide surrounding areas with the support, continuity, driving force and example, all of which improve the economic and social conditions of residents.

Shanghai is located in the middle of the Yangtze River Delta area, one of the most urbanized regions in China, ranked the world's sixth largest urban agglomeration. As China's primate city, Shanghai has joined ranks

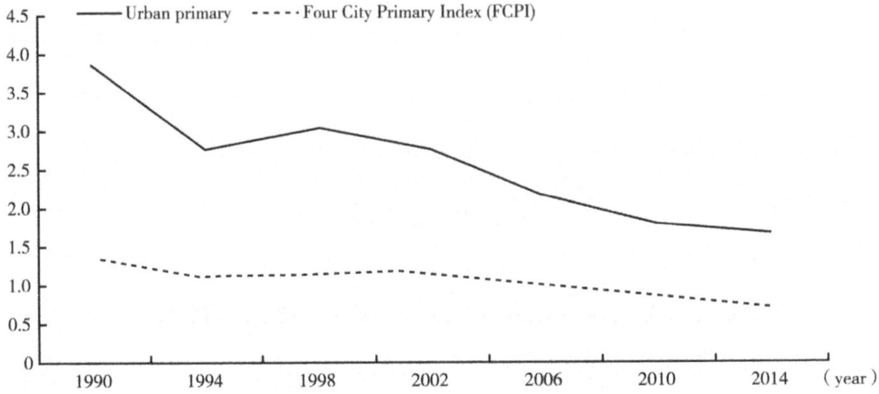

Figure 3.1 GDP Primacy of Cities in the Yangtze River Delta from 1990 to 2014

of international metropolises, and represents development direction of world's major advanced cities. Therefore, studying Shanghai's economic impact on surrounding areas as a core city is of great significance.

By comparing GDP primacy[1] of cities in the Yangtze River Delta (Figure 3.1), we can see that these cities' GDP has increased steadily in recent years, however, Four City Primacy Index (FCPI) and Shanghai's primacy have been declining continuously. This indicates that a GDP growth rate is lower in regional core cities than in neighboring cities. From the GDP point of view, cities in the Yangtze River Delta are becoming less uneven in economic development level.

1.2 *Review of International Studies*

The concept of growth poles allows talents, technologies, energies, funds and other factors to be concentrated in developed regions, due to polarization effect. Innovation results and economic drivers are then transferred to surrounding areas through spreading effect. Rodwin argued that growth poles are economic centers formed by spatial agglomeration of related

[1] Urban primacy = primate city's GDP/secondary city's GDP; Four City Primacy Index (FCPI) = primate city's GDP/GDP of the next four cities following the primate city.

industries, and they can promote development of surrounding hinterlands and other industries, due to their strong innovation growth capabilities and economic effects.

The "core-periphery" theory is a relatively systematic and comprehensive model. The theory constructs a complete dual economic system, which includes the core and periphery. Dual structure is prominent in early stages of economic development. Core regions are generally considered dominant and have relatively favorable development conditions, while periphery regions are usually dominated, and have relatively backward conditions for development and economy.

1.3 *Review of Domestic Research*

Wu Liangyong (1996) explored sustainable development of China's megalopolises by studying Beijing, Shanghai and Guangzhou, and proposed a possible development path for these cities, to develop from single core metropolises to megalopolitan areas.[2] Shi Yishao (1999) reviewed China's program of construction of satellite towns, and recommended a model by which satellite towns are built in China's megalopolises, by studying successful cases of innovation in spatial organization models, adopted by major cities across the world.[3]

The three mechanisms of regional economic impact was summed up, namely, by point, by line and by surface, thereby the economic impact theory of regional economic development was systematically expounded. The two economic impact mechanisms of finance are as follows: one is bottom-up economic impact that naturally shapes financial growth poles by the power of market, and the other is top-down economic impact that facilitates and promotes growth using the power of government. A selected number of indicators were used to measure the size of urban

---

[2]Wu Liangyong: Towards the 21st century — The future of sustainable development in China's megalopolitan areas — Taking Beijing, Shanghai and Guangzhou as examples. *City Planning Review*, 1996 (4).

[3]Shi Yishao: From monocentric city to polycentric city — Spatial organization model of megalopolitan development in China. *Urban Planning Forum*, 1999 (3).

economic impact which resulted in analysis and comparison of Shanghai and Beijing's urban economic impact using factor analysis.

2. *Analysis of Core Factors for Development of Core Cities*

Every great economic paradigm requires three elements — communication media, driving energy and transportation system — and each of these interact with the other as a whole.

Core cities are closely connected with surrounding cities and economic hinterlands through "agglomeration" and "economic impact". Industries, capital, talents, raw materials, science and technology, information and other resources in an economic region are constantly concentrated in the core city because of its economies of scale, market benefits, talent benefits and infrastructure benefits. The core city's economic productivity level continues to improve thanks to polarization effect, and rapid economic growth further strengthens the core city's role in driving regional economic growth.

2.1 *Core Elements for Development of Core Cities in the Industrial Economy Era: Resources and Spatial Distance*

Industrial economy features transition from closed management to professional labor division, and focuses more on collaboration among people. As opposed to agriculture, machinery industry integrates capital, manpower, material, and scientific and technological strength, and represents economies of scale with agglomeration effect. It objectively requires production to be organized based on socialization, specialization and cooperation, and needs industrial agglomeration, convenient transportation, and good public infrastructure, as well as a large consumer population and free market circulation. During industrialization, enterprises tend to be geographically concentrated in one area, leading to spatial concentration of economic factors such as labor and capital. Such concentration facilitates specialization and cooperation among similar enterprises and results in fierce competition, thus promoting enterprise innovation.

2.2 *Core Elements for Urban Development in High-Speed Railway Era: Resource and Time Distance*

High-speed rail is a modern means of transportation characterized by large flow, high density and public popularity. It promotes large-scale transfer and flow of passengers among cities, thus creating exchange of capital, technology and information among cities it connects. It also indirectly facilitates development of various economic activities in cities along high-speed rail lines.

High-speed rail allows economic factors to flow very quickly, thus shortening distance between cities. Distance here refers to time distance that replaces spatial distance. High-speed rail contributes to a city's development in the long run, and creates a huge impact on the city rather than just one or two programs.

2.3 *Core Elements for Core Cities in the "Internet Plus" Era: Innovation Resources and Time-Space Network*

The Internet of Things platform connects people, devices, logistics networks, natural resources, consumption habits, production lines, recycling flows and all aspects of economic and social life, through various software and sensors, providing a large amount of data for all nodes (i.e. business, home, means of transportation) in a timely and effective manner. In turn, modern technology methods analyze Big Data to dramatically increase production efficiency and cut marginal production and sales costs throughout the economy. Thus, free access to the Internet is important for improving collaboration among people, core cities in urban agglomerations comprehensively influence and drive the development of surrounding cities and areas, and such influence is transferred through different factors.

3. *Economic Impact of Core Cities on Surrounding Areas*

3.1 *Economic Impact on Surrounding Areas*

- Related industry effect

  Initial development of urban industries is not complicated, but with continuous segmentation of industrial structure, urban industrial systems become increasingly complex and complement each other to a certain extent. Functions of urban systems are continuously enhanced among these industries, accelerating agglomeration effect of urban economy. Taking an industry for example, from a horizontal perspective, it includes manufacturers that provide complementary products, or other enterprises that can provide related skills and technical support. From a vertical perspective, it includes related enterprises in the industrial chain, such as those engaged in product service, component production and equipment.

- Gradient transfer effect

  In the development process of an urban agglomeration economy, urban agglomeration diseconomy greatly increases costs of industrial development, and consumes marginal output congestion costs for industries. High energy-consuming and labor-intensive industries that use more energy and raw materials, adversely impact the environment, and yield products with low added value, will lose their place in a city due to higher land costs, rising labor costs and increasing new expenses.

- Industrial agglomeration effect

  Industrial agglomeration refers to the situation where an industry and its related industries or different types of industries support one another, and aggregate in a geographical area. Urbanization effect amounts to agglomeration effect generated among different enterprises from different industries, and among different behavioral subjects. It refers to positive and negative effects caused by overall environment of economic activities, on the results of economic subjects' activities in a region.

- Urban agglomeration linkage effect

  Urban agglomerations and industrial clusters are closely linked; and the former provides a main gathering place for the latter's development. An outstanding economic environment for urban agglomerations provides a strong impetus for development of industrial clusters, which in turn helps urban agglomerations play a multiplier effect. There are also some differences between the two. Industrial clusters help enterprises take root in local places, and emphasize development of large, medium and small-sized enterprises in urban agglomerations, rather than focus on large-sized enterprises alone.

3.2 *Mechanisms by which the Impact is Realized*

The economic impact of core cities on surrounding areas can be realized through a number of different mechanisms, such as by point, by line, by surface and by network. Opening up of economy and free flow of resources are important conditions for a core city's economic impact on surrounding areas, which is realized mainly through transportation, information, and interpersonal relationship networks (Figure 3.2).

- Economic impact by point

  Large and medium-sized cities situated in the center impose their economic impact on surrounding areas. By virtue of high concentration of science and technology, capital and manpower, as well as high level of economic development and modernization, large and medium-sized cities are relatively more advanced in all aspects as opposed to surrounding areas; however, they most often lack natural resources and labor force.

  Natural resources and labor force are often subject to one-way economic impact. However, technologies often flow from core cities to surrounding areas, and capital is bound to flow to areas with high investment efficiency. In other words, capital mainly flows from surrounding underdeveloped areas to core cities.

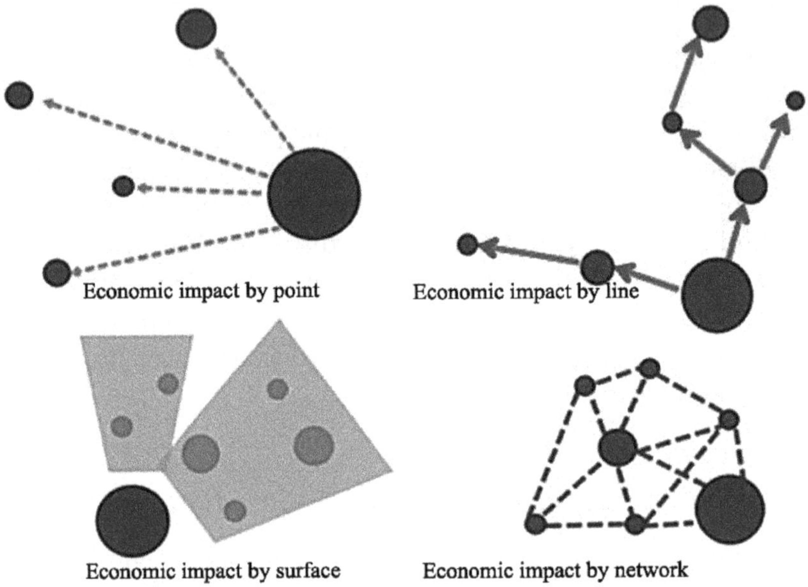

Figure 3.2 Four Mechanisms of Economic Impact

- Economic impact by line

  Lines associated with this mechanism have many advantages, including frequent flow of people among different regions, convenient transportation, fast flow of economic resources, and relatively more open information industry economy. Fewer transaction costs incurred on the lines lead to higher efficiency of economic impact. From a transmission point of view, flow of natural resources in this mechanism varies.

- Economic impact by surface

  Development and mutual influence of the above two mechanisms eventually create a center, and at its core, it relies on high economic impact level of economic development and modernized construction of cities, or areas situated on the lines. Small cities form a source of economic impact in the center of these areas, but there is a wider gap between them and big cities with strong economic impact. This mechanism enables economic impact by surface as it extends its reach to surrounding areas, and these cities influence each other.

- Economic impact by network

  Functional layout of urban networking space is a regional spatial structure formed by networking of various factors through exchange and integration, while core urban areas, counties (cities), and core towns act as network nodes. Core cities composed of main cities, sub-cities and clusters impact and drive small and medium-sized cities through factor flow network, while small and medium-sized cities impact and drive broad areas within their coverage through the network, thereby forming a functional system that features free flow of factors and optimal allocation of resources in the region, thereby achieving coordinated development of regional economy and society.

4. *Measurement of the Size and Reach of the Economic Impact of Core Cities on Surrounding Areas*

4.1 *Model Method*

Breaking-point theory used to analyze interaction between different cities or regions is required to measure changes in the reach of a core city's economic impact on surrounding areas. This theory combines the size of the city's economic impact with the city size and distance from its neighboring city, in order to measure the reach and size of the city's economic impact. Reilly W. J. (1929)'s law of gravitation is similar to Newton's law of universal gravitation. Converse P. D. (1930) proposed the following calculation formula based on Reilly's theory:

$$\begin{cases} d_A = \dfrac{D_{AB}}{1+\sqrt{P_B/P_A}}, \\ d_B = \dfrac{D_{AB}}{1+\sqrt{P_A/P_B}}. \end{cases}$$

d_A and d_B are distances from breaking point to city A and city B, respectively. D_{AB} is the linear distance between city A and city B. P_A and P_B are populations of city *A* and city *B*, respectively. The formula uses urban population to indicate a city's size and attractiveness, and the latter is truly reflected by its overall strength. Hence, the urban centrality strength indicator system that replaces the population as an evaluation indicator should be selected for quantitative evaluation, as it reflects the city's overall strength.

In the field strength formula, F_A is the size of city *A*'s economic impact at breaking point, P_A is city *A*'s size, and d_A is the distance from city *A* to the breaking point.

$$F_A = \frac{P_A}{d_A^{\,2}}.$$

4.2 *Empirical Analysis*

In this section, principal component analysis is used to measure urban centrality strength. An indicator system is established to evaluate urban competitiveness by selecting 35 indicators (Table 3.1) in terms of economic development, social, science and education development, residents' quality of life, infrastructure, etc. Principal component analysis of SPSS software is used to obtain and sort comprehensive scores (Table 3.2) of indicators for cities situated in the Yangtze River Delta.

To ensure the original data's order, original data columns are processed for data conversion using the [1, 8.255] mapping interval. Map of urban centrality strengths is displayed in Figure 3.3.

In this case, spatial distance is used as economic distance, mainly based on the following reasons: In the service economy of the Yangtze River Delta, expressways, railways, flights and waterways on which the flow of people, logistics and commerce rely, extend in all directions, forming an intensive transportation network. Inter-city transportation conditions do not vary greatly among cities other than Zhoushan. Time distance is directly proportional to spatial distance. After transportation infrastructures are operational, the one-city effect is increasingly apparent.

Table 3.1 Urban Centrality Strength Indicator System

Indicator category	**Specific indicators**
Economic development and benefits	Gross GDP, GDP per capita, total retail sales of social consumer goods, local financial revenue, total investment in fixed assets, total use of foreign capital in the year, gross industrial amount per capita, realized profit per RMB100 gross output, contribution of non-agricultural industries to GDP, gross industrial output per capita, profit per RMB100 assets and unemployment rate.
Social, science and education development	Total urban population, proportion of urban non-agricultural population in total population, proportion of population receiving subsistence allowance among total population, natural population growth rate, proportion of scientific research and education expenses in financial expenditure, number of college students per 10,000 people, number of people with intermediate technical titles and above per 10,000 employees and number of doctors per 10,000 people.
Residents' quality of life	Total wages per capita, savings per capita at year end, domestic power consumption per capita, domestic water consumption per capita, household gas penetration rate, number of Internet users, and number of mobile phone users.
Infrastructure and environment	Built-up area, number of public buses per 10,000 people, greening rate of built-up area, industrial SO_2 removal rate, total business volume of postal and telecommunications services, urban road area, compliance rate of industrial waste-water discharge, and environmentally-safe disposal rate of domestic garbage.

Breaking points from Shanghai to 15 cities in the Yangtze River Delta are calculated by substituting each of the 15 cities' urban centrality strengths into the breaking-point formula (Table 3.3).

Calculation results show that field strengths of breaking points from Shanghai to Suzhou, Wuxi, Changzhou, Hangzhou and Nanjing

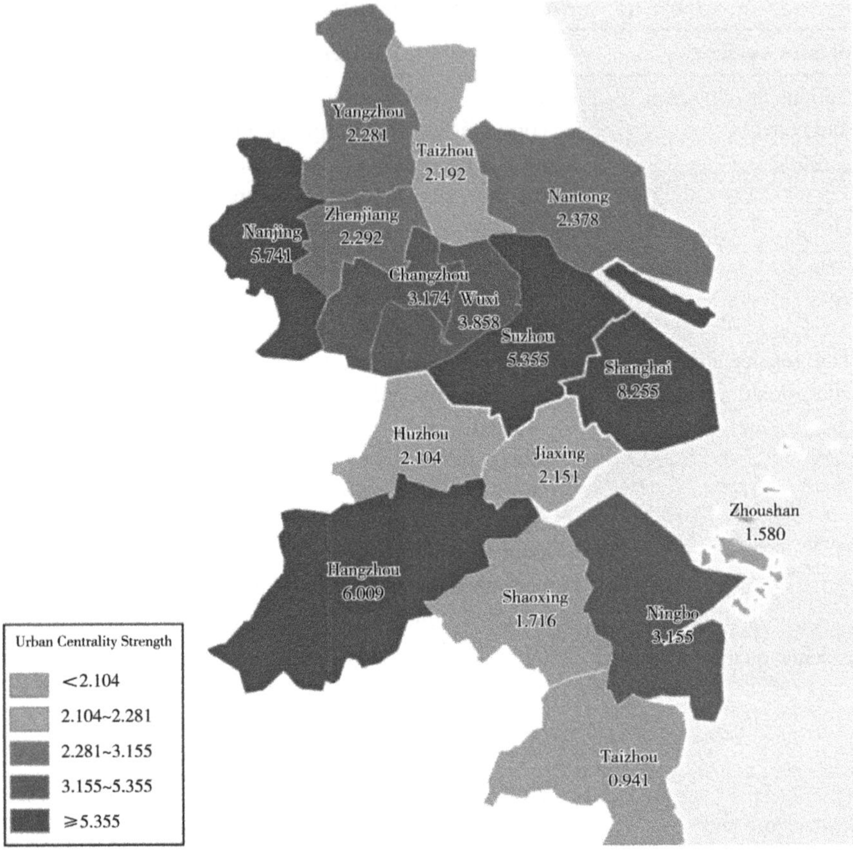

Figure 3.3 Urban Centrality Strengths of 16 Cities in the Yangtze River Delta

are relatively stronger than those from Shanghai to other cities in the Yangtze River Delta. This is because these cities boast better social and economic development effects, as well as higher development of science, education, culture and health. These cities also rank among the top in terms of comprehensive score, among 16 cities in the Yangtze River Delta. Field strengths of breaking points from Shanghai to Jiaxing and Huzhou are obviously stronger than those from Shanghai to other cities of similar size (Table 3.4). As the two cities are closer to

Table 3.2 Ranking of Urban Centrality Strengths of 16 Cities in the Yangtze River Delta

City	Comprehensive score	Urban centrality strength	Ranking
Shanghai	5.432	8.255	1
Hangzhou	3.186	6.009	2
Nanjing	2.918	5.741	3
Suzhou	2.532	5.355	4
Wuxi	1.035	3.858	5
Changzhou	0.351	3.174	6
Ningbo	0.332	3.155	7
Nantong	−0.445	2.378	8
Zhenjiang	−0.531	2.292	9
Yangzhou	−0.542	2.281	10
Taizhou (Jiangsu)	−0.631	2.192	11
Jiaxing	−0.672	2.151	12
Huzhou	−0.719	2.104	13
Shaoxing	−1.107	1.716	14
Zhoushan	−1.243	1.58	15
Taizhou (Zhejiang)	−1.882	0.941	16

Shanghai, they have an innate advantage as they are subject to Shanghai's economic impact.

5. *Changes in the Size of the Economic Impact of Core Cities on Surrounding Areas*

5.1 *Definition of Core Concept*

On the one hand, traditional industries in a core city constantly move to hinterlands as technological progress drives industrial upgrade in the city; on the other hand, the city's gradual loss of economies of scale leads some resources to migrate to surrounding areas due to rising land prices

Table 3.3 Breaking Points from Shanghai to 15 Cities in the Yangtze River Delta

City	Distance away from Shanghai (km)	Breaking-point distance (km)
Shanghai	—	—
Nanjing	301.00	136.87
Suzhou	84.00	41.27
Wuxi	126.00	56.76
Changzhou	165.00	70.37
Zhenjiang	237.00	91.77
Nantong	585.00	229.07
Yangzhou	402.00	155.42
Taizhou (Jiangsu)	466	177.97
Hangzhou	203	102.66
Ningbo	374	157.31
Jiaxing	110	38.96
Huzhou	170	58.71
Shaoxing	266	87.68
Zhoushan	368	112.64
Taizhou (Zhejiang)	580	160.13

Table 3.4 Field Strengths of Breaking Points from Shanghai to Other Cities in the Yangtze River Delta

Nanjing	0.044064034	Hangzhou	0.078331089
Suzhou	0.484689959	Ningbo	0.033356272
Wuxi	0.256230069	Jiaxing	0.543791189
Changzhou	0.166724033	Huzhou	0.239465128
Zhenjiang	0.098028744	Shaoxing	0.107378012
Nantong	0.015731505	Zhoushan	0.065064104
Yangzhou	0.034172674	Taizhou (Zhejiang)	0.032194659
Taizhou (Jiangsu)	0.026061652		

and living costs. This is how the core city imposes its economic impact on surrounding areas. The core city's productivity level continues to improve and it achieves rapid economic growth thanks to polarization effect. This growth further strengthens the position of the core city as a source of economic impact on surrounding areas.

5.2 *Model Method*

There are many methods for measuring the size of a core city's economic impact on surrounding areas. Linear regression method is used in this section, where we considered relevance between utilization level of foreign capital (economic extraversion index) and GDP growth, among several cities situated in the Yangtze River Delta with high economic development in urban agglomeration. We selected four cities (Shanghai, Suzhou, Hangzhou, and Nanjing) with high urban centrality strengths among cities in the Yangtze River Delta, based on research results described in the last section, and analyzed their GDP and actual amount of foreign capital attracted in the past. We converted data into proportional coefficients using 2008 as a benchmark. This conversion makes the data more concise and intuitive.

5.3 *Empirical Analysis*

There are many ways to measure economic development. Here, we analyzed GDP as an important indicator and made the following assumption: A core city has huge economic impact within an urban agglomeration and its economic growth drives or undermines neighboring cities' economic development in varying degrees. We did regression of the above-mentioned data and verified how reasonable it is through testing.

We calculated GDP proportional coefficients using the cities' GDP data with 2008 as a benchmark, as displayed in Figure 3.4. Sampling the Yangtze River Delta's urban agglomeration data from 2008 to 2014, we measured changes in the size of economic impact of Shanghai, Suzhou, Hangzhou and Nanjing, as core cities, on surrounding areas (Figure 3.5).

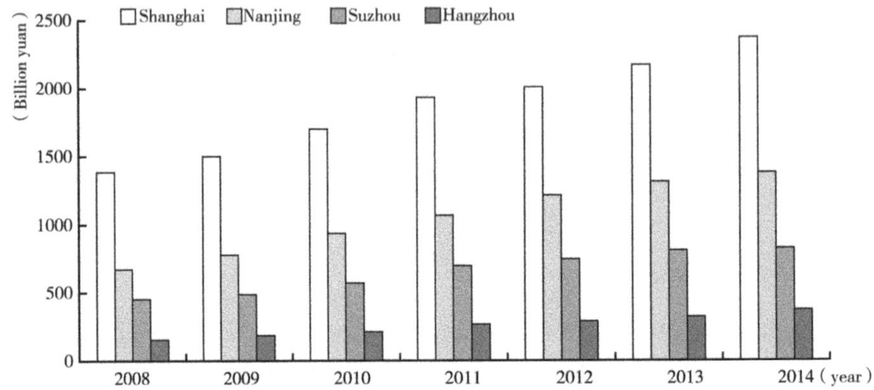

Figure 3.4 GDP of Four Major Cities in the Yangtze River Delta from 2008 to 2014

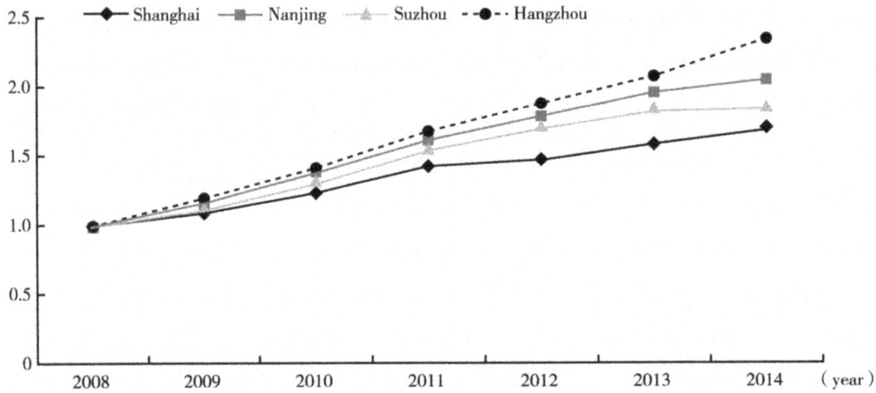

Figure 3.5 Changes in GDP Proportional Coefficients of Four Major Cities in the Yangtze River Delta

We used Stata to do regression of the above data and obtain estimated coefficients. Due to space constraints, we cannot have a more detailed discussion of all regression results; hence, we only listed the unary linear regression of Nanjing and Shanghai as an example.

Based on software results: $ynj = 1.518029 \times ysh - 0.5002283$ and it passed the prominence parameter test. Results are explained as follows: Nanjing's economic growth maintained a rising trend with slope of

Source	SS	df	MS		
Model	0.94463514	1	0.94463514	Number of obs	= 7
Residual	0.010870662	5	0.002174132	*F* (1, 5)	= 434.49
				Prob > *F*	= 0.0000
Total	0.955505802	6	0.159250967	R-squared	= 0.9886
				Adj R-squared	= 0.9863
				Root MSE	= 0.04663

Y	Coef.	Std. Err.	*t*	*P*>|*t*|	[95% Conf.	Interval]
Shanghai	1.518029	0.0728268	20.84	0.000	1.330822	1.705236
_cons	-0.5002283	0.1002451	-4.99	0.004	-0.7579165	-0.2425401

1.518029 and intercept of –0.5002283 from 2008 to 2014. In other words, Shanghai's GDP growth by 1% will drive Nanjing's GDP growth by 1.518029%. Linear regression results between Shanghai and other cities in the Yangtze River Delta were similarly calculated:

$$\text{Suzhou: ysz} = 1.292587 \times \text{ysh} - 0.2680489$$
$$\text{Hangzhou: yhz} = 1.854225 \times \text{ysh} - 0.8644467$$

Based on the above results, we can see that Shanghai as a core city, has strong economic impact on surrounding areas. Based on our regression results, when Shanghai's GDP grows by 1%, Suzhou's GDP grows by 1.292587%, Hangzhou's by 1.854225%, and Nanjing's by 1.518029%. The core city's growth has driven growth of peripheral economic areas at a higher speed, proving that our assumption of a core city's economic impact on surrounding areas can be validated from the GDP growth angle.

Amid China's current labor-intensive but capital-poor economic conditions, ability of foreign capital to spread and flow has become an important factor for a core city's economic impact on surrounding areas. Table 3.5 shows actual utilization of foreign capital in major cities in the Yangtze River Delta.

Using the same method, we converted the above data into proportional coefficients and then used Stata for linear regression, obtaining the following calculation results:

Our regression results show that data of cities in the Yangtze River Delta have good relevance and higher stability. Shanghai's economic impact has widely benefited surrounding cities, showing that Shanghai

Table 3.5 Actual Utilization of Foreign Capital in Five Major Cities in the Yangtze River Delta (Unit: USD 100 million)

City	2008	2009	2010	2011	2012	2013	2014
Shanghai	100.84	105.38	111.21	178.71	151.85	167.80	181.66
Suzhou	25.17	21.96	23.13	37.69	91.65	86.98	81.20
Hangzhou	33.12	38.80	43.56	59.89	49.78	52.76	63.35
Ningbo	25.17	21.96	23.13	37.69	28.50	32.75	40.25
Nanjing	22.61	22.82	26.76	47.09	41.30	40.33	32.91

Table 3.6 Regression Results of Actual Utilization of Foreign Capital in Four Cities

City	Coefficient	Intercept	Passed the test
Suzhou	2.622423	−1.618253	No
Hangzhou	0.9013602	0.1982885	Yes
Ningbo	0.7578671	0.1178445	Yes
Nanjing	1.033288	0.0172564	Yes

has been increasingly "decentralized" in the Yangtze River Delta Economic Zone, and the Yangtze River Delta Economic Zone is developing toward a structure of multiple core cities with economic impact on surrounding areas (Table 3.6).

6. *Conclusions and Suggestions*

6.1 *Main Conclusions*

By comparing GDP primacy of cities situated in the Yangtze River Delta, we found that these cities' GDP has increased steadily in recent years; however, FCPI and Shanghai's primacy have been declining continuously. This indicates that GDP growth of a regional core city is slower than that of its nearby cities. Considering GDP alone, cities in the Yangtze River Delta fall in a "decentralization" trend. Shanghai's economic impact has widely benefited surrounding cities, due to which Shanghai has become increasingly "decentralized" in the Yangtze River Delta Economic Zone, and the Yangtze River Delta Economic Zone is developing toward a structure of multiple core cities with economic impact on surrounding areas.

6.2 *Policy Recommendations for Shanghai to Improve its Economic Impact on Surrounding Areas*

6.2.1 Actively respond to the "decentralization" trend and improve its economic impact on surrounding areas

In the "Internet Plus" era, basic goal of enhancing Shanghai's economic impact on surrounding areas, amounts to decentralization supported by "Internet Plus" technologies. Specific efforts include shifting from inward agglomeration to outward diffusion, avoiding excessive population concentration, providing equal public services, changing excessive agglomeration, balancing regional economic development, and reducing differences between urban and rural areas and among different regions through "decentralized" development model featuring urban–rural balance. This helps ensure equal strengths in infrastructures, job opportunities, social security and medical conditions among large, medium and small-sized cities, and between urban and rural areas. It also leads to formation of Yangtze River Delta urban agglomerations characterized by moderate size, resident-friendly environment, reasonable distribution and balanced development. To achieve this goal, "cross-industry" theme should be added to Shanghai's roadmap to enhance its economic impact on surrounding areas. Shanghai should break through space limitations on the administrative division and industry restrictions on sector categories, and leverage "Internet Plus" technologies.

6.2.2 Achieve spatial cross-industry development and optimize resource flow model

Shanghai's cross-regional development is driven by the "pole", and Shanghai's position as a regional economic growth pole has not changed. In the "Internet Plus" era, the "point-to-area" development model of regional growth pole is shifting to the "network linkage" model of regional balanced development. The reach of Shanghai's economic impact on surrounding areas is no longer confined to the Yangtze River Delta, and extending the reach of its economic impact in a more flat and borderless manner is a spatial path for Shanghai's urban development in the "Internet Plus" era.

6.2.3 Reconstruct industrial development pattern and enhance value creation ability

Cross-industry integration between the Internet and traditional industries is an important development direction for "Internet Plus". At its core, integration is aimed at comprehensively applying the Internet's innovation achievements to various economic and social fields, and improving real economy's innovation capability to achieve a change in thinking, technology and model, in both economy and society. Therefore, Shanghai has to capitalize on diversified and mixed industrial forms, and break through traditional industrial barriers, to enhance and expand the city's economic impact on surrounding areas in the "Internet Plus" era.

To realize cross-industry integration, Shanghai should strengthen the "Internet Plus" approach on cross-industry integration, enhance industries' value creation ability, and improve industries' cross-industry economic impact, based on original advanced manufacturing industry and modern service industry.

6.2.4 Leverage platform's interconnection effect and support technological innovation and upgrade

The "Internet Plus" era is strongly represented by constant changes in new generation information technologies, such as mobile Internet, cloud computing, Big Data, Internet of Things, etc. With accelerated application of fiber-optic broadband networks and rapid development of fourth-generation mobile communication technology, new-generation information networks are becoming more integrated, intelligent and convergent. This has led to a big leap toward realizing collaborative innovation between traditional and emerging industries, optimal allocation of integrated online and offline resources, and economic sharing featuring re-engineering of business models.

II. Changes in Core Cities' Functions

Cyberspace comprising of resilient elements, such as computers, smart phones, e-commerce platforms, cloud services, and network infrastructure, has changed the setting of location and distance by traditional spatial economics. Cities such as Detroit that deviate from global industrial chain and information superhighway are marginalized. Cities such as Silicon Valley and Tsukuba that are positioned as information network hubs and enjoy geo-spatial advantages are upgraded to new core cities typical to the "Internet Plus" era. Against the backdrop of globally dispersed manufacturing and services, global cities such as New York and London that are home to high-end service industries, join the ranks of global core cities.

1. *Impact of the "Internet Plus" Era on Urban Functions*

A prominent imbalance takes place in spatial distribution of economic activities, as evidenced by the fact that 50% of global economic activities are concentrated in metropolises, whose land area accounts for 1.5% of global land area. Based on existence of increasing returns to scale and transportation costs in production, as well as consumer preferences for diversified products and transportation costs, the "new economic geography" theory proposes a theoretical framework to interpret the function of urban agglomeration, wherein agglomerations have larger production and market sizes and higher factor prices. Under optimum conditions, higher factor prices in agglomerations tend to lead to higher labor productivity; or else, driven by profit maximization, manufacturers would choose areas with lower factor prices.

1.1 *Mechanisms for Realizing Urban Agglomeration's Function*

Urban agglomeration's function is to improve productivity and this is achieved by three mechanisms. The first is sharing mechanism, that is, a city has a better function of input sharing. Manufacturers get returns to scale and reduce average costs, while suppliers provide specialized products and services based on differentiated customer demands. The second is matching mechanism, that is, a city has a better function for matching production factors. It is easier for businesses to find necessary inputs and workers with specific skills, which in turn is more likely to help workers find suitable jobs. Lastly, the third is learning mechanism, that is, a city has more learning opportunities. Spatial agglomeration is conducive to knowledge spillovers and promotes learning and innovation between enterprises and workers, and also among different sectors.

1.2 *Impact of the "Internet Plus" Era on Economic Growth*

The "Internet Plus" concept has effectively expanded a city's size and enhanced the city's quality, making itself a new driver for urban development, following industrialization. Based on data collected in 2010 and 2013, McKinsey Global Institute (MGI) proposed an iGDP indicator to compare and measure a country's Internet economy size. The iGDP indicator uses expenditure method for calculating GDP. It adds up all activities linked to creation and use of Internet networks and services: consumption by individuals (including hardware, software, Internet access, and e-commerce), public expenditure (including infrastructure), business investment in Internet technologies, and the country's trade balance in Internet-related goods and services. In 2010, China's Internet economy was just 3.3% of its GDP, lagging behind most advanced economies. But by 2013, China's iGDP rose to 4.4%, indicating that Chinese Internet economy's contribution to its GDP ranked fifth after the United Kingdom, South Korea, Japan, and Sweden, surpassing the United States, France, Germany, Canada, and Italy (Figure 3.6).

MGI selected six representative sectors and predicted the Internet's contribution to GDP growth for each of the six sectors by using 2025 GDP projections from IHS (Information Handling Services) as baseline. They estimated productivity gains by assessing the cost base affected by the Internet, adoption rate, and potential cost savings. They further estimated new market creation by assessing market penetration of new

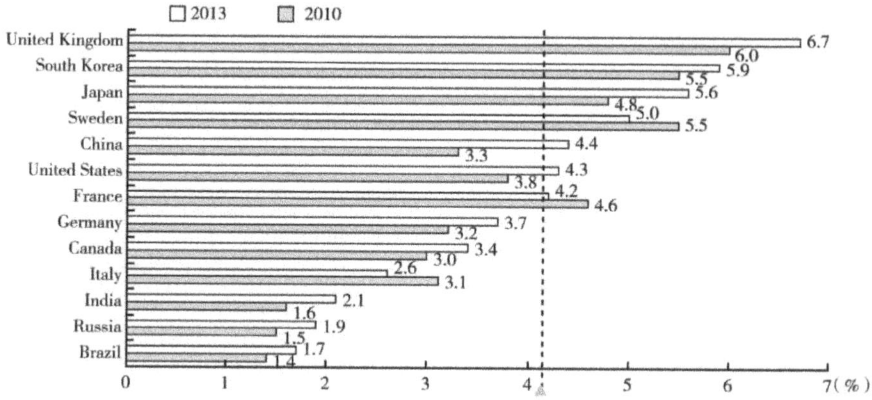

Figure 3.6 iGDP Indicator: Internet-related Expenditure as % of Respective Country's GDP

Notes: C2C (consumer-to-consumer) e-retailing category in most countries primarily consists of secondary-market transactions conducted by individuals and is negligible. In China, however, it contains sales achieved by small enterprises and micro-businesses that have not yet been registered. If C2C is included, China's iGDP would be 7%, much higher than that of any G7 country.

Source: McKinsey Global Institute. China's Digital Transformation: The Internet's Impact on Productivity and Growth (2014).

offerings, ratio of incremental market growth vs. existing market, and value addition of the new market. Given the finance sector's new capabilities to allocate capital more effectively, the prediction is that the Internet's contribution to China's GDP growth will reach 7–22% from 2013 to 2025 (Figure 3.7).

1.3 *Impact of the "Internet Plus" Era on Urban Agglomeration's Function*

Online shopping has sparked e-retail's explosive growth, creating new consumption bases. Impact of the "Internet Plus" on urban agglomeration's function is reflected in transformation from consumer-oriented, to entrepreneurship and innovation, and it can be seen in transition from GDP-driven political achievement philosophy, to orienting toward O2O public products and services. The "Internet Plus" and its effects can also

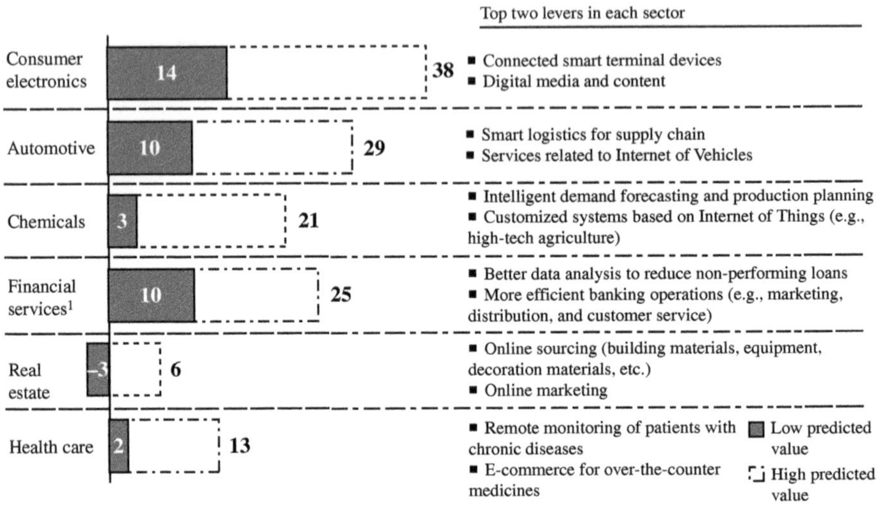

Figure 3.7 The Internet's Contribution to GDP Growth for Six Representative Sectors, from 2013 to 2025

Note: Effects of capital reallocation on the economy are not included.
Source: McKinsey Global Institute. China's Digital Transformation: The Internet's Impact on Productivity and Growth (2014).

be seen in the shift from extensive connotative growth based on cheap factor costs to smart growth based on productivity, innovation, and consumption. The "Internet Plus" influences urban agglomeration's function in terms of three dimensions — "new driver-new model-new pattern".

1.3.1 New driver for urban development: Informatization–globalization–deindustrialization

Informatization promotes globalization, leading to separation of production services from manufacturing and assembly. When developed countries move manufacturing to developing countries' cities, their local cities enter the de-industrialization process with rapid growth and constant upgrade of production services. Through "learning–interaction–innovation", global industrial networks and innovation incubators, together with face-to-face communications that contribute to social honesty and reciprocal exchange of information have, by means of synergy, promoted spatial reconstruction of cities and regions. This has led to intensive clustering of "data–information–knowledge-personalized information".

1.3.2 New model for urban transportation: Hub airport–high-speed railway–expressway–rail transit

An anchor airport symbolizes a global city's high-level position, and functions as a central hub for intercontinental air traffic and short-distance high-speed traffic. High-speed railway connects node cities as a new means of transportation, offering such advantages as high speed, large capacity, better convenience, low energy consumption, less pollution, and smaller area. An expressway network is a primary transportation mode suitable for a 2-hour commute circle thanks to its "flexibility and accessibility". Subway or light rail is a major rapid public transport mode for travelling from city outskirts to central business districts.

1.3.3 New pattern for urban system: Mono-centric–multi-polarization–networking

The traditional centripetal urban spatial structure is transforming into a low-density, multi-core urban spatial structure. One evident trend is formation of networked urban complexes consisting of multiple cities and small towns, through networks of private vehicle transportation and communications, such as metropolitan areas in the US. The other significant trend is expansion of multi-core urban areas into mega-urban areas such as Paris Region, Greater London and so on.

2. *Research on Law of Global Urban Function Changes*

In a globalized world bestrewn with diversified urban expansion patterns and increasingly profound economic integrations, cities and regions not only experience significant structural changes, but also undergo accelerated dispersion of economic development, signaling obvious regional characteristics. Thus, localization and regionalization are concurrent drivers along with globalization.

2.1 *Industrial Gradient Transfer and Traditional Flying Geese Paradigm*

Urban industrial transformation and urban spatial restructuring are closely related. Theoretical research on industrial transfer can be traced back to the "flying geese paradigm" developed during 1930s. The traditional "flying geese paradigm" epitomizes economic development in East Asia, with Japan portrayed as the "lead goose". It uses a ladder-type system of industrial division of labor, featuring "technology-intensive/high value-added industries — capital technology-intensive industries — labor-intensive industries".

Reduction in transportation and information exchange costs brought about by technological progress has led to continuous increase in scale of international production, investment, trade and personnel activities. To stay competitive in the world, multinationals outsource low value-added production processes to countries with lower labor and land costs, or increase outward foreign direct investment to establish production plants overseas. This leaves only R&D, design and marketing, management of innovative products, as well as other high value-added processes to their respective countries. Industrial transfer as a trend has expanded from manufacturing to services.

2.2 *Deepening of International Division of Labor and Post-Flying Geese Paradigm*

As the process and result of resilience capital accumulation and development in geographic space, a city takes on increasingly important and continuously updated functions in the process of globalizing management, finance, services, production and communications. In essence, a global city can control few key sectors of global economy, such as corporate headquarters, international finance, global transportation and communications, advanced business services, and so on. At its core, the global city follows the trend of deepening international division of labor, and focuses on global integration, management and control in the context of dispersed production space (Figure 3.8).

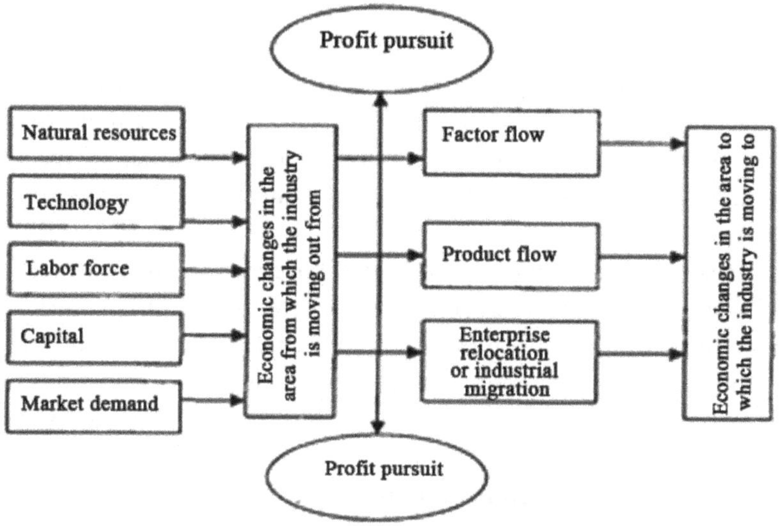

Figure 3.8 Globalization-driven Coexistence of Vertical and Horizontal Division of Labor in Manufacturing

In the global production network, regional economic factors reveal a new threshold for spatial agglomeration and a new diffusion screening model, through restructuring of division of labor, construction of transportation infrastructure, and communication information technology platform. Globalization enables increasing integration and interdependence of regional economies based on division of labor. A core city's agglomeration function grows more complex and heterogeneous based on the measure of how embedded it is in the network. The traditional "flying geese paradigm", which was dominated by vertical international division of labor, has gradually given way to the "post-flying geese paradigm" after East Asia's economic crisis in 1997. The new paradigm emphasizes not only differences among economies, but also global economy's role as a community.

2.3 *Global City Regions and How the Flying Geese Paradigm Has Evolved*

A global city region is spatially characterized by a diversified, multi-core internal structure, sprawling suburbs, and continuous hinterland systems.

The global city region's hierarchical structure includes a core metropolitan area, a hinterland metropolitan area, and several towns. As the center of the core metropolitan area, the global city has a highest order of magnitude and threshold for agglomeration. However, the city region's overall order of magnitude is determined by agglomeration effect of the core metropolitan area and supporting power of hinterland urban agglomeration systems.

An urban hierarchy that is established based on the order of magnitude of a city's functions is engendering differentiated, poly-centric city networks influenced by informatization, globalization, and de-industrialization. City networks that consist of multiple nodes and connections on a global spatial level, remain a central-peripheral urban hierarchy on a regional level. The "network + hierarchy" spatial structure indicates that local city regions form agglomerations with clear structures and definite labor division through functional networks, and are then linked to global networks through functional organizations (Figure 3.9).

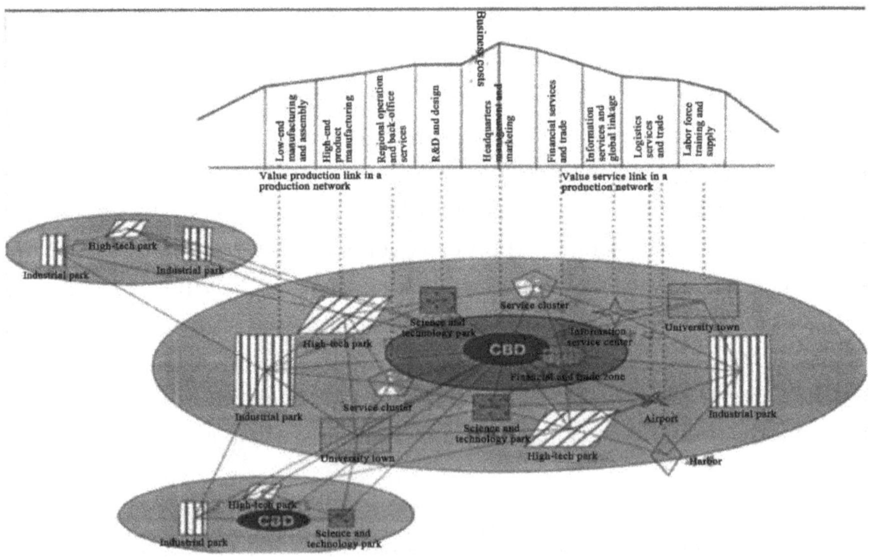

Figure 3.9 From Global Production Networks to General Model of Spatial Organization for Production in Metropolitan Areas

3. *Analysis of Changes in Domestic Core Cities' Functions*

2007 saw large-scale industrial transfer in China's southeastern coastal regions, especially in the Pearl River Delta, due to rapidly rising land and housing prices, increasing labor costs, and higher pressure on energy conservation and emission reduction. In 2010, Foxconn moved inwards into Central China, from Shenzhen to Henan and from Kunshan to Chongqing, and established a production and R&D base in Hunan, leading to upstream and downstream industrial chain transfer. The number of employees in Foxconn's Shenzhen factory reduced from nearly 400,000 to a little more than 100,000. At the end of 2008, an RMB 4 trillion stimulus package was announced in response to the international financial crisis, and more than half of it was put in railways, highways, airports and other major transportation infrastructure. In 2009, investment in transportation infrastructure in eastern, central and western regions increased by 17.79 times, 26.09 times and 35.19 times, respectively, and growth in western and central regions far exceeded than in the eastern region. Eastern coastal cities experienced economic slowdown and industry hollowing-out probably because of move-out of traditional industries and lagging development of high-end industries. The key is to promote industrial structure adjustment and industrial upgrade, rather than just focusing on industrial and labor transfer.

3.1 *Functional Changes in Domestic, Large and Medium-sized Cities Based on Industrial Transfer and Innovation Capability*

The changes in China's urban hierarchy reflect the effect of regional industrial transfer on a large scale. In 2012, Jones Lang LaSalle listed Chengdu, Chongqing, Dalian, Hangzhou, Nanjing, Shenyang, Suzhou, Tianjin, and Wuhan as Tier 1.5 cities in the *Top 50 Chinese Emerging Cities*. As per the *Top 60 Chinese Emerging Cities* listed in 2015, Tier 1.5 cities' status as regional commercial centers was strengthened, and Tianjin, Chongqing, Chengdu and Wuhan ranked among world's fastest growing major cities. Xi'an joined the ranks of Tier 1.5 cities as one of the fastest growing cities, and Dalian was relegated to the ranks of Tier 2 cities.

The "Internet Plus" provides new growth opportunities for Tier 2 and Tier 3 cities, and imposes new requirements for Tier 1 cities' agglomeration functions. By analyzing Big Data of e-commerce enterprises, we can see that location of large-scale e-commerce enterprises is closely related to innovation and entrepreneurship abilities of cities and regions they are situated in. Shenzhen-based Tencent Open Platform evaluated innovation and entrepreneurship abilities of Chinese cities in 2014, by using total revenue statistics of third-party developers collected from March 2013 to March 2014; and Beijing, Guangzhou and Haikou ranked the top three (Figure 3.10). Hangzhou-based AliResearch released the *Report on Development Indices of China's E-Commerce Demonstration Cities 2014*, which showed that Shenzhen's e-commerce application level ranked first

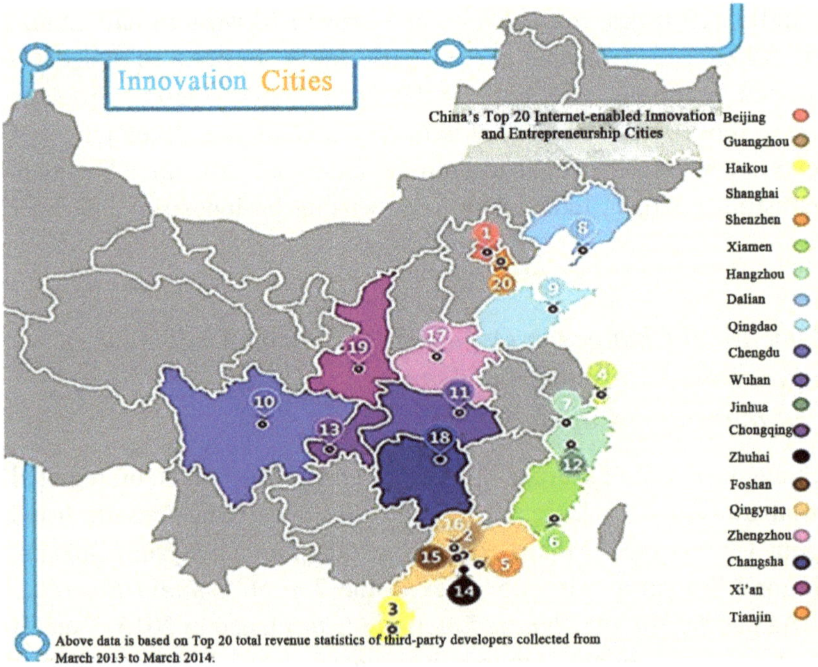

Figure 3.10 China's Top 20 Internet-enabled "Innovation and Entrepreneurship" Cities in 2014

in the country, and Hangzhou's e-commerce service level ranked No. 1 in the country.

In terms of urban and regional innovation environment evaluation, Tsinghua University's TusPark Innovation Institute released the *Research Report on Evaluation of China's Urban Innovation and Entrepreneurship Environment in 2014*, which used eight primary indicators, namely, government support, industrial development, talent environment, R&D environment, financial support, intermediary service, market environment, and innovation awareness. The report evaluated urban innovation and entrepreneurship environment by taking 154 cities in Mainland China whose GDP exceeded RMB120 billion, as samples. However, municipalities directly under central government were excluded to remove outliers (Table 3.7).

By comparing municipalities directly administered by the central government, with cities in the control group, we can see that Beijing and Shanghai ranked first and second, respectively, but each had its advantages. Beijing ranked first in six primary indicators, i.e. talent environment, R&D environment, financial support, intermediary services, market environment and innovation awareness, while Shanghai ranked first in government support and industrial development (Table 3.8).

3.2 *Changes in Spatial Equilibrium of Three Urban Agglomerations Based on Central Geographical Interpretation*

As the focus of regional developmental strategy, urban agglomeration functions as a regional economic growth pole. China's three urban agglomerations, namely, the Beijing–Tianjin–Hebei Region, the Yangtze River Delta and the Pearl River Delta, are not only three growth poles that have been driving China's economic development and industrial upgrade, but are also pilot and demonstration areas for interconnected-type smart urbanization development in the "Internet Plus" era.

In terms of the three urban agglomerations' initial endowment and spatial pattern, the Yangtze River Delta is oriented toward labor-intensive industries, and is urbanized through high concentration of urban population,

Table 3.7 China's Top 20 Cities for Innovation and Entrepreneurship Environment

Ranking	City	Administrative level	Province
1	Shenzhen	City with independent budgetary status	Guangdong
2	Guangzhou	Provincial capital	Guangdong
3	Hangzhou	Provincial capital	Zhejiang
4	Wuhan	Provincial capital	Hubei
5	Chengdu	Provincial capital	Sichuan
6	Suzhou	Prefecture-level city	Jiangsu
7	Xi'an	Provincial capital	Shaanxi
8	Nanjing	Provincial capital	Jiangsu
9	Dalian	City with independent budgetary status	Liaoning
10	Ningbo	City with independent budgetary status	Zhejiang
11	Zhengzhou	Provincial capital	Henan
12	Changsha	Provincial capital	Hunan
13	Shenyang	Provincial capital	Liaoning
14	Qingdao	City with independent budgetary status	Shandong
15	Wuxi	Prefecture-level city	Jiangsu
16	Jinan	Provincial capital	Shandong
17	Dongguan	Prefecture-level city	Guangdong
18	Hefei	Provincial capital	Anhui
19	Taiyuan	Provincial capital	Shanxi
20	Fuzhou	Provincial capital	Fujian

Source: Tsinghua University's TusPark Innovation Institute. Research Report on Evaluation of China's Urban Innovation and Entrepreneurship Environment in 2014. Tsinghua University (2014).

presenting a multi-core, multipolar, clustered spatial development path. The Beijing–Tianjin–Hebei Region is oriented toward capital-intensive industries such as iron, steel and chemicals, and is urbanized through expansion of urban built-up areas, showing a unipolar spatial development path. In this region, capital is invested efficiently in park land, production materials, and transportation costs. The Pearl River Delta is oriented toward labor-intensive industries and outward-looking economy, and is urbanized through expansion of population concentration and urban built-up areas, exhibiting a clustered path from pole-core development to point-axis

Table 3.8 Comparison between Municipalities Directly Administered by Central Government and Relevant Cities in Terms of Innovation and Entrepreneurship Environment

	2012		2013		
City	**Score**	**Ranking**	**Score**	**Ranking**	**Ranking change**
Beijing	85.87	1	100.00	1	0
Shanghai	83.25	2	90.77	2	0
Shenzhen	85.01	3	77.26	3	0
Guangzhou	76.20	4	66.65	4	0
Tianjin	70.37	5	64.11	5	+2
Suzhou	75.61	6	60.10	6	−1
Hangzhou	74.44	7	60.04	7	−1
Wuhan	64.29	8	59.17	8	+3
Chengdu	58.16	9	57.15	9	4
Chongqing	65.25	10	56.93	10	0

Source: Tsinghua University TusPark Innovation Institute. Research Report on Evaluation of China's Urban Innovation and Entrepreneurship Environment in 2014. Tsinghua University (2014).

development. The population's urbanization rate is close to 100% in Guangzhou, Shenzhen, and Foshan, and migrant laborers are employed to reduce labor costs.

From the perspective of the three urban agglomerations' spatial center of gravity and equilibrium type, the Yangtze River Delta is an urban agglomeration with center-core staggered deviation: Shanghai is an alpha core city located on the eastern side of the geometric center of gravity, posing a significant impact on agglomeration function and connectivity for the entire region. The Pearl River Delta is an urban agglomeration with center-core superposition: centers of gravity of Guangzhou — Tier 1 core city, and the entire agglomeration's other cities are distributed adjacent to geometric center of gravity, hence, this agglomeration more or less conforms to spatial equilibrium characteristics reflected by a central place. The Beijing–Tianjin–Hebei Region is an urban agglomeration with center-core staggered centering: centers of gravity of Beijing — alpha

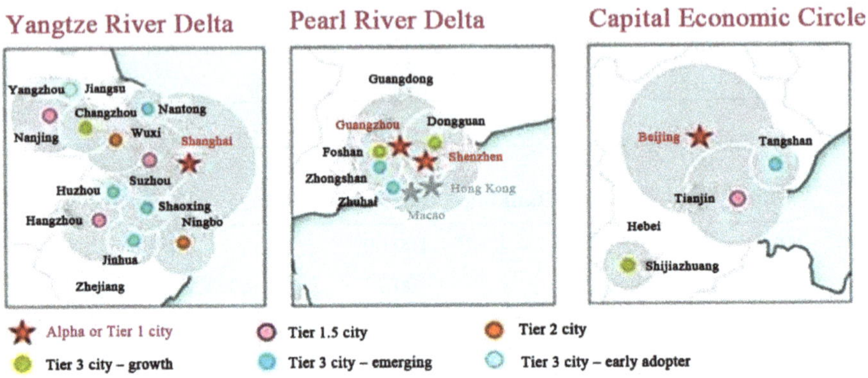

Figure 3.11 Spatial Patterns and Urbanization Paths of China's Three Urban Agglomerations

core city, and the entire agglomeration's other cities are situated on both sides of the geometric center of gravity's central axis. Inter-city economic connectivity is weaker than administrative monopoly within the urban agglomeration (Figure 3.11).

4. *Defining Shanghai's Urban Functions*

In 2014, China's e-commerce market transactions amounted to RMB13.4 trillion, an increase of 31.4% over the same period last year. In terms of integration, a new market governance structure that involves e-commerce platforms, government regulatory authorities, and enterprises engaged in online sales, has emerged. In terms of the integration model, mobile e-commerce and O2O extend from consumption to entrepreneurship, accelerating online and offline integration. Cross-border electronic transactions have developed rapidly and cross-border online shopping has become a new economic growth point. In terms of integration space, e-commerce service enterprises are mainly concentrated in the Yangtze River Delta, the Pearl River Delta, Beijing and other economically developed regions, and their concentration levels continue to increase. E-commerce channels are penetrating into Tier 3 and Tier 4 cities as well as rural markets, and are conducive to revitalizing local economy. China's top 10 most dynamic cities in 2014 included Beijing, Shenzhen, Shanghai, Ningbo, Hangzhou, Nanjing, Chengdu, Chongqing, Tianjin, and Xiamen, in that order (China E-Commerce Research Center, 2015).

In July 2015, the *Guiding Opinions of the State Council Concerning Actively Promoting "Internet Plus" Action Plan* not only set out a new strategy of institutional support and implementation for ministries, but also proposed new requirements for local governments at all levels in terms of positioning of urban functions. Based on laws, mechanisms, paths and levels of changes in core cities' functions, Shanghai has positioned its urban functions in the "Internet Plus" era as follows: Based on digitalization, networking and intelligence, Shanghai will focus on informatization to boost construction of "Four Centers" and promote in-depth integration between informatization and urban development, by taking the opportunity to build China (Shanghai) Pilot Free Trade Zone. In keeping with "Internet Plus" development requirements, Shanghai will restructure its innovation system, stimulate innovation vitality, nurture emerging industries, and build innovative public services models. In doing so, it will forge "twin engines" featuring entrepreneurship and innovation, and increase public products and public services. Simply put, Shanghai will remake itself into an e-City driven by "twin engines" by relying on "4+1" construction (Figure 3.12).

III. Evolution of Urban Morphology in Core Cities

Urban morphology is an external spatial embodiment of endogenous factors for urban development, and its evolution is considered the result of combined effects of urban population, economy, society, and so on.

In the "Internet Plus" era, a city's industrial base and functional zoning are constantly changing, and urban space can be creatively reorganized, resulting in new features of urban morphology.

1. *Mutual Integration of Functional Zoning in Cities*

The social and economic development in any city engenders new roles for it that overshadow some old ones, resulting in the spatial expansion and

Figure 3.12 Changes in e-City's Informatization Function in the "Internet Plus" Era

outward movement of so many of its functions, which drive the spatial reorganization of the city's functional zoning.

1.1 *Adjustment in Industrial Structure Makes a CBD's Status More Prominent*

Evolution of urban morphology is closely related to periodic characteristics of industrial development and cyclical nature of economic development (Figure 3.13). In the era of innovative economy, urban industrial structure is being upgraded at a rapid rate, and the manufacturing industry can demarcate between R&D and manufacturing, production and marketing, as well as sales and logistics. Many traditional limitations such as transportation costs can be overcome through optimal location selection, and information accessibility grows even more important. A central business district (CBD) gains a higher status for headquarters economy, and helps make urban spatial configuration become more refined.

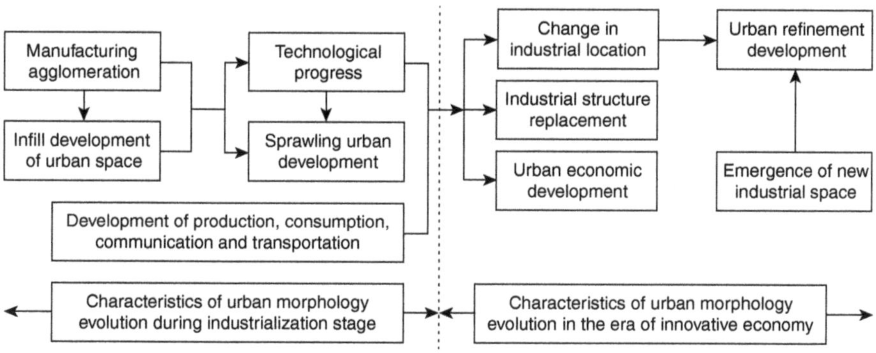

Figure 3.13 Characteristics of Urban Morphology Evolution in Different Stages

1.2 *Changes in Consumption Patterns Promote Coexistence of Large Concentration and Small Dispersion of Urban Commercial Centers*

The Internet's popularity has led to a precipitous rise in online shopping, which in turn has led to spatial changes to a city's commercial space. While the proportion of traditional retail brick-and-mortar stores continues to decline, and large shopping malls characterized by one-stop shopping represent the city's new business model, there are numerous small retail stores that provide instant goods supply, complementing large shopping malls, making many things convenient for local residents. Thus, a commercial space pattern featuring large concentration and small dispersion has taken shape.

In addition, a business model featuring online and offline integration is rapidly developing. Offline brand experience has become a new type of business that follows development trend of "Experience is King". Online marketing models driving offline consumption, or online sales and offline delivery, have made the city's commercial space pattern become more flexible and diverse.

1.3 *Telecommuting's Popularity Diversifies Residential Community Selection*

In the era of innovative economy, e-commerce, online shopping, telecommuting and flexible work system are all popular options that allow people to select residential locations with more freedom with respect to both

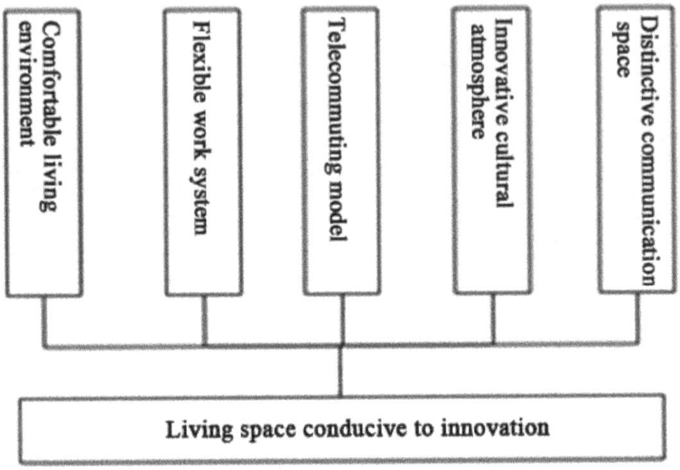

Figure 3.14 Conditions for Residential Location in the Innovation Era

space and time. Comfort, air quality, cultural environment and other resident-friendly factors are gaining more prominence (Figure 3.14).

From the perspective of urban morphology, a community's status as a basic unit of the city has been elevated. A large residential community not only provides basic life functions, but also serves as a place to work, for information exchange, and cultural communication. Diversified community functions enrich urban morphology and make it more distinctive.

1.4 *Central Activities Zone and Central Intelligence District Emerge as New Spatial Elements in Innovative Cities*

A central activities zone (CAZ) extends the CBD conceptualization and emphasizes on quality and content. ACAZ has five elements, namely, shopping experience, casual dining, composite office, cultural display, and creative innovation. With emphasis on lasting vitality, and flexible and diversified space, it incorporates multiple functions such as leisure and entertainment culture, business administration, tours and sightseeing, and high quality residence, and all these elements make a CAZ vibrant and attractive.

A central intelligence district's (CID) core functions are knowledge creation and R&D transformation. Numerous information and resource agencies are highly concentrated in the CID, where subjects are involved

Table 3.9 Basic Types of Urban Innovation Space

Type	Industrial park	High-tech industrial park	Science and technology park
Theoretical origin	Industrial agglomeration	Knowledge spillover	Innovation space
Goal	Infrastructure sharing to reduce transaction costs	Industry-university-research combination, to promote cooperation between universities, scientific research institutions and enterprises	Technology and R&D, to improve innovative capabilities of universities and research institutions
Function	Realize economies of scale for manufacturing	Transform scientific research results into products	Develop innovative economy

in well-developed horizontal cooperation for innovation. These agencies can be developed from science cities, university towns, science and technology parks, and so on, and what they have in common is information and technology. Solid infrastructure, a large number of high-tech professionals, and an innovative atmosphere are key factors for successful development of the CID (Table 3.9).

2. *Fuzzy Outer Boundaries of Cities*

2.1 *Close Ties Among Cities and Accelerated Metropolitan Integration Process*

Due to spatial separation between R&D and production in manufacturing industry in the informatization era, division of labor is more refined within the same industry, and industrial clusters can exhibit virtualization characteristics. These changes have led to more frequent flow of factors among cities, and rapid increase in information exchange and material flow. The original economic zone concept based on administrative boundaries is gradually fading and has been replaced with wide, universal linkages among cities. Cities have become more interdependent, and have accelerated metropolitan integration process (Table 3.10).

Table 3.10 Characteristics of Spatial Relations in Different Stages of Urban Development

Development stage	Urban function	Urban construction	Urban morphology	Spatial relations
Agricultural society	Commodity trading, handicraft production	Simple and extensive	Small size	Relatively closed, urban and rural separation
Industrialization stage	Commercial trading, large-scale mechanized industrial production	Comprehensive infrastructure	Size expansion, quantity increase	Wider gap, urban, and rural dual structure
Post-industrialization stage	Center of service sector, functional diversification	Prominent modernization features, fast construction speed	Formation of functional zoning, sprawling metropolises	Close linkage, urban, and rural integration
Innovative economy era	Information flow, management, and innovation services	Intelligence, landscaping, and comfort	Decomposition of metropolises, and development of small and medium-sized cities	Narrow gap, spatial integration

2.2 *Cities Linked Together Through High-tech Industrial Belts*

A belt made up of high-tech industries is formed when high-tech companies incubated in university parks develop into clusters in peripheral cities, and then expand further along inter-city transportation lines until a sizable area with relatively dense concentration of them is formed. In the Internet age and an innovation-driven economy, such spatial relations among cities defined by economic linkages and serving the interest of economic coordination will become increasingly common (Figure 3.15).

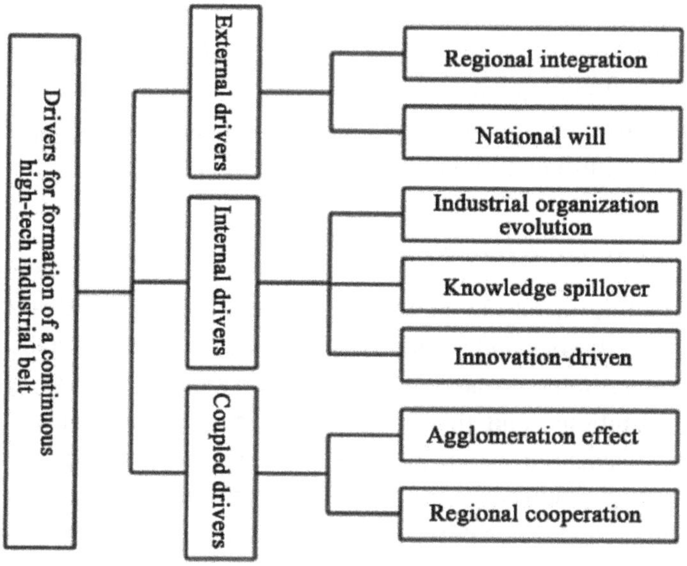

Figure 3.15 Formation Mechanism of a Continuous High-tech Industrial Belt[4]

---

[4]This figure is created based on relevant information drawn from Macro Management Consulting's report on *Research on Urban Innovation Space*. *Source*: Baidu Library. Available at: http://wenku.baidu.com/link?url=HfbUyyjMthwpWVvq4XHo9WWeDgyFKQsctimt2SNKM4bX74n_GjUZOd1JFTpT3humQk5QCghaw382ibXTAvW8xUTeyRe-tPvSH35qW2ea_KS.

3. *New Choices for Core Cities*

3.1 *Developing Compact Cities*

A compact city is a type of urban morphology featuring high density with mixed functional elements. It advocates reduction in energy use and less reliance on private cars, and supports public transport and other green means of transportation. Achieving these goals entails more accessible public service facilities and more effective municipal facilities and infrastructure.

In the era of innovative economy, urban development depends more on scientific and technological innovation, as well as R&D and creative industries. Importance of land cost decreases in enterprise location selection, while location condition requirements such as transportation conditions, scientific research atmosphere and cultural environment gain greater prominence. Also, as scientific and technological innovation enterprises yield high-added value and have the ability to incur high business costs and improve urban land output level, a compact city concept is more conducive to rebirth and revitalization of a core city.

3.2 *Highlighting a CID's Role and Status*

As an upgrade to a CBD, a CID can leverage the city's advantages in innovation capabilities and service functions. A CID can be established in an area that is home to colleges and universities as well as scientific research institutions, and this can be done by transforming traditional business or residential areas, into a knowledge and innovation-oriented community that pursues quality of life and features a mixed layout for both residential and office purposes. An innovation hub can be introduced in the CID, and is expected to incorporate a central district, a high-tech park, living, and working areas, and sports and leisure center, thereby creating a new public community. Thus, the core city can maintain sufficient vitality and keep its leading position in innovation.

3.3 *Seeking Innovation in Commercial Center Construction*

A core city must seek innovation in positioning of its commercial center to maintain commercial vitality. As combining culture and commerce is a new trend, cultural elements are integrated into commerce, so that consumers can enjoy quality culture while shopping and enjoying leisure activities. Better consumption experience attracts more consumers.

In addition, innovative breakthroughs should be made in the commercial center's construction. The core city's commerce serves not only local residents, but also tourists from all over the country and even the world as part of the tourism link. A commercial center with unique construction features often becomes the city's iconic building.

3.4 *Making Sure Newly Constructed Residential Areas are Resident-friendly*

In the Internet era, due to increased integration of living and office space, there is more emphasis on resident-friendly environment in residential areas. Quality is primarily taken into account in site selection, planning and construction of residential areas, and all these elements should be conducive to innovation. Lower floor area ratio, beautiful buildings, rich colors, and green energy are essential elements. In addition, there are also other basic considerations such as public transport development, reduction of vehicle exhaust emissions, alleviation of urban traffic congestion, and improvement in commuting conditions, which are necessary for residential construction in the new era.

3.5 *Optimizing Planning for Storage Space Construction*

In an Internet economy trade, i.e. the flow of value is spatially separated from logistics, i.e. the flow of things. The greater virtual presence, improved convenience and lowered resource costs made possible by the Internet have burst the traditional boundaries of commercial transactions.

These changes meet the needs of modern logistics, which is characteristically large in both geographical reach and operational scale. Thanks to the availability of more accurate and timely information, the level of precision in delivery has greatly increased. "Door-to-door", "warehouse-to-warehouse" or even "line-to-line" delivery, which was never possible before, is now commonplace. The Internet has transformed the complex logistics industry and helped it achieve optimum efficiency. Site selection and planning for storage space play a decisive role. In addition to building large warehouses in the suburbs, a logistics distribution networks with sensible layout should be established inside the city in order to improve logistics services in terms of speed and precision.

References

Converse P. D. *Elements of Marketing*, Englewood Cliffs, 1930.

Kong Fan'e. A study of division and change of Guangzhou's urban Hinterland, *Urban Studies*, 2006 (4).

Reilly W. J. *Methods for the Study of Retail Relationships*, University of Texas, 1929.

Chapter 4

Shanghai's Industrial Transformation and Upgrade Path

Manufacturing is the foundation of a country's economy, boosts social development, and fundamentally drives growth and innovation in various sectors. In fact, in today's world, especially after the financial crisis, both developed and developing countries have formulated reindustrialization strategies to revive and revitalize manufacturing, making it a key factor in global economic competition once again. As some have put it, "the order of the day is to refocus on the development of industry and manufacturing, which are sources of value creation".[1] As the re-shoring trend continues for high-end manufacturers in developed countries and developed and developing countries vie to host middle and low-end manufacturing plants, China's manufacturing industry is being squeezed on both sides. How should we respond to the situation? Many have suggested further promoting the use of the Internet in general and development of intelligent

[1] Wen Jicong. "*Internet Plus Manufacturing*" *Drives the Made in China 2025 Initiative*. Available at: http://www.ce.cn/xwzx/gnsz/gdxw/201507/08/t20150708_5877874.shtml.

manufacturing in particular. Under the international division of labor model, only by enhancing their own intelligent manufacturing capabilities can Chinese manufacturers attract more opportunities to cooperate with multinationals and become better places to work. The reality, however, is that the country has still much catching-up to do when it comes to the capability for independent innovation, product competitiveness, management, as well as intelligent manufacturing capability to which these are closely linked. Therefore, transforming and upgrading China's manufacturing industry means creating conditions to accelerate transformation to intelligent manufacturing. After all, "Internet Plus Manufacturing" presents a new model for value realization. Shanghai is home to a large manufacturing industry; however, it urgently needs to be transformed and upgraded. This prominent contradiction between size and strength, a defining characteristic of where things stand at this point in time is seen mostly clearly in the separation between production and market, and persistent stagnation and backlog throughout the supply chain. It would be imperative for manufacturers in Shanghai to shift toward intelligent manufacturing.

I. From Manufacturing to Intelligent Manufacturing: Value Realization Model for Manufacturing in the "Internet Plus Industry"

Revolutionary breakthroughs and cross integration of new energy, new materials, information technology, biotechnology and other important fields and frontier directions, are bringing about a new round of industrial innovation, which significantly affects global manufacturing and its development model. In particular, in-depth integration of new-generation information technology with manufacturing is leading to profound changes in manufacturing model, organizational model for production, and industrial form, with intelligent manufacturing and service-oriented manufacturing becoming a new development trend. How value creation and value distribution are created in manufacturing is also changing.

1. *"Internet Plus Manufacturing" not Subject to the "Smiling Curve"*[2]

The "smiling curve" divides an industrial chain into three segments, namely, R&D and design, production and manufacturing, and marketing and services. Production and manufacturing constitute the low-profit portion of the industrial chain (Figure 4.1). Therefore, manufacturers always anticipate to move towards R&D and design and brand marketing. In the international division of labor system, enterprises in developed countries tend to occupy high-end positions in R&D and design, and marketing and service segments in the industrial chain, while manufacturers in developing countries are squeezed into the production and manufacturing

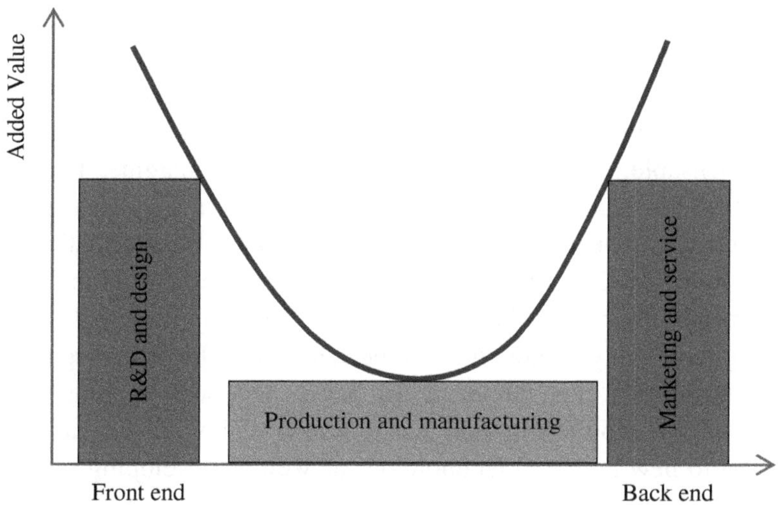

Figure 4.1 "Smiling Curve"

[2]This section is written with reference to: Wang Xiwen. *Industry 4.0, Internet Plus, and Made in China 2025: The Future Direction of Transformation and Upgrade of China's Manufacturing*, *National Governance Weekly*, 2015 (23); and Wang Xiwen. *The Internet Plus Industry Helps China's Manufacturing Get Rid of the Smiling Curve*. Available at: http://www.ca800.com/news/d_1nto2d6lvav23.html. (If any part of the rest of this chapter cites these documents, then the source is referred to as Network Information).

segment, constituting the low-profit portion in the industrial chain. Moving to the industrial chain's high-end positions in the international industrial division of labor system and extending to both ends of the "smiling curve", are important goals for manufacturers in developing countries.

In general, both ends (R&D and design, and marketing and service) of the entire industrial chain command higher added value, while the middle area (production and manufacturing) generates lowest added value. While a lot is "Made in China", most of it is in the mid-section of the "smiling curve", occupied by production and manufacturing companies that are labor-intensive and low-yield in terms of added value.

R&D and design and marketing and service activities at both ends of the "smiling curve" are relatively profitable and their profit models are usually sustainable. Production and manufacturing in the bottom middle area can only maintain relatively weak profitability, and due to low levels of technology and relatively low entry threshold, competition is more intense in production and manufacturing and companies in these areas are often dispensable, putting further squeeze on profit margins. Therefore, staying at the bottom of the "smiling curve" is not a long-term plan for manufacturing industry, which needs immediate transformation and upgrade; however, China's manufacturing industry still has a long way to go before moving out of the bottom of the "smiling curve". There has been long-term study on how this can be achieved. It has been argued that moving traditional manufacturing to R&D and service ends of the "smiling curve" would eliminate the dilemma of low added value, and upgrading to new high-end technologies as well as developing manufacturing-related services was the only way forward. However, this process is accompanied by many challenges and is unlikely to achieve the desired result of exiting the bottom of the "smiling curve".

The "Internet Plus Industry" era ensures this problem no longer lingers on, as traditional models of value creation and distribution in manufacturing are changing. The Internet platform enables enterprises, customers and stakeholders to participate in all aspects of manufacturing such as value creation, delivery, and realization. "Internet Plus Industry" provides not only "information sharing", but also "physical sharing", thus creating new models of value creation and sharing. In other words, with development of "Internet Plus Industry", all components of the value chain will create, deliver and share value together. As a result, "Internet Plus Industry" will thoroughly reconstruct the value chain, i.e. the "smiling curve" of manufacturing. Customization leaves front-end R&D and design to end customers, who directly place orders with enterprises. Customization weakens back-end sales, thereby leveling the "smiling curve", which is re-integrated into the value ring.

Therefore, bidding farewell to the "smiling curve" represents an inevitable trend of future manufacturing industry development in the "Internet Plus Industry" era.

2. *The "Internet Plus" Era Changes Manufacturing Resource Allocation*[3]

2.1 *Customer Centric*

Explosive development of the Internet, especially the mobile Internet, has driven consumers to shift from passive consumption to active consumption, due to which dominance of an enterprise's value chain has been transferred from manufacturers and distributors to consumers who extensively participate in the entire production and value creation process in real time. The open network platform encourages dispersed producers and consumers, to extensively and frequently communicate and interact in real time, and fully stimulates potential for social innovation, thereby meeting consumers' personalized needs as well.

2.2 *Cloud Manufacturing Resources*

A variety of manufacturing resources and capabilities are virtualized, service-oriented, and added into a pool of cloud manufacturing resources for unified, centralized, intelligent operations and management, by integrating existing concepts and technologies such as networked

[3]This section is written with reference to: Tong Youhao. *The "Internet Plus" Promotes the Transformation and Upgrade of Manufacturing*. Available at: http://cyyw.cena.com.cn/2015-06/15/content_281046.htm.

manufacturing, ASP platform, the Internet of Things, and manufacturing grids. The network and cloud manufacturing service platform provides users with standard, shareable, safe, reliable, quality and low-cost manufacturing life cycle services that are available at any time and used when required.

2.3 *Production Process Flexibility*[4]

"Flexibility" refers to the supply chain's flexibility to respond promptly to market demand, be it multi-style small batches, or big batches for reorder and replenishment. Standard and controllable quality is ensured for either small or big orders, which are delivered promptly at almost the same costs. A flexible supply chain's biggest benefit for enterprises is to seize sales opportunities without inventory risks.

2.4 *Intellectual Resource Socialization*

By relying on the Internet, a manufacturing company can publish its demand for R&D creativity, and extensively collect knowledge and ideas from customers and external personnel through its own or existing "crowdsourcing" platform, which greatly expands sources of creativity.

3. *The "Internet Plus" Era Changes Production Model and Manufacturing Management*[5]

In-depth development of "Internet Plus Manufacturing" is changing innovation, production, sales, profit and organizational models for manufacturers.

---

[4] AliResearch: *Research Report on the "Internet Plus"*, March 2015.

[5] This section is written with reference to: Tong Youhao: *The "Internet Plus" Promotes the Transformation and Upgrade of Manufacturing*. Available at: http://cyyw.cena.com.cn/2015-06/15/content_281046.htm.

3.1 *Rapid Development of Collaborative Innovation*

The Internet enables integration of advantageous resources of all parties, to form a cross-field, network-based collaborative innovation platform that helps achieve breakthroughs in core technologies. Some enterprises establish innovation networks using the Internet, in order to provide other partners with opportunities for mutual learning, information sharing and collaborative innovation. These networks allow sharing, integration, utilization and re-creation of information, knowledge and innovative resources to meet the needs of all parties, realize knowledge appreciation and value creation, and improve quality and efficiency of industry–university–research collaborative innovation.

3.2 *Intelligent Manufacturing as a New Production Model*

With the help of sensors and strategically placed machines throughout the production process that are connected to the network, the manufacturing industry utilizes the Internet and data analysis technologies at the machine and equipment level to improve machine intelligence and equipment performance. At the factory level, it enables planning, optimizing and scheduling production resources among several workshops and production lines for specific production tasks, based on the supply chain situation and market demand. At the human and machine level, it allows all manufacturing systems and equipment to be interconnected with people, and focuses on enhancing efficiency and providing better services in order to achieve interaction between people and intelligent manufacturing systems, promote digitalized, networked and intelligent production and manufacturing development, enhance value chain's high-end components, and promote transformation of traditional manufacturers.

3.3 *Personalization and Customized Production*

The Internet reduces interaction costs between manufacturers and users. It enables manufacturers to respond to users' specific needs rapidly. Scale effect is no longer a key factor in industrial production which is changing from centralized control to decentralized control. With intelligent computing and flexible manufacturing, manufacturers are able to realize large-scale, personalized custom production, and reduce or even eliminate inventory based on consumers' personalized needs, by refining and re-combining production information control modules, as well as new manufacturing processes.

3.4 *Popularity of Network Marketing*

With the mobile Internet's vertical development and mobile terminals' fast spread, e-commerce has rapidly extended its reach from consumption to manufacturing. In terms of marketing, the simpler offline promotion model or yesteryear has gradually been replaced by O2O omni-channel marketing model. Industrial apps, e-commerce platforms, O2O, mobile social marketing, search matching and other Internet services have gradually penetrated into procurement, fabrication, logistics, marketing, delivery, and services.

3.5 *Optimization of Organizational System*

Development and in-depth application of the Internet, emergence of e-commerce, further integration of international and domestic markets, refined market segmentation, and higher personalized demand and service requirements, have increased competition among manufacturers. Products and services are more finely targeted toward specific consumer needs, industrial strategies have changed, the organizational structure has become more decentralized, and coordinated manufacturing has emerged as an important production organization model.

4. *The "Internet Plus" Era Optimizes Value Realization Path for Manufacturing*[6]

Integrating manufacturing with advanced computing, analysis tools, low-cost sensing and higher networking levels enables optimization of the

[6]This section is written with reference to: Tong Youhao. *The "Internet Plus" Promotes the Transformation and Upgrade of Manufacturing*. Available at: http://cyyw.cena.com.cn/2015-06/15/content_281046.htm.

value realization path for manufacturing, as evident from improved product and equipment technology, increasingly prominent service turn of manufacturing, and enhanced profitability.

4.1 *Higher Technological Content in Products and Equipment*

Information technology, especially the Internet's features such as high driving force, high penetrability, high multiplication and high innovativeness, show that the process of applying the Internet amounts to the process of integration with traditional manufacturing products and equipment, to generate new scientific and technological achievements and engender new productive forces. Relying on Big Data and Internet technologies, product manufacturing has undergone three changes: a shift from mechanical products to intelligent products, from intelligent products to smart-connected products, and from supply of products to supply of product-based services.

4.2 *The Service Turn of Manufacturing*

As the applications of the Internet continue to deepen and the customer-first service mentality take root, manufacturers have been turning into service providers. Increasingly, manufacturers are producing output in the form of services. Products sales are no longer the only source of revenue, which now includes service provision, too. The new "product sales and service provision" profit model is more sustainable.

4.3 *Enhanced Profitability of Manufacturing*

As global economic integration deepens and technology transfer develops rapidly, the Internet will continue to bring about wide range of benefits to the world. For example, Internet's industry data analysis capabilities, address challenges facing railways such as speed, reliability and transport capacity.

II. Intelligent Manufacturing Capability and Equilibrium Effect of a Core City's Manufacturing Industry Under International Industrial Division of Labor

1. *Study Background*

Under the international industrial division of labor, China's manufacturing has developed rapidly and sustainably in the past decade and grown in comprehensive strength, thanks largely to low labor costs and market scale. It has not only made important contributions to domestic, economic and social development, but has also become an important force in the world economy. Nevertheless, major adjustments in international industrial division of labor has brought severe challenges to China's manufacturing. For example, re-shoring of high-end manufacturing in developed countries have intensifying competition among middle and low-income countries for middle and low-end manufacturing have left China's manufacturers squeezed on two sides. On the one hand, in a reversal of earlier trend, an increasing number of high-end manufacturing factories have been relocated back in developed countries. As many countries trying to revitalize their manufacturing sector, it is once again becoming the pivot in global economic competition. In developed countries, re-shoring is the latest trend in manufacturing. On the other hand, by virtue of their comparative advantages in resource endowment and labor supply, Vietnam, India and other Southeast Asian countries have become more competitive in mid- and low-end manufacturing, attracting a growing number of factories in the labor-intensive manufacturing sector with the promise of low costs. Some multinational investors are investing and setting up factories directly in emerging economy countries, while some others are considering moving their factories from China to these countries.

It is believed that this situation is caused by Chinese manufacturers' weak intelligent manufacturing capabilities. Traditional industrialization's technical characteristics are reflected in the use of mechanization, electrification and automation, in realizing mass production and bulk sales. In the context of the current complicated international environment and fierce international competition, traditional production (manufacturing) must be upgraded to intelligent production (intelligent manufacturing), to enhance China's manufacturing status in the global industrial value chain, and boost China's manufacturing strength, which is now big but not strong.

As mentioned above, intelligent manufacturing is important for building manufacturing strength, marks a new path toward industrialization, and development model; it is instrumental for creating new industrial competitive advantages and for seizing opportunities in the industrialization process. However, the level of informatization is still not high in China, and there is huge potential for intelligent manufacturing capabilities to improve. At present, China is still lagging behind developed countries in terms of construction and application of information infrastructure. Therefore, it is best to accelerate integration of new-generation information technologies and manufacturing technologies, adopt intelligent manufacturing as the main direction, enhance intelligence levels of enterprises' R&D, production, management and services, and transform China's manufacturing model from "Made in China" to "Made by Intelligent Manufacturing in China".[7]

It is believed that intelligent manufacturing capability directly determines how far local manufacturers can cooperate with multinationals under international industrial division of labor. In general, multinationals are responsible for designing manufacturing blueprints (R&D or innovation), while local enterprises are responsible for implementing existing blueprints (manufacturing) under international industrial division of labor. On the one hand, multinationals are willing to involve local manufacturers in blueprint design if their intelligent manufacturing capability is strong enough, to maximize local enterprises' efforts while substituting their design efforts, and increase probability of design's success. On the other hand, local manufacturers' participation in design translates into additional costs to multinationals: proprietary information may be leaked when local manufacturers execute contracts; and the blueprint designs by

[7]Planning Department of the Ministry of Industry and Information Technology: *Interpretation of the "Made in China 2025" Initiative (IV): China's Task of Building a Strong Manufacturing Power is Arduous and Urgent.* Available at: http://www.miit.gov.cn/n11293472/n11293832/n11294042/n11481465/16595213.html.

the local manufacturers and their parent multinationals may not be strongly intersubstitutable. When local manufacturers manage to succeed where multinationals have failed in designing blueprints, the latter are often required to make adjustments, incurring additional costs. In sum, for multinationals, the question about involvement of local manufacturers in blueprint design is necessarily one about trade-offs manufacturing.

Local manufacturers' intelligent manufacturing capabilities determine blueprint design substitutability between two parties, to a large extent. Local manufacturers with strong intelligent manufacturing capabilities understand customer needs faster, which aids in designing corresponding blueprints based on customer needs, and also they are able to better under multinational enterprises' demands and innovation processes, thereby enabling them to provide blueprint designs that meet requirements in information exchange process with multinationals. Therefore, local manufacturers with strong intelligent manufacturing capability can provide blueprint designs similar to those desired by their parent multinationals. In those cases where multinationals adopt local manufacturers' blueprint design, or vice versa, no high adjustment costs result, a situation agreeable to both parties. Analysis shows that stronger intelligent manufacturing capability encourages multinationals to involve local manufacturers in designing blueprints. Moreover, the equilibrium result is that local manufacturers with strong intelligent manufacturing capability are paid more by multinationals and have opportunities to work with more multinationals. In addition, improvement in intelligent manufacturing capability also creates higher benefits for local manufacturers.

Most literatures on organizational economics related to the international industrial division of labor and cooperation, emphasize on integration and non-integration. For example, Grossman and Helpman (2002a, 2002b) emphasized on determining whether integration leads to a trade-off between specialized income and search costs. Arora and Merges (2004) emphasized on integration and outsourcing decision-making by determining the trade-off between high-powered incentive effect and rent dissipation. Antras (2005) emphasized on production outsourcing by determining the trade-off between specialized income and sunk costs. Lai *et al.* (2009) emphasized on R&D outsourcing by determining the trade-off between revenue generated from innovation speed and information leakage costs. Obviously, the aforementioned literature only demonstrates traditional "make or buy" problem, but does not extend its theoretical reach to the degree of cooperation under contract conditions of international industrial division of labor.[8]

2. *Model*[9]

2.1 *Basic Assumptions and Explanations*

When a multinational works with a Chinese local manufacturer to make products, under the principle of the international industrial division of labor, the latter is responsible for implementing the multinational's blueprint design in the cooperation process. In the "Internet Plus Industry" background, multinationals consider involving Chinese enterprises in designing blueprints by determining their intelligent manufacturing capabilities. The following assumptions have been proposed to facilitate analysis:

Assumption 1. Many local manufacturers are found in a region (core city or peripheral city) in China, but each of them can cooperate with only one multinational at the most. In the context of "Internet Plus Industry", local manufacturers are most likely to design blueprints that are required by multinationals based on their ability to understand and extract customer (common) requirements quickly and accurately, based on diverse needs and feedback from customers.

In such cases, any multinational that involves a local manufacturer in blueprint design would gain two advantages: (i) increased probability of successful blueprint design; and (ii) partial substitution of multinational's creative efforts by local manufacturers. However, involving local manufacturers in designing blueprints generates two additional costs for multinationals: (a) Information leakage by local manufacturers,

[8]Refer to Fei Fangyu *et al.* (2009) for more detailed literature review of contents in this part.

[9]The framework of this model is established by reference to relevant discussions of Puga and Trefler (2005, 2010, 2014).

resulting in higher payment costs for multinationals; (b) Multinationals and local manufacturers are required to share information in the blueprint design process, and there may be cases where some local manufacturers leak information by (i) selling it to the principal's competitors; or (ii) entering directly into the principal's industry as a competitor (Lai *et al.*, 2009), both of which would lead to economic losses to the multinational.

Assumption 2. The local manufacturer's creative effort is observable but unverifiable.

Based on the above assumption, irrespective of whether a local manufacturer manages to design a blueprint or not, it could claim to be the blueprint's designer and leak information. In such cases, it is difficult to disentangle the relative contribution of each party's effort, and it is assumed that the court would grant the local manufacturer an income $\mu\pi$ and the multinational $(1 - \mu)\pi$, where π refers to profits realized after the blueprint is implemented. In other words, if the local manufacturer is involved in blueprint design, it would get the outside option value of $\mu\pi$. At this time, the multinational would make fixed payment $\mu\pi$ to the local manufacturer, in order to avoid information leakage by the latter. If the local manufacturer is not involved in the blueprint design, it could only receive fixed payment T (assuming $T < \mu\pi$).

Secondly, the local manufacturer's involvement in blueprint design could result in adjustment costs to both parties. In such cases where both the multinational and local manufacturer are working on blueprint design, it is assumed that even if the local manufacturer does not manage to design a blueprint, and instead the multinational manages to do so, the latter's adjustment effort would be 0, whereas the local manufacturer would exert adjustment effort to implement the blueprint; it is only in cases where the local manufacturer manages to design the blueprint, that the multinational would exert adjustment effort to implement the blueprint. We use $\eta \in (0, 1)$ to express the local manufacturer's intelligent manufacturing capability, as well as to measure the degree of substitutability of blueprints designed by both parties. We assume that adjustment effort a_i is a decreasing function of intelligent manufacturing capability i and creative effort e_i.

Assumption 3. Adjustment efforts by the multinational and local manufacturer can be expressed as:

$$a_i = \begin{cases} 0 & \text{if } i\text{'s blueprint is implemented,} \\ (1-\eta)(1-e_i) & \text{if } j\text{'s blueprint is implemented.} \end{cases}$$

Assumption 4. Preferences of the multinational and local manufacturer is a Cobb–Douglas function over consumption and leisure, and is homothetic for all goods. Thus, the indirect utility function for the relevant party i is $u_i = (y_i/P)^{\alpha} l_i^{\beta}$, where y_i is i's income, l_i is i's leisure, and P is the relevant price index. To demonstrate, we assume $\alpha = \beta = 1$; $P = 1$. We also assume that the principal and agent are each endowed with one unit of leisure (so, $l_i = 1 - e_i - a_i$).[10] Additionally, it is assumed that each design blueprint yields the same profit π, and probability of a blueprint being successfully designed by each party lies in effort level e_i.

Lastly, for convenience, this model's time structure is explained further. It is assumed that the multinational could automatically match the Chinese local manufacturer. Upon matching the two parties, the local manufacturer's intelligent manufacturing capability follows the cumulative distribution function $F(\eta)$.[11] Before the multinational accurately understands the local manufacturer's intelligent manufacturing capability, the two parties enter into an initial contract stipulating that the local manufacturer shall be responsible only for implementing the blueprint designed by the multinational, and receive payment T from the multinational. The two parties can accurately understand the intelligent manufacturing capability η over a period of time. If the local manufacturer's intelligent manufacturing capability η is weak, the multinational would design the blueprint on its own, and the local manufacturer would continue to implement the blueprint (if successfully designed); if the local manufacturer's intelligent manufacturing capability η is strong, the

[10]Here, we draw on relevant rules set out by Puga and Trefler (2010, p. 68) on utilities (and leisure endowments) of the principal and agent.

[11]The multinational is able to accurately evaluate the local manufacturer's intelligent manufacturing capability η only after working with it.

multinational would involve the local manufacturer in blueprint design, for which the latter would receive payment $\mu\pi$. At this point, the two parties would amend the initial contract (provided the local manufacturer's incentive compatibility condition is satisfied). The new contract would specify that as long as the multinational succeeds in designing the blueprint, the local manufacturer would implement this blueprint regardless of whether it has managed to design its own blueprint. Only when the multinational fails to design the blueprint and the local manufacturer succeeds in designing the blueprint, will the latter implement its own blueprint design. If both parties fail to design successful blueprints, they would obtain zero incomes. In this framework, the multinational and local manufacturer would choose effort levels e_F and e_D. In conclusion, the time structure shown in Figure 4.2 can be used.

2.2 *Multinational's Option to Involving the Local Manufacturer in Blueprint Design*

2.2.1 The two parties' effort levels under the initial contract

Under the initial contract, when the local manufacturer only implements the blueprint designed by the multinational, but is not involved either in the design or design process ($e_D = 0$), it obtains income T. The multinational's main problem is choosing the effort level e_F to maximize its expected utility level $e_F = \arg\max \mathrm{EU}_F$, which yields:

$$\mathrm{EU}_F = e_F(\pi - T)(1 - e_F).$$

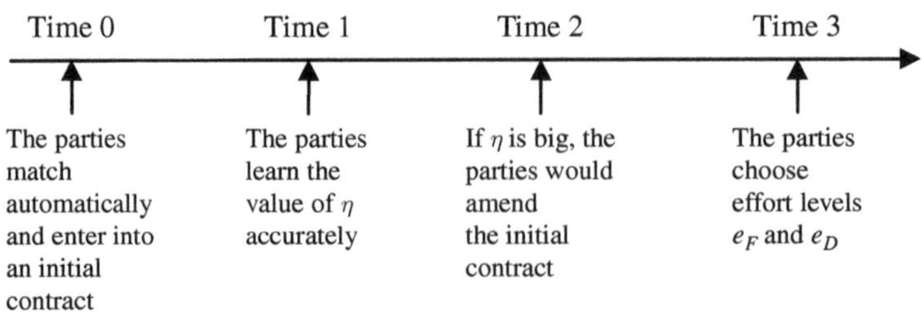

Figure 4.2 Time Structure

In the above equation, e_F is the probability of a multinational successfully designing the blueprint, $(\pi - T)$ is its income, and $(1 - e_F)$ is its leisure. The local manufacturer's income is T and leisure is $1 - (1 - \eta) = \eta$; it obtains income T and leisure η with probability e_F. Thus, the local manufacturer's expected utility is:

$$\mathrm{EU}_D = e_F T\eta .$$

In summary, the multinational and the local manufacturer's effort levels are:

$$e_F = 1/2, \quad e_D = 0.$$

2.2.2 The two parties' effort levels under the amended contract

Under the amended contract, both parties are working on the blueprint design (the agent is involved in design). The multinational's effort level is $e_F = \arg\max \mathrm{EU}'_F$, where,

$$\mathrm{EU}'_F = e_F(1-\mu)\pi(1-e_F) + (1-e_F)e_D(1-\mu)\pi(1-e_F)\eta . \qquad (1)$$

In Eq. (1), the principal designs the blueprint with probability e_F to obtain income $(1 - \mu)\pi$ and leisure $(1 - e_F)$. When only the local manufacturer designs the blueprint (with probability $(1 - e_F)e_D$), the multinational will obtain income $(1 - \mu)\pi$ and leisure $(1 - e_F)\eta$. If both parties fail to design the blueprint, the utility is 0. Similarly, the local manufacturer will choose effort level $e_D = \arg\max \mathrm{EU}'_D$, where,

$$\mathrm{EU}'_D = e_F\mu\pi(1-e_D)\eta + (1-e_F)e_D\mu\pi(1-e_D). \qquad (2)$$

Equations (1) and (2) yield the reaction functions of the two parties over one another's effort level:

$$e'_F(e_D) = \frac{1-2\mu e_D}{2(1-\mu e_D)}, \quad e'_D = \frac{1-(1+\mu)e_F}{2(1-e_F)}.$$

Thus, we can yield the creative effort levels of both parties under Nash equilibrium:

$$e_F^{'} = \frac{1}{2+\mu}, \quad e_D^{'} = \frac{1}{2(1+\mu)}.$$

Obviously, $e_F^{'} < e_F$, $e_F^{'} > e_F = 0$. When the local manufacturer is involved in blueprint design, it will partially substitute the multinational's effort. In addition, under the initial contract, the probability of a blueprint being successfully designed is $e_F = 1/2$, while under the amended contract, the probability is $e_F^{'} + (1 - e_F^{'})e_D^{'} = \frac{3}{2(2+\eta)}$. Obviously, $\frac{3}{2(2+\eta)} > \frac{1}{2}$. In other words, the probability of the blueprint being successfully designed increases after the local manufacturer is involved in its design.

2.2.3 The multinational's decision on whether to amend the initial contract

The multinational can decide whether to amend the initial contract based on its utility level, provided the local manufacturer's incentive compatibility condition is satisfied. Based on the above discussion, the multinational's expected utilities in two cases are (IC is the initial contract and AC is the amended contract):

$$\mathrm{EU}^{\mathrm{IC}} = \frac{1}{4}(\pi - T),$$

$$\mathrm{EU}^{\mathrm{AC}} = (1-\mu)\pi\frac{(1+\eta)}{2(2+\eta)}.$$

When

$$\mathrm{EU}^{\mathrm{AC}} = \mathrm{EU}^{\mathrm{IC}},$$

$$\eta^* = \frac{2(\mu - T/\pi)}{1 - 2\mu + T/\pi}. \tag{3}$$

Thus, if $\mathrm{EU}^{\mathrm{AC}} > \mathrm{EU}^{\mathrm{IC}}$, then $\eta > \eta^*$, and the multinational will amend the initial contract and involve the local manufacturer in blueprint design;

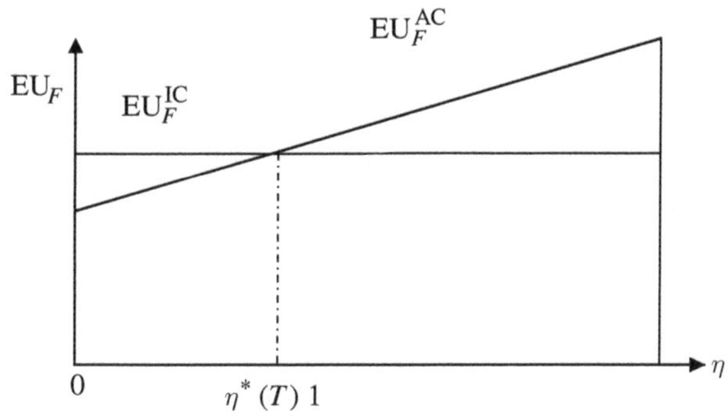

Figure 4.3 Multinational's Option to Involve the Local Manufacturer in Design (Whether or Not to Amend the Initial Contract)

if $EU^{AC} \leq EU^{IC}$, then $\eta \leq \eta^*$, and the multinational will not amend the initial contract, but shall only allow the local manufacturer to implement the blueprint. Figure 4.3 specifically describes the multinational's decision on whether to amend the initial contract.

Proposition 1. *If and only if* $\eta > \eta^*$, *the multinational will involve the local manufacturer in blueprint design.*

The straightforward meaning of Proposition 1 is that the local manufacturer cannot be involved in blueprint design unless its intelligent manufacturing capability exceeds threshold η^*, which explains why Chinese manufacturers in some fields can be involved in blueprint design, while those in some other fields can only implement blueprints designed by multinationals. Where mobile phone design is concerned, accurately grasping consumer habits is an important part of technological innovation, and domestic demand and design capability promote one another (Li Bo, 2005). In fact, Nokia had 40% of its mobile phone R&D work done in Beijing. However, due to lack of intelligent manufacturing capabilities in the biomedicine field, even several successful enterprises are just engaged in synthesis of compound structures designed by principals, but are not involved in the design process. Thus, improving Chinese enterprises' intelligent manufacturing capabilities will allow them to have more opportunities to participate in the design process.[12]

[12]Through involvement in design process, local manufacturers can also learn cutting-edge international technological development, and keep up with latest foreign research

In the context of the "Internet Plus", China's large domestic consumption market with a population of 1.3 billion is becoming the largest foundation for improvement in China's intelligent manufacturing capabilities. "Internet Plus Manufacturing" is customer-centric and enables quick response to customers' needs through local manufacturers' intelligent manufacturing capabilities, as well as the above-mentioned idea that domestic demand and design capability promote one another. In other words, intelligent manufacturing capability is a must in the "Internet Plus" era. Therefore, as long as Chinese manufacturers embrace the "Internet Plus" at a faster pace, they can enhance their intelligent manufacturing capabilities, and be more involved in the design (creation) process under the principle of the international industrial division of labor.

It should be noted that the incentive compatibility condition that ensures the agent's participation in the innovation process, is automatically met under our assumptions. Substituting the two parties' effort levels into the expected utility function of the local manufacturer yields:

$$\mathrm{EU}_D^{\mathrm{IC}} = \frac{T\eta}{2}, \tag{4}$$

$$\mathrm{EU}_D^{\mathrm{AC}} = \frac{\mu\pi}{4}\frac{(1+2\eta)^2}{(1+\eta)(2+\eta)}. \tag{5}$$

Thus, incentive compatibility condition that ensures agent participation in the innovation process is $\mathrm{EU}_D^{\mathrm{AC}} > \mathrm{EU}_D^{\mathrm{IC}}$. As $\frac{d\mathrm{EU}_D^{\mathrm{IC}}}{d\eta} > 0$, $\frac{d\mathrm{EU}_D^{\mathrm{AC}}}{d\eta} > 0$ and $\mathrm{EU}_D^{\mathrm{AC}}$ is the concave function of η (easy to prove), and incentive compatibility condition must be met when $\mathrm{EU}_D^{\mathrm{AC}}\Big|_{\eta=1} > \mathrm{EU}_D^{\mathrm{IC}}\Big|_{\eta=1}$. From Eqs. (4) and (5), $\mathrm{EU}_D^{\mathrm{AC}}\Big|_{\eta=1} = \frac{T}{2}, > \mathrm{EU}_D^{\mathrm{IC}}\Big|_{\eta=1} = \frac{3\mu\pi}{8}$. From the assumption $\mu\pi > T$, $\mathrm{EU}_D^{\mathrm{AC}}\Big|_{\eta=1} > \mathrm{EU}_D^{\mathrm{IC}}\Big|_{\eta=1}$ is automatically met.

From Eq. (3), $\frac{\partial\eta^*}{\partial\mu} = \frac{2(1-T/\pi)}{(1-2\mu+T/\pi)^2} > 0$ (from the assumption $\mu\pi > T$). μ is the ratio of realized profits (π) to be obtained by the local manufacturer after implementing the blueprint in case of information leakage. Thus, smaller μ results in greater intensity of intellectual property protection.

---

and development, which in turn will further foster their intelligent manufacturing capabilities.

From $\frac{\partial \eta^*}{\partial \mu} > 0$, greater intensity of intellectual property protection results in lower threshold η^*, which provides local manufacturers more opportunities to participate in blueprint design, thereby establishing Corollary 1.

Corollary 1. *Greater intensity of intellectual property protection results in more opportunities for local manufacturers to participate in blueprint design.*

Corollary 1 has a strong policy implication. The government must strengthen intellectual property protection in order to allow local manufacturers to be more involved in the innovation process. This can overcome barriers to innovation (less involvement in design) that result from information leakage, to a large extent.

2.3 *Equilibrium Effect when Comparing Different Intelligent Manufacturing Capabilities*

2.3.1 More specific assumptions

Given two Chinese cities, city 1 and city 2, city 1 is a core city and city 2 is a peripheral city. The two cities have the same number of enterprises n, which are engaged either in the secondary industry (assuming that the secondary industry is limited to manufacturing) by working with multinationals, or in the primary industry (such as aquaculture). Suppose income T_0 of enterprises in the primary industry follows the law of diminishing marginal returns of labor ($T_0 < 0$): the more enterprises enter the primary industry, the smaller T_0 is. Moreover, the two types of enterprises have the same expected utilities (assuming that enterprises in the primary industry have one unit of leisure). Let x_1 and x_2 be the number of manufacturers in the core city and peripheral city, respectively, thus

$$\begin{aligned} T_0(n - x_1) \times 1 &= \mathrm{EU}_D(T_1, F_1), \\ T_0(n - x_2) \times 1 &= \mathrm{EU}_D(T_2, F_2). \end{aligned} \tag{6}$$

Let F_1 and F_2 be the cumulative distribution functions of the two cities' intelligent manufacturing capabilities, respectively. Suppose the core city has stronger intelligent manufacturing capability than the peripheral city, or F_1 first-order stochastic dominates F_2, for any $\eta \in (0, 1)$, $F_1(\eta) \leq F_2(\eta)$, and the existence of $\eta \in (0, 1)$ makes the strict inequality $F_1(\eta) < F_2(\eta)$ hold. First-order stochastic dominance implies that for any non-decreasing function g, $\int_0^1 g(\eta)dF_1(\eta) > \int_0^1 g(\eta)dF_2(\eta)$ holds.

Based on the above analysis, when a multinational chooses to cooperate with an enterprise in the core city, the expected utilities of the two parties are:

$$\mathrm{EU}_i = \int_0^{\eta^*} \mathrm{EU}_i^{\mathrm{IC}} dF_1(\eta) + \int_{\eta^*}^1 \mathrm{EU}_i^{\mathrm{AC}} dF_1(\eta), \qquad i = F, D. \tag{7}$$

For both parties ($i = F, D$), we have the following definition:

$$g_i(\eta, T) = \begin{cases} \mathrm{EU}_i^{\mathrm{IC}} & 0 < \eta < \eta^*, \\ \mathrm{EU}_i^{\mathrm{AC}} & \eta^* \leq \eta < 1. \end{cases} \tag{8}$$

Thus, if the multinational chooses to cooperate with an enterprise in the core city, its expected utility is

$$\begin{aligned} \mathrm{EU}_F &= \int_0^1 g_F(\eta, T_1) dF_1(\eta) = \int_0^{\eta^*} \frac{1}{4}(\pi - T_1) dF_1(\eta) + \int_{\eta^*}^1 (1-\mu)\pi \frac{(1+\eta)}{2(2+\eta)} dF_1(\eta) \\ &= \frac{1}{4}(\pi - T_1) F_1(\eta^*(T_1)) + (1-\mu)\pi \int_{\eta^*}^1 \frac{(1+\eta)}{2(2+\eta)} dF_1(\eta). \end{aligned} \tag{9}$$

For a manufacturer in the core city (as also for a manufacturer in the peripheral city), its expected utility is

$$\mathrm{EU}_D = \int_0^1 g_D(\eta, T_1) dF_1(\eta) = \int_0^{\eta^*} \frac{T_1 \eta}{2} dF_1(\eta) + \int_{\eta^*}^1 \frac{\mu\pi}{4} \frac{(1+2\eta)^2}{(1+\eta)(2+\eta)} dF_1(\eta). \tag{10}$$

2.3.2 Comparison of payment levels in an equilibrium

Assume that the core city and peripheral city are no different for the multinational (their expected utilities are the same), i.e.

$$\mathrm{EU}_F(T_1, F_1) = \mathrm{EU}_F(T_2, F_2). \tag{11}$$

Moreover, suppose each city has manufacturers that only implement blueprints, there is η that approaches 0, and there is also η bearing a large value ($\eta \to 1$) that satisfies $F_1(\eta) < F_2(\eta)$. In this case, we can compare payment levels in equilibrium.

Proposition 2. *Suppose* $F_1 \succ_{\text{FOSD}} F_2$ *(*F_1 *first-order stochastic dominates* F_2*), then in an equilibrium, payment* T_1 *received by the core city's manufacturer which cooperates with the multinational, is higher than payment* T_2 *received by the peripheral city's manufacturer which cooperates with the multinational.*

Proof. Suppose (contrary to Proposition 2) $T_1 \le T_2$, differentiating Eq. (9) for T and combining the definition of η^* yield

$$\frac{\partial \text{EU}_F}{\partial T} = \left[\frac{\pi - T}{4} - (1-\mu)\pi \frac{(1+\eta^*)}{2(2+\eta^*)}\right] \frac{dF(\eta^*)}{d\eta^*} \frac{\partial \eta^*}{\partial T} - \frac{1}{4}F(\eta^*) = -\frac{1}{4}F(\eta^*) < 0$$

(by assumption, $F(\eta^*) > 0$). Thus, $T_1 \le T_2$ means $\text{EU}_F(T_1, F_1) \ge \text{EU}_F(T_2, F_1)$. According to Eq. (7), $g_F(s, T_2)$ is a non-decreasing function. Since $F_1 \succ_{\text{FOSD}} F_2$ and there exists $\eta(\eta \to 1)$, this makes the strict inequality $F_1 < F_2$ hold, $\text{EU}_F(T_2, F_1) = \int_0^1 g_F(\eta, T_2) dF_1(\eta) > \int_0^1 g_F(\eta, T_2) dF_2(\eta) = \text{EU}_F(T_2, F_2)$. Combining $\text{EU}_F(T_1, F_1) \ge \text{EU}_F(T_2, F_1)$ yields $\text{EU}_F(T_1, F_1) > \text{EU}_F(T_2, F_2)$, which violates Eq. (11). Hence, $T_1 > T_2$. □

The straightforward meaning of Proposition 2 is that the multinational is more willing to work with a manufacturer with stronger intelligent manufacturing capability $\left(\frac{dg_F(\eta)}{d\eta} \ge 0\right)$. As the core city's intelligent manufacturing capability first-order stochastic dominates the peripheral city's, and the multinational's expected utilities are the same, the multinational will pay more to the core city's manufacturer than to the peripheral city's.

2.4 *Comparison between Degree of Involvement in Blueprint Design and Number of Principals*

The core city's intelligent manufacturing capability first-order stochastic dominates the peripheral city's, which significantly impacts the degree to which manufacturers in the two cities are involved in blueprint design.

Proposition 3. *Suppose $F_1 \succ_{\mathrm{FOSD}} F_2$, then, threshold $\eta^*(T_1)$ of involvement of the core city's manufacturer in blueprint design is lower than threshold $\eta^*(T_2)$ of involvement of the peripheral city's manufacturer in blueprint design.*

Proof. From Eq. (3),

$$\frac{\partial \eta^*(T)}{\partial T} = \frac{2/\pi(\mu-1)}{[1-2\mu+T/\pi]^2} < 0 .$$

Since $T_1 > T_2$, $\eta^*(T_1) < \eta^*(T_2)$. Obviously, in this case, the core city's manufacturer will be more involved in blueprint design. Furthermore, even if the core city's manufacturer has the same intelligent manufacturing capability as the peripheral city's manufacturer, the former will also have greater opportunities to participate in blueprint design (as discussed in Corollary 2). □

Corollary 2. *Assume that the core city's manufacturer has the same intelligent manufacturing capability as the peripheral city's manufacturer, and that its intelligent manufacturing capability meets the condition $\eta^*(T_1) < \eta < \eta^*(T_2)$, in which case, only the core city's manufacturer can participate in blueprint design.*

Although it may seem like the core city's manufacturer has relatively stronger intelligent manufacturing capability than the peripheral city's manufacturer, the multinational pays more to the former than to the latter. Thus, we need to compare the number of multinationals (principals) that cooperate with the core city, with the number of multinationals (principals) that cooperate with the peripheral city in equilibrium.

Proposition 4. *Suppose $F_1 \succ_{\mathrm{FOSD}} F_2$, then, in equilibrium, the core city will cooperate with more multinationals than the peripheral city, i.e. $x_1 > x_2$.*

Proof. Differentiating Eq. (17) for T yields

$$\frac{\partial \mathrm{EU}_D(T_1,F_1)}{\partial T_1}$$

$$= \frac{1}{2}\int_0^{\eta^*} \eta\, dF_1(\eta) + \frac{T}{2}\eta^* \frac{dF(\eta^*)}{d\eta^*}\frac{\partial \eta^*}{\partial T_1} - \frac{\mu\pi}{4}\frac{(1+2\eta^*)^2}{(1+\eta^*)(2+\eta^*)}\frac{dF_1(\eta^*)}{d\eta^*}\frac{\partial \eta^*}{\partial T_1}$$

$$= \frac{1}{2}\int_0^{\eta^*} \eta\, dF_1(\eta) + \left(\mathrm{EU}_D^{\mathrm{IC}}\Big|_{\eta=\eta^*} - \mathrm{EU}_D^{\mathrm{AC}}\Big|_{\eta=\eta^*}\right)\frac{dF_1(\eta^*)}{d\eta^*}\frac{\partial \eta^*}{\partial T_1}.$$

Since $\mathrm{EU}_D^{\mathrm{IC}} < \mathrm{EU}_D^{\mathrm{AC}}$ and $\frac{\partial \eta^*(T)}{\partial T} < 0$, $\frac{\partial \mathrm{EU}_a(T, F_1)}{\partial T} > 0$. From Proposition 2, $T_1 > T_2$, hence $EU_D(T_1, F_1) > EU_D(T_2, F_1)$. From specific values of $\mathrm{EU}_D^{\mathrm{AC}}$ and $\mathrm{EU}_D^{\mathrm{IC}}$ and from Eq. (8), $g_a(s, T_2)$ is increasing function over s. Since $F_1 \succ_{\mathrm{FOSD}} F_2$, $\mathrm{EU}_D(T_2, F_1) = \int_0^1 g_D(\eta, T_2) dF_1(\eta) . > \int_0^1 g_D(\eta, T_2) dF_2(\eta) = \mathrm{EU}_D(T_2, F_2)$. Combining $\mathrm{EU}_D(T_1, F_1) > \mathrm{EU}_D(T_2, F_2)$ yields $\mathrm{EU}_D(T_1, F_1) > \mathrm{EU}_D(T_2, F_2)$. From Eq. (6), $T_0(n - x_1) = EU_D(T_1, F_1) > \mathrm{EU}_D(T_2, F_2) = T_0(n - x_2)$, i.e. $T_0(n - x_1) > T_0(n - x_2)$. Since $T_0 < 0$, $x_1 > x_2$. □

The straightforward meaning of Proposition 4 is that, since the expected utility of the core city's manufacturer is higher than that of the peripheral city's manufacturer, and with difference in industries that the enterprises in respective cities are engaged in not making any difference, enterprises engaged in the primary industry in a core city have higher expected utilities than those engaged in the primary industry in a peripheral city. In other words, the core city has fewer enterprises engaged in the primary industry (and more engaged in manufacturing) than the peripheral city, or has more enterprises that cooperate with multinationals.

Combining the above conclusion $\mathrm{EU}_D(T_1, F_1) > \mathrm{EU}_D(T_2, F_2)$ with Eq. (6), the following corollary can be derived that is directly related to intelligent manufacturing capability's benefit generation effect.

Corollary 3. *Suppose $F_1 \succ_{\mathrm{FOSD}} F_2$, then, in any equilibrium, utility gained by each enterprise in the core city is greater than that gained by each enterprise in the peripheral city.*

Corollary 3 holds great practical significance to China in enhancing its intelligent manufacturing capability, and in adapting to the international industrial division of labor trend. Current international and domestic environments determine that Chinese manufacturers will continue to play a role in implementing blueprints under international industrial division of labor principle for a period of time in future. As long as China improves its intelligent manufacturing capability and takes active part in international industrial division of labor, it can create international division of labor, in which manufacturers' participation shifts from low-end to middle and high-end in the global production network's industrial chain (shift from implementation to design, and from manufacturing to creation), and more importantly, provide Chinese manufacturers with greater benefits, while enabling them to obtain more opportunities for cooperation.

2.5 *Basic Conclusion and Highlights*

In this section, the relationship between a Chinese manufacturer's intelligent manufacturing capability and the degree of its involvement in blueprint design under international industrial division of labor principle, and the equilibrium effect when comparing different intelligent manufacturing capabilities in a core city and a peripheral city is studied. Intelligent manufacturing capability is generalized as the similarity between a local manufacturer's blueprint design and one that is designed by a multinational. A local manufacturer cannot be involved in blueprint design unless its intelligent manufacturing capability exceeds a threshold, failing which, it can only implement the blueprint designed by the multinational. Intelligent manufacturing capability threshold turns smaller with increasing intensity of intellectual property protection. Thus, greater intensity of intellectual property protection will result in more opportunities for local manufacturers to participate in blueprint design.

It is assumed that the core city's intelligent manufacturing capability first-order stochastic dominates the peripheral city's; hence, in an equilibrium, the core city's manufacturer receives higher payment than the peripheral city's manufacturer; the threshold of the intelligent manufacturing capability required by the core city's manufacturer to participate in blueprint design is lower than that required by the peripheral city's manufacturer; and the core city gets more opportunities to cooperate with multinationals and obtains higher benefits than the peripheral city. In this sense, intelligent manufacturing capability has become an important assessment indicator for multinationals to cooperate with local Chinese manufacturers. Therefore, it is necessary for Chinese manufacturers to embrace the "Internet Plus" at a faster pace, and improve their intelligent manufacturing capabilities.

III. "Industry 4.0" and "Made in China 2025": Current Situation of and Challenges to Shanghai's Manufacturing Industry

A new round of scientific, technological and industrial revolution is making new progress in new-generation information technologies that focus on in-depth integration with manufacturing, as well as in new energy, new materials and biotechnology. All these developments are giving rise to far-reaching changes in the industry as well as new production concepts such as the Industrial Internet, Industrial Big Data and Industry 4.0.

1. *"Industry 4.0"*[13]

"Industry 4.0" originated from the German government's High-Tech Strategy, which was jointly funded by the German Federal Ministry of Education and Research and the Federal Ministry of Economic Affairs and Energy, with an estimated investment of €200 million. "Industry 4.0" is aimed at increasing the level of intelligent manufacturing, building adaptive, resource-efficient and ergonomics-based smart factories, and integrating customers and business partners in business and value processes. "Industry 4.0" is based on a cyber-physical network system and the Internet of Things.

"Industry 4.0" refers to intelligent manufacturing in the Internet era. Compared to the three industrial revolutions featuring mechanization, electrification and automation, "Industry 4.0", which is called "The Fourth Industrial Revolution", is a new model of personalized, digitalized, intelligent manufacturing that is enabled by real-time communication among people, equipment and products. The core of "Industry 4.0" is integration between production and manufacturing through the Internet of Things and service networks, and its essence lies in information management. However, "Industry 4.0" intelligence is no longer limited to production factories and has extended its reach to society, so its true essence is prompt information collection, exchange and collaboration. "Industry 4.0" embraces an innovation space that is far greater than the space that accommodates various e-commerce activities, and emphasizes "smart factory" and "intelligent production". Its true significance lies in realizing in-depth integration between information and automation technologies, and its most direct purpose is to maintain manufacturing industry's competitive advantage in the

---

[13]This part of introduction is written with reference to the article found in Baidu Baike. Available at: http://baike.baidu.com/link?url=70z-8Sc3Us-5LeqxR-XvYyjpF1M2g3F6D2gE6jgrj0eFA4da0AwyOdfzLpVY2v2nbm_8NQoi5blJWxQnaSgQvHk8ViNF_CFuWRE-v7GSMZu.

world. "Industry 4.0" does not refer to intelligent transformation of a single factory, but transformation and upgrade of entire society, and it entails government planning and coordination. It makes comprehensive use of physical information systems to transform the basic model from centralized control to decentralized, enhanced control meant to establish a highly resilient, personalized and digitalized production mode for products and services.

As mentioned earlier, China's manufacturing industry is currently facing unprecedented challenges — a "two-way pressure" caused by the return of high-end manufacturing to developed countries and transfer of low-end manufacturing to low-cost countries. Moreover, according to the *2015 Study Report on Industry 4.0* issued by analysis, although China is the world's largest manufacturing economy, modernization and informatization development levels vary in different regions with low degree of standardization. China's manufacturing industry is now experiencing unbalanced growth; it is stuck with the dilemma that it has not comprehensively realized Industry 2.0 (mass production and mechanization) and Industry 3.0 (industrial automation), and now has to face Industry 4.0 (in-depth integration of industrial automation and informatization).[14] In this scenario, China's manufacturing needs to be urgently transformed and upgraded. Therefore, it is pragmatic to study and learn from Industry 4.0, build smart factories, and promote in-depth integration of informatization and industrialization, to transform and upgrade China's manufacturing.

2. "*Made in China 2025*"

On May 19, 2015, the State Council officially issued the "Made in China 2025" initiative, defining intelligent manufacturing as China's main orientation for building strong manufacturing capabilities. The initiative proposed the guiding principle of in-depth informatization and industrialization integration, with a focus on developing intelligent equipment and products, application of intelligence to production processes, cultivation of new production modes, overall improvement in enterprise intelligence levels in terms of R&D, production, management and services, and implementation of major intelligent manufacturing projects.

---

[14] Analysis: *2015 Study Report on Industry 4.0*, May 2015.

Based on the general concept of adhering to new industrialization with Chinese characteristics, the "Made in China 2025" initiative aims to promote innovative development of manufacturing, improve quality and efficiency, speed up integration between new-generation information technologies and manufacturing, promote intelligent manufacturing, and meet the demand for major technological equipment, as required for economic and social development as well as national defense construction. These efforts are aimed at strengthening industrial base capacity, improving comprehensive integration levels, enhancing multi-level talent systems, promoting industrial transformation and upgrade, and achieving a historical leap from a "big manufacturing economy" to a "strong manufacturing economy". It should be emphasized that the main guideline of the initiative is integration between new-generation information technologies and manufacturing; the main orientation is intelligent manufacturing; and the essence is a shift from resource-driven manufacturing to information-driven manufacturing.

3. *Current Situation of and Challenges to Shanghai's Manufacturing Industry*

Chinese manufacturers' key core technologies are still controlled by others, as evidenced by the fact that a large number of key components, system software, and high-end equipment are basically imported, which adversely affects its independent innovation capabilities. In terms of product quality, China's manufacturing has weak competitiveness and lacks world-renowned brands. Furthermore, leading manufacturers do not give sufficient impetus to their development potential. In some countries and regions, "Made in China" has become synonymous with poor quality, seriously damaging China's reputation and image. Informatization of China's manufacturing is generally changing from single business coverage to comprehensive integration; however, informatization levels are still not high. Intelligent equipment's penetration rate has improved, but the value of intelligent manufacturing has not yet been sufficiently extracted.

Furthermore, in terms of management, institutional mechanisms and management models in the industrial era are ill-adapted to the new model of "Internet Plus Manufacturing" as reflected by the ill adaptation between traditional production relations and emerging production relations, between cross-industry integration accelerated by manufacturing and industrial management featuring segmentation, and between developing basic information resource sharing and business collaboration demands and regulatory methods.

Lastly, although "Made in China" has a large domestic market as its major advantage, it is now in a delicate situation where it lags behind pacemakers, and is followed by pursuers in the international environment. While on the one hand, some Western developed countries are implementing "Industry 4.0" upgrade programs, making it harder for China to catch up with them as they have a strong industrial base; on the other hand, Southeast Asian countries and other emerging economies are capitalizing on their cheap labor and low business cost advantages, due to which, some of China's traditional manufacturing capacities are being transferred to such countries. In a sense, China is threatened from both sides in the field of international competition, where China is vying with developed countries in high-end manufacturing, and with developing countries in middle and low-end manufacturing.[15]

The biggest problem for Shanghai's manufacturing is not poor technological level or low productivity, but the separation between production and market, as well as stagnation and backlog in all aspects of the supply chain, such as overcapacity, idle equipment, long production cycle, slow new product development, poor product marketability, inventory backlog, and other issues. Therefore, transforming and upgrading Shanghai's manufacturing does not lie in technological transformation featuring "local optimization", but the overall efficiency of the supply chain, i.e. market demand, sales, production and procurement, which is applicable to both consumer goods and industrial products. It is heartening to see that the Internet provides excellent conditions to evaluate the problem from a systematic perspective.

As one of the eight pilot zones for integrating informatization and industrialization identified by the Ministry of Industry and Information Technology, Shanghai has seen enhanced information technology application levels in enterprises in recent years, improvement in innovation capabilities and

---

[15]NetEase Finance: *Opportunity for Reform of "Made in China*." Available at: http://money.163.com/15/0520/03/AQ1E0ELD00253B0H.html.

industrial levels, and optimization of industrial structure and integrated environment. Shanghai has figured in the top ranks for many years in a row, in the Ministry of Industry and Information Technology's evaluation of regional integration between informatization and industrialization.

However, some bottlenecks now hinder further development of intelligent manufacturing in Shanghai, such as undefined technology roadmap, undetermined development strategy, imperfect industrial technology system, higher focus on hardware as opposed to software, and weak industrial technological service ability. Currently, Shanghai's enterprises are engaged in scattered, low-level application of intelligent manufacturing, and their technologies have high external dependence. They have relatively insufficient self-innovation and absorption capabilities, and are weak in key technologies. A lot of important equipment, core technologies and key components are mainly imported, and they lag behind development of advanced materials, 3D printing and other cutting-edge areas. High-end intelligent manufacturing equipment developed with independent technologies has not yet been introduced to the market, and no high-end intelligent software is used in various types of complex product design and enterprise management. A wide gap still exists between developed countries and China in terms of computer-aided design, resource planning software, e-commerce and other key technological areas.[16]

IV. Transformation and Upgrade Path and Policy Suggestions for Manufacturing Industries in Core Cities Under "Internet Plus Industry"

1. *Transformation and Upgrade Path*

Acting blindly would be a big mistake for manufacturers. They should put aside their glorious history of manufacturing, embrace new technologies

[16]Shanghai Investment Attraction Website: *Shanghai "Internet Plus Manufacturing" Conference 2015 held in Shanghai*. Available at: http://www.zhaoshang-sh.com/jjkx/2015/11-3/1511314215J29CJ73E4IIGECJ97GHE.html.

Chapter 5

National Strategy to Build Shanghai into an International Financial Center

I. Shanghai Financial Center Function and National Strategy

N. S. B. Gras (1922), an American economic historian, elaborated upon different stages of urban development. He expounded that the first stage of urban development is commerce, the second is industry, the third is transportation, and the fourth is finance. Financial development is the highest stage of urban development, and finance is more concentrated than commerce, industry, and real estate. Thus, final stage of urban development is the development of a financial center (Pan, 2010).

Construction of a financial center is conducive to a city's economic development, thereby increasing urban function and demand capacity, which directly leads to development of other related cities and has a direct economic impact on other cities. Furthermore, construction of a financial center helps resource allocation globally, and supports economic development of the city, region and even country, thus having an indirect economic impact on other cities.

1. *Financial Center's Agglomeration and Mechanisms of Economic Impact*

Based on the principles of urban agglomeration development, it becomes important to leverage a core city's agglomeration effect, economic impact and leading role in finance, logistics, trade, exhibition, information, and high-end manufacturing. Based on the principles of growth of a global megalopolis, the city's core lies in the central business district (CBD), and drives overall urban development through CBD's economic impact.[1]

A financial center's agglomeration effect and economic impact on surrounding cities constitute a closed-loop mechanism by which hinterland economy supports construction of financial center, which subsequently supports development of hinterland cities, leading to sound interaction.

1.1 *Financial Center's Agglomeration Mechanism*

1.1.1 Supporting effect

Supporting effect is embodied in six aspects of connotative development, especially when it comes to making "big, strong, new, good, practical and beautiful" achievements. "Big" refers to connotative development expanding financial and shipping center's impact level. "Strong" refers to connotative development improving financial and shipping center's core competitiveness. "New" refers to connotative development promoting institutional and product-related innovations in the financial and shipping center, such as introducing trade of new elements such as carbon emission permits. "Good" refers to connotative development improving residents' welfare levels, by creating a good environment for the financial and shipping center. "Practical", refers to connotative development upgrading China's position in international division of labor and

[1]Guo Chu. Capitalize on economic impact and leading role of a core city. *Guangzhou Daily*, April 13, 2013, p. A3.

enhancing local currency's international status, thereby consolidating the financial and shipping center's foundation. "Beautiful" refers to connotative development improving national image, improving relationships between man and nature, and enhancing financial and shipping center's international image.

1.1.2 Multiplier effect

A well-known feature of long-term economic development is that financial assets grow faster than gross output growth. Thus, when economy grows, financial services sector generally grows faster than national output.

In Shanghai, for example, total added value achieved by Shanghai's financial industry was RMB718.45 billion during "11th Five-Year Plan" period, with an average annual growth rate of 23.4%, which was 10.6% and 8.4% higher than GDP growth and growth of tertiary industry's added value in the same period, respectively. It accounted for 10.4% and 18.5% of Shanghai's GDP and tertiary industry's added value, an increase of 2.3% and 2.9%, respectively, over the "10th Five-Year Plan" period. It contributed 14.7% to GDP growth, an increase of 11.4% over the "10th Five-Year Plan" period, ranking among the best in various tertiary industry sectors.

1.2 *Financial Center's Mechanisms of Economic Impact*

Financial center's economic impact is reflected in the fact that the financial center's development drives development of other cities through a variety of transmission mechanisms.

1.2.1 Mechanism of direct economic impact

The mechanism of direct economic impact works in a manner that financial center's development leads to improvement in its economic level and increase in purchasing power, thereby expanding demand for other cities or increasing their production capacity, and thus directly fueling their development. It includes a "demand-pull mechanism" and an "industrial transfer mechanism".

"Demand-pull mechanism" works in a manner that the financial center's development leads to improvement in its economic level and increase in its purchasing power, thereby expanding demand for other cities or increasing their production capacity, and thus directly fueling their development.

"Industrial transfer mechanism" functions in a way that financial industry's development in the financial center, results in transfer of traditional industries to other cities. Thus, financial center creates a mechanism of direct economic impact on other cities. Based on international experience, when urban development reaches a certain stage, its core functions will be partially transferred externally. This is a common practice to deal with housing, transportation, environment and other "metropolis problems", and to promote orderly urban division of labor and development of urban agglomerations.[2] In turn, it also drives other related cities' economic development (Figure 5.1).

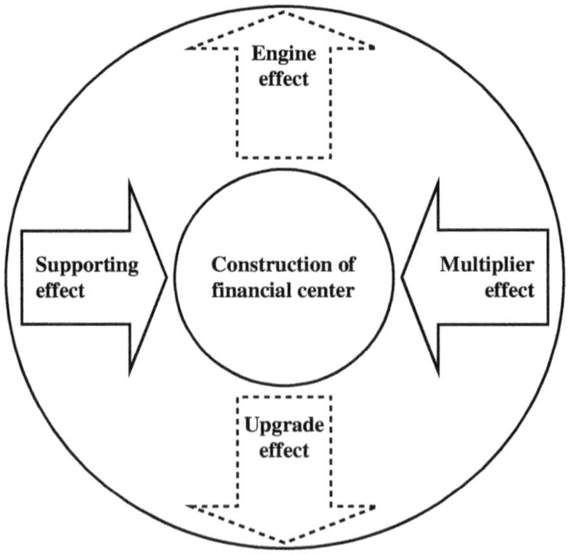

Figure 5.1 "Agglomeration and Mechanisms of Economic Impact" for Interactive Development between Financial Center and Other Cities

1.2.2 Mechanism of indirect economic impact

The mechanism of indirect economic impact is reflected by the financial center's ability to optimize resource allocation through finance, thereby promoting other cities' development through "engine effect" and "upgrade effect".

The core of finance lies in optimal allocation of capital-based resources based on four dimensions of time, space, risk and income. Effective finance should create a Pareto improvement of the entire society and thus, should be "conducive to construction of a good society" (Shearer, 2015). International financial center's construction will enhance a city's ability to allocate resources globally, thereby improving level and quality of economic growth in the city, region and even country, indirectly driving other cities' development. This indirect leading effect is mainly embodied in "engine effect" and "upgrade effect" of the financial center's construction based on overall economic growth.

Engine effect. Financial industry can effectively reduce transaction costs in international finance and trade as it has a long value chain and wide range of related industries; hence, development of financial and shipping industries can boost country's economic growth, industrial structure upgrade and economic growth globally. To some extent, financial and shipping industries have an "engine effect" on overall economic growth.

For example, London's 311,000 strong workforce, account for a little more than 1% of the UK workforce; however, they make significantly higher contributions to UK's prosperity in terms of output, taxes and overseas income, due to London's international financial services industry's vitality and efficiency, with contributions to UK's output and taxes around 4%. In addition, London handles 54% of the EU's financial wholesale services.

Upgrade effect. Upgrade effect is the positive effect of a financial center's construction on upgrading and optimizing the industrial structure, and enhancing a country's innovation capability and international status. Financial center's construction is conducive to mobilizing advantageous factors and resources globally, and improving total factor productivity, to promote industrial structure's upgrade and drive connotative development.

2. *Shanghai Financial Center's Economic Impact Network*

Shanghai financial center's economic impact constitutes an omni-directional economic impact network that is enabled by point, by line, by surface and by network. "Economic impact by point" refers to Shanghai financial center's effect on Shanghai's economic development. "Economic impact by line" refers to Shanghai financial center's effect on Yangtze River Economic Belt's economic development. "Economic impact by surface" refers to Shanghai financial center's effect on national economic development. "Economic impact by network" refers to Shanghai financial center's effect on global economic development.

2.1 *Shanghai Financial Center's Economic Impact on Shanghai's Economic Development ("Economic Impact by Point")*

According to *Statistical Communique on Shanghai's National Economic and Social Development in 2014*, Shanghai achieved gross domestic product (GDP) of RMB2.356094 trillion in 2014, an increase of 7.0% over the previous year at comparable prices. Specifically, the financial industry's added value was RMB326.843 billion, an increase of 14% over the previous year, and accounted for 13.9% of the GDP, an increase of 2.1% since 2010. Table 5.1 shows the proportion of added value of Shanghai's financial industry to Shanghai's GDP for 10 years from 2005 to 2014.

As shown in the table, from 2005 to 2014, Shanghai's financial industry's added value increased every year, and Shanghai's financial industry's added value proportion in the GDP grew, marking gradual increase in financial industry's pulling effect on Shanghai's overall economic development.

2.2 *Shanghai Financial Center's Economic Impact on Yangtze River Economic Belt ("Economic Impact by Line")*

A world-class urban agglomeration is an important functional area to participate in international division of labor and improve international

Table 5.1 Proportion of Added Value of Shanghai's Financial Industry to Shanghai's GDP (2005–2014) Unit: RMB100 million

Year	2005	2006	2007	2008	2009	2010	2011	2012	2013	2014
Shanghai's GDP	9247.7	10572.2	12494.0	14069.9	15046.5	17166.0	19195.7	20181.7	21602.1	23560.9
Added value of Shanghai's financial industry	689.9	799.4	1195.7	1442.6	1817.9	1931.7	2240.5	2450.4	2823.3	3268.4
Proportion of added value of financial industry to GDP	7.46%	7.56%	9.57%	10.25%	12.08%	11.25%	11.67%	12.14%	13.07%	13.87%

Source: Data collected from *Statistical Communique on Shanghai's National Economic and Social Development* over the years.

competitiveness. In Yangtze River Economic Belt's construction, urban agglomeration has been identified as an important functional area to optimize development pattern and enhance international competitiveness. Yangtze River Delta urban agglomeration is the most developed urban agglomeration in China, and is China's only urban agglomeration which is listed as one of the world's six major urban agglomerations. Shanghai is the undisputed primate city in Yangtze River Delta urban agglomeration, and shoulders strategic mission of following major national strategy, promoting coordinated development in Yangtze River Delta, and enhancing its economic impact on the Yangtze River Economic Belt, in its construction.

Acting as the Yangtze River Economic Belt's leader, Shanghai also exerts an important role of financial impact. For example, Shanghai encourages social capital to participate in Yangtze River Delta Collaborative Development Fund, and has established a professional operating team and a market-oriented operating mechanism to ensure that the Fund works properly and safely, benefiting all parties.[2]

2.3 *Shanghai Financial Center's Economic Impact on Overall Economic Development of the Country ("Economic Impact by Surface")*

This economic impact can be further deconstructed into three forces: "Shanghai's magnetic force" that creates interactive development between Shanghai and Yangtze River Delta urban agglomeration, and promotes country's overall economic development; "Shanghai's driving force" that effectively enhances China's ability to allocate resources globally and achieves country's overall economic development; and "Shanghai's pulling force" that improves China's position in international financial system and boosts country's overall economic development. The three forces work in synergy to integrate various types of financial resources and

---

[2] Xue Yanjie and Wang Zhen. How does Shanghai act as a good "Leader" in the Yangtze river economic belt. *Jiefang Daily*, April 15, 2015, p. 11.

factors in Shanghai, Yangtze River Delta, China, and the world, boosting China's economic development.

(1) Shanghai's magnetic force: Shanghai financial center is the "magnetic center" of local economic development, and Shanghai achieves its own productivity growth and connotative development through agglomeration and scale effect. Shanghai financial center has an economic impact on surrounding cities and drives connotative development of urban agglomerations. The economic impact is embodied in promotion of peripheral urban agglomerations' connotative development, through subcontracting and spillover economy.

    Based on the principle of a financial and shipping metropolis, a core city does bring about strong "economic impact" on neighboring cities. For example, London is now the "trademark" and "pivot" of UK's financial services industry, whose financial brand effect and subcontracting effect characterized by its pursuit of low costs have produced strong economic impact. London has led to comprehensive development of UK's financial services industry, and Edinburgh's financial development is particularly outstanding. Edinburgh's rise reflects the charm of a mature financial center, and this is also London's charm.[3] In addition, 16% of sales achieved by small and medium-sized enterprises surrounding London come from transactions with enterprises within London.[4]

(2) Shanghai's driving force: Financial and shipping center mobilizes advantageous factors and resources worldwide, reduces transaction costs, encourages all kinds of innovation, and promotes industrial upgrade, thus acting as an important driving force for the country to achieve connotative development.

(3) Shanghai's pulling force: A financial center's construction can enhance the country's rule-making influence and pricing power over

[3]Chu Minwei, He Ying and Zhu Delin. Blue book on the construction of Shanghai International Financial Center in 2008. *Shanghai People's Publishing House*, 2008, p. 177.
[4]Study Report of the City of London: *The City of London's Supply Chain and its Relations with the City Fringes*. Retrieved from http://www.cityoflondon.gov.uk.

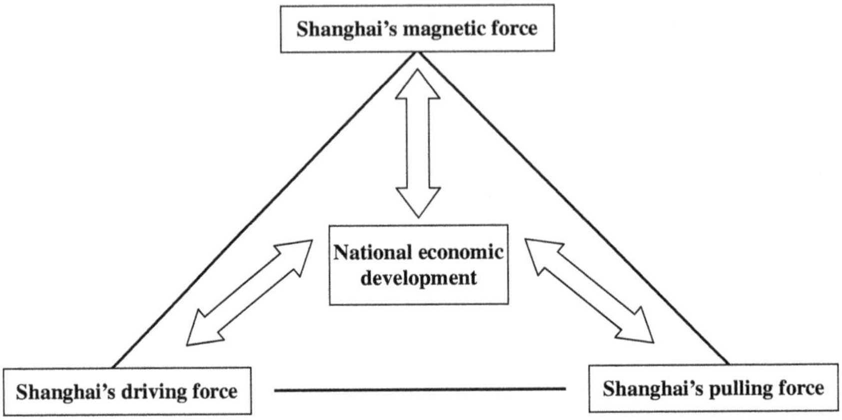

Figure 5.2 Interactive Relationship between "Shanghai's Forces" and National Economic Development

global goods and factors, and thus help the country raise its position in division of labor in international industry and value chain. Shanghai financial center's construction enhances the city's rule-making and pricing influence in international market. It is known as "Shanghai's influence", which is also referred to as "Shanghai's pulling force".

Figure 5.2 shows interactive relationship between "Shanghai's forces" and national economic development.

2.4 *Shanghai Financial Center's Economic Impact on Global Economic Development ("Economic Impact by Network")*

Shanghai financial center's construction plays a spillover and leading role in global economic development, known as "economic impact by network".

At present, Silk Road Economic Belt construction and 21st Century Maritime Silk Road (the "Belt and Road") is China's major national strategy. The National Development and Reform Commission, Ministry of Foreign Affairs and Ministry of Commerce jointly issued *Vision and Actions on Jointly Building Silk Road Economic Belt and 21st Century*

Maritime Silk Road, in March 2015, stating that it is the aim to allow people of countries situated along the "Belt and Road" to share results of the strategy. This chapter will further analyze Shanghai financial center's "economic impact by network" by taking the "Belt and Road" as an example.

3. *Shanghai Financial Center's Financial Support to the "Belt and Road"*

3.1 *Current "Belt and Road" Financial Development Situation*

3.1.1 Countries and regions situated along the "Belt and Road" are relatively weak financially

There are over 60 countries situated along the "Belt and Road" and most of these are emerging and developing countries and fall into different stages of economic development, with widely prevalent regional financial suppression. In many of these countries, development of capital markets is slow, and good quality enterprises lack safe and efficient direct financing channels. Countries situated along the "Belt and Road" have limited overall financial strength, and there is no funding and financing support for these countries to enable them to build interconnection infrastructure.

3.1.2 The "Belt and Road" has strong financial development requirements

Specifically, economic and trade cooperation is the foundation and pilot action for the "Belt and Road" construction, and the key lies in large-scale infrastructure construction in initial stages. Subsequently, cooperative development and resource and energy utilization, as well as a full range of trade services will become the focus, which will bring about investment opportunities in multiple industrial chains and across multiple industries.

According to Ministry of Commerce's statistics, between 2004 and 2013, the value of trade between China and countries situated along the

"Belt and Road" grew by 19% annually on average. China's direct investment in these countries increased by 46% annually on average, much higher than total annual average growth in foreign trade and outward foreign direct investment during the same period. In 2013, value of trade with countries situated along the "Belt and Road" accounted for 1/4 of total value of China's foreign trade.

Financial support must keep pace in the context of steady progress and increasing scale of economic and trade cooperation between China and countries situated along the "Belt and Road".

3.2 *Three Levels of Financial Support for the "Belt and Road"*

3.2.1 Financial support at international level

Firstly, international and regional financial institutions need to be established to satisfy capital needs for infrastructure construction related to the "Belt and Road". For example, Asian Infrastructure Investment Bank (AIIB) and Silk Road Fund have been setup to provide important financial support mechanisms for constructing the "Belt and Road". In addition, New Development Bank BRICS, Shanghai Cooperation Organization Bank and AIIB are also important financial support platforms.

Secondly, regional financial cooperation systems need to be established. It may be necessary to consider deepening pragmatic cooperation between SCO Interbank Consortium and China–ASEAN Interbank Consortium. This will enhance Silk Road Fund and AIIB's role, expand scale and scope of a bilateral currency swap, increase settlements in local currency in cross-border trade, and reduce exchange rate risks and settlement costs in intra-regional trade and investment.

Thirdly, international investment and finance systems need to be established. With AIIB and Silk Road Fund as forerunners, it is important to fully mobilize various types of investment funds of relevant countries and regions, establish relevant financial operation mechanisms, and encourage decisive role of market mechanism based on respect for rights and interests of all parties. For example, international long-term investment bonds can be issued in the international market.

3.2.2 Financial support at national level

Firstly, there should be active efforts to internationalize the Renminbi. China is an important trading partner for countries situated along the "Belt and Road". China's investment in these countries drives export of goods and services, expands Renminbi's capital export, and increases Renminbi's use in global resource allocation, and production and sales, thereby promoting Renminbi's regionalization and internationalization. In turn, Renminbi's greater internationalization provides a new choice of international currency for countries situated along the "Belt and Road", thereby reducing exchange rate risks and transaction costs.

Secondly, foreign exchange reserves should be utilized in the "Belt and Road". The "Belt and Road" has changed China's long-term dependence on purchase of government bonds issued by the United States and other developed countries to use foreign exchange reserves, broken through restrictions on indirect investment, and strengthened China's ability to allocate resources globally (especially in Asia).

Thirdly, development-oriented finance and policy-based finance's role should be exerted. Development-oriented and policy-based banks are more likely to encourage financing and financial advisers' role, and provide low-cost financing for domestic and foreign enterprises as well as large projects, while large commercial banks with overseas branches tend to facilitate financing by offering guarantees or loans through fund settlement or internal and external institutional linkage. Policy-based financial institutions should be encouraged to accelerate development of operations in countries and regions situated along the "Belt and Road", and domestic provinces located along the "Belt and Road" should be allowed to establish pilot regional policy-based banks.

3.2.3 Financial support at domestic level

First, there is commercialized operation of financial institutions. Commercial financial institutions are encouraged to "go global". Secondly, there is involvement of domestic residents' savings in the "Belt and Road" for investment, and an overseas investment fund for the "Belt and Road" can be considered to raise investment funds from people all over the country.

3.3 *Shanghai Financial Center's Support to the "Belt and Road" Initiative — A Roadmap*

3.3.1 Background of Shanghai financial center's support to the "Belt and Road" initiative

In March 2015, National Development and Reform Commission, Ministry of Foreign Affairs and Ministry of Commerce jointly issued *Vision and Actions on Jointly Building Silk Road Economic Belt and 21st Century Maritime Silk Road*, stating that "it is necessary to accelerate construction of China (Shanghai) Pilot Free Trade Zone and support Fujian in building a core area for the 21st Century Maritime Silk Road, by leveraging the high degree of openness, strong economic strength, and large economic impact of the Yangtze River Delta, Pearl River Delta, Western Taiwan Straits Economic Zone, and Bohai Economic Rim". Therefore, there is enough room for Shanghai to support the "Belt and Road" initiative, and for this, financial support is an important driving force.

3.3.2 Economic impact mechanisms for Shanghai financial center's support to the "Belt and Road" initiative

Economic impact mechanisms for Shanghai financial center's support to the "Belt and Road" initiative include direct economic impact and indirect economic impact mechanisms.

(i) **Indirect economic impact.** Firstly, indirect economic impact mechanism is reflected by financial support provided by Shanghai's financial market for projects related to the "Belt and Road" initiative. From the stock market's perspective, indirect economic impact is evident by the fact that Shanghai's stock market provides a platform for enterprises of countries situated along the "Belt and Road" to issue Renminbi-denominated bonds, stocks and funds. For example, Shanghai Stock Exchange and China Securities Index Co., Ltd.

formally launched SSE the "Belt and Road" theme index on June 24, 2015. Secondly, Shanghai financial center can seek further financial cooperation with major financial centers of countries situated along the "Belt and Road" with respect to settlement and clearing, credit guarantee, risk sharing, and other aspects.[5]

(ii) **Direct economic impact.** This is characterized by "go global" and "bring in" strategies that are jointly implemented. "Go global" strategy means that Shanghai-based financial institutions such as banks and insurance companies will provide financial products and services in countries and regions situated along the "Belt and Road", to attract and bring together financial institutions in these countries and regions. "Bring in" strategy means Shanghai's financial market issues bonds, stocks and funds related to the "Belt and Road".

4. *"New Thoughts" on How Shanghai Can Leverage its Financial Impact in the "Internet Plus" Era*

4.1 *Change in Shanghai Financial Center's Economic Impact Mechanisms in the "Internet Plus Finance" Era*

An important background in the current economic development is the arrival of the "Internet Plus" era. "Internet Plus" as a strategy is intended to bring all industries including traditional ones within the fold of Internet, using Internet platforms and information and communication technologies, thereby creating a new ecosystem in a new field. "Internet Plus" represents a new way of life, a new production mode, and a changing trend in social form in future, and is an irresistible trend of the times.

In the "Internet Plus Finance" era, the financial center's economic impact extends beyond traditional geographical boundaries, and service time, space and quality is rapidly upgraded. This provides an opportunity for Shanghai financial center to catch up with and even surpass others in international financial center competition. As Internet Finance goes beyond time and space limitations and geographical boundaries,

---

[5]Zhang Jun. The implementation program for Shanghai's promotion of the "Belt and Road" initiative has taken initial shape. *Jiefang Daily*, May 15, 2015, p. 2.

development of Internet banking allows Shanghai's financial industry to cover China and even the world, with the help of the mobile Internet platform, providing Shanghai a shortcut in its journey to become a global financial center. Internet Finance is the biggest opportunity for Shanghai to "breakthrough corners" while constructing the financial center (Yu, 2015).

4.2 *New Thoughts on How Shanghai Financial Center Leverages its Economic Impact in the "Internet Plus" Era*

4.2.1 Leveraging financial impact with the "Internet Plus" concept

In the Internet era, national strategy of building Shanghai into an international financial center is endowed with a new connotation based on the times. If traditional financial industry takes the initiative to use "Internet Plus" concepts and achieves innovation-driven transformation and development, it provides a strong impetus in constructing Shanghai's international financial center.

In August 2014, the Shanghai Municipal People's Government issued *Several Opinions on Promoting Healthy Development of Internet Financial Industry in the City*, advocating "a more inclusive attitude to support Internet financial innovation".

4.2.2 Serving national strategy at four levels — "economic impact by point, economic impact by line, economic impact by surface, and economic impact by network", and fostering a more powerful "synergy" of economic impact through strategic interaction

At the level of economic impact by point, Shanghai seeks to link with national strategies such as building "Four Centers", creating a globally influential center for scientific and technological innovation, and establishing Pilot Free Trade Zone. For example, with the help of Pilot Free Trade Zone, Shanghai has promoted pilot application of financial open innovation in free currency convertibility, investment and trade facilitation, financial market opening, and other aspects. Bilateral investment in China and overseas, expansion of free trade account functions, and "international board" for financial markets are likely to be breakthroughs that will be made in future.

At the level of economic impact by line, Shanghai is actively focusing on being involved in integrating the Yangtze River Economic Belt and the Yangtze River Delta, fulfilling the strategic mission of enhancing its economic impact on the Yangtze River Economic Belt.

At the level of economic impact by surface, Shanghai is steadily advancing Renminbi's internationalization and process of building Shanghai into an international financial center.

At the level of economic impact by network, Shanghai is actively serving the "Belt and Road" initiative and leveraging the role of finance in supporting this strategy.

II. Establishing Shanghai as a Commodity Pricing Center

1. *Commodities and Their Pricing*

After joining the World Trade Organization, China has deepened its integration into the global economy. As the world's factory, China's demand for primary products such as energy and raw materials has grown rapidly, and it ranks first in the world in consumption of many commodities. Due to resource constraints and mounting environmental crisis in China, local supply of some commodities has not been able to meet their growing demand, leading to increased import of such commodities, such as petroleum, copper, iron ore, soybeans, etc. Since 1995, when China became a net importer of primary products, the volume of primary product imports has increased year-on-year, and the trade deficit for commodities continues to grow.

Although China has become the world's largest commodity importer, it has so far failed to establish an internationalized trading center, and does not hold pricing power for commodities because of capital account control, non-internationalization of the Renminbi and many other reasons. Due to lack of pricing power for commodities, China has been exploited by foreign financial institutions, affecting China's real economy. The futures market plays a central role in international pricing of commodities (Tang *et al.*, 2006). The lack of an international futures trading center is why China has lost commodity pricing power. Therefore, China should actively promote internationalization of Chinese futures market, and vigorously develop its multinational futures companies (Dong and Wang, 2006). Crude oil futures on Shanghai International Energy Exchange Corporation and iron ore futures on Dalian Commodity Exchange are two kinds of internationalized futures that China is now striving to promote.

2. *Establishing Shanghai as a Commodity Pricing Center*

2.1 *Position of Shanghai's Future Market*

As per figures provided by the Futures Industry Association (FIA) on the world's 75 derivatives exchanges, the top five exchanges with highest trading volume in 2014, are Chicago Mercantile Exchange Group Inc. (CME Group), Intercontinental Exchange (ICE), Eurex Exchange, National Stock Exchange of India Ltd. (NSE), and the BM&F BOVESPA, just as they were in 2013 (Zhang, 2015). The Shanghai Futures Exchange, Dalian Commodity Exchange, Zhengzhou Commodity Exchange, Hong Kong Exchanges and Clearing Limited, China Financial Futures Exchange, and Taiwan Futures Exchange ranked 9th, 10th, 13th, 14th, 18th, and 19th, respectively, which shows that Shanghai Futures Exchange has occupied a leading position in the domestic commodity future market.

2.2 *Shanghai Gold Exchange*

After Shanghai Gold Exchange was established in October 2002, China's gold market, together with its currency, securities and foreign exchange markets have completely shaped China's financial market system. It provides a spot trading platform for participants in China's gold market, enables matching supply and demand for gold production and consumption enterprises, and realizes smooth transition from monopoly purchase and distribution of gold, to market transaction.

The Shanghai Futures Exchange provides a platform for gold futures trading, and Shanghai Gold Exchange offers a platform for spot trading of gold, and they are the main players helping China strive for international pricing power in gold.

2.3 *China (Shanghai) Pilot Free Trade Zone and Commodity Pricing*

The *Overall Plan of China (Shanghai) Pilot Free Trade Zone* clearly put forward the necessity to "explore building an international commodity trading and resource allocation platform in the zone". Based on the current commodity trading situation in Shanghai, emphasis is on constructing a commodity trading platform for gold and crude oil in China (Shanghai) Pilot Free Trade Zone ("Shanghai FTZ").

2.3.1 Gold

As a hedge commodity, gold is an important investment commodity globally. The Shanghai Gold Exchange is China's only and world's largest physical gold exchange. In May 2014, the People's Bank of China approved establishment of an international gold board to be operated by Shanghai International Gold Trading Center Co., Ltd., a subsidiary of the Shanghai Gold Exchange, in the Shanghai FTZ. In June 2014, the Shanghai International Gold Trading Center was established in the Shanghai FTZ, which allowed China's gold market to have a say in global gold pricing. The international gold board launched by the Shanghai Gold Exchange is known as "Shanghai Gold", and allows foreign investors to trade.

2.3.2 Crude oil

In November 2013, Shanghai International Energy Exchange Limited was established in the Shanghai FTZ. In December 2014, China Securities Regulatory Commission approved Shanghai International Energy Exchange Limited to trade in crude oil futures, marking the countdown to the listing of China's crude oil futures. The operation of crude oil futures will promote petroleum market system reform, provide an effective risk management tool for crude oil supply chain enterprises, guide reasonable resource allocation through a market-oriented pricing mechanism, and improve petroleum industry's international competitiveness and its ability to resist price risks.

2.4 *Economic Impact of Commodity Pricing Center on the "Belt and Road" Initiative*

2.4.1 The "Belt and Road" initiative

The "Belt and Road" runs through Asia, Europe and Africa, with one end connected to the active East Asian economic zone, and the other end connected to the developed European economic zone; countries situated in the vast central hinterland have huge economic development potential. The Silk Road Economic Belt in particular connects China to Europe (the Baltic Sea) via Central Asia and Russia, links China to the Persian Gulf and the Mediterranean Sea via Central Asia and West Asia, and extends from China to Southeast Asia, South Asia and the Indian Ocean. The 21st Century Maritime Silk Road focuses on the route from China's coastal ports to the Indian Ocean via the South China Sea, and extends to Europe; and the route from China's coastal ports to the South Pacific via the South China Sea.

Hu and Liu (2015) pointed out that implementing the "Belt and Road" initiative serves three purposes: industrial transfer, resource control along the "Belt and Road", and formation of China-dominant trade rules; these three purposes aim to comprehensively enhance China's commodity pricing power from different aspects.

2.4.2 The "Belt and Road" initiative and energy

The "Belt and Road" initiative was proposed against the backdrop that China's surrounding regions need a new economic engine to fuel economic prosperity, due to weak global economic recovery and change in global energy structure. China's rise has led to growth in energy consumption, while the growing energy independence in the United States has reduced their dependence on Middle East energy. The Ukrainian crisis has pushed Russia to shift its energy strategy to China. Therefore, with the world energy markets gradually shifting focus to China, it has become the center of energy geopolitics.

Successful shale oil development marks the success in United States' energy independence strategy, allowing the US to rapidly change from being the largest energy importer, to an energy independent country and even a net exporter of crude oil in future. The Middle East needs to find a substitute for the US as a crude oil importer in order to diversify its export markets, while China has to ensure stable and sustainable supply of crude oil from the Middle East, so as to overcome the restrictions imposed by the United States on China's maritime transport channels. As the largest crude oil exporter, the Middle East has joined hands with major crude oil importers such as China, Central Asia and Russia, with the aim to promote RMB-denominated crude oil trading, and to include crude oil futures launched by Shanghai International Energy Exchange Limited, following the North Sea Brent Crude launched by the London Intercontinental Exchange and the WTI Crude launched by the New York Mercantile Exchange, in the pricing benchmark basket for futures contracts, thereby enhancing China's crude oil pricing power (Hu and Liu, 2015).

2.4.3 The "Belt and Road" initiative and base metals

(i) **Steel.** Due to high infrastructure investment requirements for the "Belt and Road", equipment manufacturing related to energy, high-speed rail and nuclear power will enhance steel demand tremendously. More than 70% of the 64 countries situated along the "Belt and Road" are net steel importers and key target markets for China's steel export.

2015 saw domestic crude steel production capacity of about 1.15 billion tons, with annual production estimated at 820 million tons, capacity utilization of only 71.30% and excess capacity of about 300 million tons. The "Belt and Road" strategy encourages steel mills to go global. Steel mills can establish factories overseas, transfer production capacity and boost steel export, in order to ease domestic overcapacity, and they can also capitalize on good mineral resources in some foreign regions to reduce costs. In addition, the Asia–Europe

High-speed Railway Program and other infrastructure investment programs related to the "Belt and Road" initiative will greatly boost steel demand.

(ii) **Copper.** At present, China is the world's largest metal consumer, and it requires more than 8 million tons copper per year, which accounts for nearly half of global copper consumption. Like iron ore, China's copper has high external dependence and nearly half of the demand relies on import. However, China does not have international copper pricing power. Shanghai Futures Exchange is the world's third-largest copper futures trading market following the London Metal Exchange (LME) and the New York Mercantile Exchange (NYMEX) (Hua and Chen, 2004). As the world's largest non-ferrous metal exchange, LME's price and inventory significantly impact production and sale of non-ferrous metals worldwide. Taking into consideration competition for pricing power, no foreign exchange delivery warehouse is permitted to be set up in Shanghai FTZ, and this will surely help develop an international trading platform for copper in future.

2.4.4 The "Belt and Road" Initiative and gold

The "Belt and Road" initiative brings about benefits for gold in three aspects (Yang and Xue, 2015). First, the strategy helps countries and regions situated along the "Belt and Road" to increase their official gold holdings. In the past 6 years, central banks globally have increased gold holdings by 1,800 tons, as represented by those in many emerging countries and regions situated along the "Belt and Road" such as Russia, Kazakhstan, Azerbaijan, and Turkey. Strengthening joint development of gold cooperation schemes and improving China's gold market's physical re-export functions, can provide convenient channels for central banks in these countries and regions to purchase gold, and help them implement their strategies for increasing official gold holdings. Next, the strategy is conducive to expansion of trade impact circles for countries and regions situated along the "Belt and Road", which are known to have a tradition of cherishing and storing gold. The influence of cultural and social traditions has resulted in a robust gold consumption market chain, from West Asian countries to India and Thailand. Capitalizing on their gold demand, the

"Belt and Road" initiative is aimed at promoting cooperation and exchange in gold trade, and offers a good opportunity for China to expand trade cooperation with these countries and regions. Finally, the strategy is good for exploring new cooperation development models in resource-based industries. Many of these countries and regions have abundant mineral resources, but have inferior mining and refining techniques when compared to China; thus they have a keen need to cooperate with China. With the help of the "Belt and Road" strategic framework, China and these countries or regions can develop in-depth cooperation in gold and other mineral resources, and complement each other in terms of resources and technologies, thereby opening up win–win opportunities for all parties.

2.4.5 Internationalization of the Renminbi and commodity pricing power

Internationalization of the Renminbi is inevitably required to comprehensively enhance commodity pricing power. The "Belt and Road" initiative and establishment of AIIB can promote internationalization of the Renminbi and enhance its pricing power against commodities, and improve China's commodity pricing power (Hu and Liu, 2015). Internationalization of the Renminbi is a gradual process that should start off first with settlement, followed by reserve and then invoicing, and similarly start off with surrounding areas, then regions, and finally the world.

The "Belt and Road" initiative and AIIB will help turn the Renminbi from a settlement currency to an invoicing currency, thereby extending its reach from surrounding areas to regions. These two initiatives will facilitate basic convertibility of capital accounts in China, and boost internationalization of the Renminbi.

The "Belt and Road" initiative's implementation and AIIB's establishment will create favorable conditions for commodity pricing power competitions. Countries located along the "Belt and Road" have a wealth of resources, which are strategic resources with higher foreign trade dependence for China. In the course of trade, both sides are bound to need a large number of risk management tools, which will definitely provide a golden opportunity for developing China's futures market. If China can seize this opportunity and improve the commodity market system, including the spot market, futures market and over-the-counter market, it is entirely possible for China to win commodity pricing power.

2.4.6 "Internet Plus" commodity markets

"Internet Plus" is the innovative integration of new-generation information technologies, represented by mobile Internet, Big Data, Cloud Computing and Internet of Things, with manufacturing and service industries. "Internet Plus Commodities" will change business models and commodity market game rules, thus reshuffling the industry. It will also create upgraded versions of commodity markets, and shall enhance China's commodity pricing power (Hu and Liu, 2015).

The "Belt and Road" initiative's framework document suggests promoting cross-border fiber optic cable and other communication trunk network construction, to improve interoperability level for international communications, and to keep the information-based Silk Road open. It also proposes accelerating bilateral cross-border fiber optic cable network construction, planning intercontinental submarine fiber optic cable project construction, improving air (satellite) information channels, and expanding information exchange and cooperation. Constructing such Internet infrastructure will strongly support internationalization of China's commodity trading.

III. Financial Agglomeration and Economic Impact of China (Shanghai) Pilot Free Trade Zone

1. *Current Status and Reform Direction of Financial Agglomeration in China (Shanghai) Pilot Free Trade Zone*

1.1 *Financial Agglomeration Formation Mechanism in China (Shanghai) Pilot Free Trade Zone*

A global economy has promoted rapid flow and continuous integration of global financial resources, accompanied by high agglomeration of international financial industries in certain regions. Central business districts focused on financial industry are emerging in some cities, and play a vital role. Financial agglomeration is both a dynamic process and a static result. From a dynamic point of view, agglomeration leads to various financial institutions, resources and talents flocking to regions featuring good location advantages, strong economic base, and better governmental policy support. Financial entities in these regions influence one another, ultimately creating a financial market with a sound financial system. From a static point of view, financial agglomeration is the result of spatial movement of various financial resources; and a financial agglomeration zone takes shape when several financial institutions are highly concentrated in a particular region.

There are three forms of financial agglomeration depending on geographical range. The first is international financial agglomeration, featuring an international distribution pattern indicating an agglomeration of financial institutions and activities that varies greatly in different countries and regions. The second is national financial agglomeration, featuring a national distribution pattern, indicating an agglomeration of financial institutions and activities that are unevenly distributed in different regions of a country. The third is regional financial agglomeration, indicating an agglomeration of financial institutions and activities that are characterized by a regional distribution pattern, such as financial agglomeration in a free trade zone.

1.2 *Current Status of Financial Agglomeration in China (Shanghai) Pilot Free Trade Zone*

China (Shanghai) Pilot Free Trade Zone, also known as Shanghai FTZ for short, is a regional free trade zone set up in Shanghai by the Chinese government. It is located in the Pudong area, and is part of the Chinese free trade zone. Shanghai FTZ was formally established on September 29, 2013 with an area of 28.78 square kilometers covering four special customs supervision areas, namely, Shanghai Waigaoqiao Free Trade Zone, Waigaoqiao Free Trade Logistics Park, Yangshan Free Trade Port Area, and Shanghai Pudong Airport Comprehensive Free Trade Zone. On December 28, 2014, the Standing Committee of the National People's Congress authorized the State Council to expand Shanghai FTZ to 120.72 square kilometers.

Shanghai's economic development and progress have attracted a large number of financial institutions to Shanghai FTZ. By the end of May 2014, there were 2,297 financial institutions that had settled in Shanghai FTZ, including 57 licensed financial institutions, 321 financial leasing and equity investment financial institutions, and 1,919 financial information services, investment, asset management and other finance-related businesses. Table 5.2 shows the expected financial industry development targets in Shanghai FTZ for 2015.

Table 5.2 Expected Targets for Financial Industry Development in Shanghai FTZ for 2015

	Indicator	2012 base value	2015 target value	Description
Financial industry development	Number of financial institutions	—	3,700	100 financial institutions, 600 similar financial institutions, and 3,000 finance-related enterprises
	Size of financial leasing assets (unit: US$100 million)	25	150	Strive to achieve more than US$15 billion within the pilot period of 2–3 years, reaching more than 30% of Shanghai's financial leasing assets
	Amount of cross-border trade e-commerce transactions (unit: US$100 million)	—	2,000	Strive to achieve growth by 20%

Source: *Industrial Planning of China (Shanghai) Pilot Free Trade Zone* (Administrative Committee of China (Shanghai) Pilot Free Trade Zone).

1.3 *Main Content of Financial Reforms in Shanghai FTZ*

As per the *Overall Plan of China (Shanghai) Pilot Free Trade Zone*, Shanghai FTZ will establish a pilot financial zone under the premise of risk control, and will first carry out the following nine financial reforms in the financial zone:

(1) Realize marketization of interest rates in the financial market.
(2) Realize Renminbi capital account convertibility.
(3) Allow qualified foreign-funded financial institutions to establish foreign-funded banks, and qualified private capital and foreign-funded financial institutions to jointly establish Sino-foreign joint-venture banks.
(4) When conditions permit, establish limited license banks.
(5) Allow establishment of foreign-invested credit investigation companies.
(6) Allow qualified Chinese-funded banks to start offshore business, under the premise of improving relevant management measures and strengthening effective supervision.
(7) Encourage financial leasing by allowing financial leasing companies to concurrently engage in commercial factoring business related to their main business, and stipulating that no minimum registered capital limits should be imposed on subsidiaries with single aircraft or vessel, established by financial leasing companies.
(8) Allow foreign enterprises to participate in commodity futures trading, and allow foreign futures exchanges to designate or set up delivery warehouses for commodity futures.
(9) Collect corporate income tax at a reduced rate of 15% from project companies engaged in overseas equity investment, similar to advanced technology services industry.

Therefore, the purpose of promoting Shanghai FTZ's construction is not to have a technical upgrade of traditional preferential policies in the zone, but to conduct a trial application for in-depth reform of existing trade, investment, financial, and administrative systems. Shanghai FTZ represents another pioneering application for national reform, and its innovation will become a new standard in future.

2. *Advantages of Financial Agglomeration in Shanghai FTZ*

2.1 *Location Advantage*

At present, Shanghai is a center for international trade, shipping and finance. A model of "Four Areas and Three Ports" has been established in the Shanghai FTZ, demonstrating significant regional economic advantages. In terms of the "Four Areas", the Shanghai FTZ covers four special customs supervision areas, namely, Shanghai Waigaoqiao Free Trade Zone, Waigaoqiao Free Trade Logistics Park, Yangshan Free Trade Port Area, and Shanghai Pudong Airport Comprehensive Free Trade Zone.

2.2 *Policy Advantage*

Shanghai FTZ's establishment is an overall strategic decision concerning China's reform and opening up. As Premier Li Keqiang pointed out, its establishment can open up new space for economic growth, and it is a pilot endeavor to boost China's economic reform and improve the level of open economy. China has introduced numerous policies to support financial reforms and development. For example, the China Banking Regulatory Commission promulgated eight supporting measures to solve banking regulation issues in Shanghai FTZ, and China Securities Regulatory Commission announced several policy measures to support Shanghai FTZ's development.

Financial policy support enhances Shanghai FTZ's ability to attract more financial institutions and resources. Table 5.3 outlines measures introduced by China Banking Regulatory Commission (CBRC), China Securities Regulatory Commission (CSRC), State Administration of Foreign Exchange (SAFE), China Insurance Regulatory Commission (CIRC) and People's Bank of China (PBC), to support financial reforms, since establishment of Shanghai FTZ till February 2015.

In October 2015, the PBC, Ministry of Commerce, CBRC, CSRC, CIRC, SAFE, and Shanghai Municipal People's Government formally issued the *Program for Further Promoting the Pilot Implementation of Financial Opening and Innovation in China (Shanghai) Pilot Free Trade*

Table 5.3 List of Financial Support Policies for Shanghai FTZ (as of February 2015)

Agency	Issued on	Policy	Details
CBRC	Sep. 2013	Circular on Relevant Issues concerning Banking Regulation in China (Shanghai) Pilot Free Trade Zone	Encourages Chinese-funded and foreign-funded banks to do business in Shanghai FTZ; supports establishment of financial institutions by non-banking financial institutions and private capital in Shanghai FTZ; supports financial institutions in Shanghai FTZ to promote cross-border investment and financial services, as well as Chinese-funded banks to carry out offshore business.
	May 2014	Institutional Arrangement concerning Trial Implementation of Banking Regulation in China (Shanghai) Pilot Free Trade Zone	Specifies requirements on overall regulation of business carried out in Shanghai FTZ, risk assessment, and supervision of institutions in Shanghai FTZ; sets out provisions on special banking monitoring report system, as well as functional layout and resource support for banking in Shanghai FTZ.
CSRC	Sep. 2013	Several Policy Measures adopted in the Capital Market to Support and Promote China (Shanghai) Pilot Free Trade Zone	Approves establishment of Shanghai International Energy Exchange Limited by the Shanghai Futures Exchange; supports eligible entities and individuals to invest in both domestic and overseas securities markets; encourages securities and futures operators to set up specialized subsidiaries and engage in OTC commodity and financial derivative trading; allows Shanghai FTZ enterprises' (hereinafter referred to as FTZ enterprises) overseas parent companies to issue Renminbi-denominated bonds.

(Continued)

Table 5.3 (*Continued*)

Agency	Issued on	Policy	Details
SAFE	Feb. 2014	Circular on Supporting the Establishment of Implementation Rules for Foreign Exchange Administration in China (Shanghai) Pilot Free Trade Zone	Simplifies procedures for collecting and settling foreign exchange in current accounts as well as registering direct investment in foreign exchange; implements foreign exchange settlement for foreign exchange capital of foreign-funded enterprises; relaxes management of foreign claims and debts; improves management of foreign exchange settlement and sales; implements registration management for foreign leasing business conducted by financial leasing companies in Shanghai FTZ.
CIRC	Sep. 2013	Major Initiatives in Support of the Construction of China (Shanghai) Pilot Free Trade Zone	Encourages insurance companies to set up branches in Shanghai FTZ and carry out Renminbi cross-border reinsurance business; studies expansion scope and proportion for overseas investment by insurance institutions; supports pilot establishment of foreign-funded specialized health insurance institutions in Shanghai FTZ.
	May 2014	Circular on Further Simplifying Administrative Approval to Support the Development of China (Shanghai) Pilot Free Trade Zone	Allows Shanghai Institute of Marine Insurance to carry out pilot development of its terms, which can be independently used by member companies when reported. Cancels the need to obtain prior approval for establishing branches by Shanghai-based shipping insurance operation centers and reinsurance companies in Shanghai FTZ, and Shanghai Insurance Regulatory Bureau implements records management. Cancels the need to obtain prior qualification approval for senior executives working with insurance companies in Shanghai FTZ, and Shanghai Insurance Regulatory Bureau implements records management.

PBC	Dec. 2013	Suggestions on Financial Support for Construction of China (Shanghai) Pilot Free Trade Zone	Puts forward principled opinions on account system innovation in Shanghai FTZ, investment and financing exchange, cross-border Renminbi usage, interest rate marketization, foreign exchange management, and anti-money laundering.
	Feb. 2014	Circular on Factual Opinions of the Cross-border Renminbi Payment Business Carried out by Shanghai Payment Institutions	Payment institutions incorporated in Shanghai and having Internet payment business licenses are allowed to carry out cross-border Renminbi payment business after filing a report with the People's Bank of China, Shanghai Headquarters.
		Circular on Supporting the Expansion of Cross-border Use of Renminbi in China (Shanghai) Pilot Free Trade Zone	Provides specific norms on offshore Renminbi loans, bilateral Renminbi cash pool, cross-border centralized Renminbi collection and payments, and personal cross-border Renminbi business.
		Circular on the Removal of the Ceiling Interest Rates for Small Foreign Currency Deposits in China (Shanghai) Pilot Free Trade Zone	Removes ceiling interest rates for small foreign currency deposits (below US$3 million) of residents in Shanghai FTZ from March 1st, 2014.
		Circular on the Effective Fight Against Money Laundering and Terrorism Financing in China (Shanghai) Pilot Free Trade Zone	Requires anti-money laundering institutions to comprehensively implement all anti-money laundering and counter-terrorism financing institutional measures, as specified in the Circular.

(*Continued*)

Table 5.3 (*Continued*)

Agency	Issued on	Policy	Details
	May 2014	Rules for the Implementation of Free Trade Accounting Business in China (Shanghai) Pilot Free Trade Zone (Trial) and Rules for Prudential Risk Management of Free Trade Accounting Business in China (Shanghai) Pilot Free Trade Zone (Trial)	Sets out detailed rules on how Shanghai-based financial institutions can establish free trade accounting management system in Shanghai FTZ, open free trade (FT) accounts, use and manage funds in FT accounts, and manage and prevent business risks.
	Feb. 2015	Circular on Issuing the Rules for Implementation of Macro-prudential Management of Offshore Financing and Cross-border Fund Flows in the Free Trade Accounting Business in China (Shanghai) Pilot Free Trade Zone (Trial)	Sets out detailed rules on overseas financing management rules, accounting rules, business types and macro-control triggering mechanisms for free trade accounting business.

Source: Websites of relevant regulatory authorities.

Zone and Accelerating the Construction of Shanghai International Financial Center. The program proposes the following measures:

(1) Take the lead in realizing Renminbi capital account convertibility, study the launch of pilot overseas investment by qualified domestic individual investors, seek innovations in foreign exchange management system, and explore pilot implementation of foreign exchange convertibility within limits, in Shanghai FTZ.
(2) Further expand cross-border Renminbi usage, and encourage FTZ enterprises' overseas parent companies or subsidiaries to issue Renminbi-denominated bonds inside China.
(3) Continue to expand opening of financial services industry to both domestic and overseas markets, and support entry of private capital into the financial industry.

2.3 *Financial Advantage*

Shanghai is one of the most promising cities in China with the potential to become an international financial center. In 2012, the National Development and Reform Commission issued the *Plan of Building Shanghai into an International Financial Center during the Period of the "12th Five-Year Plan"*, with the consent of the State Council. The Plan made it clear that with the aim to become a quasi-world-class international financial center, Shanghai will not only comprehensively expand its financial services and accelerate enhancement of its financial innovation capability, but also continuously enhance international status and global influence of Shanghai's financial market, in an effort to basically establish Shanghai's status as a global center for innovation, trading, pricing, and clearing in Renminbi products, by 2015. The plan also specified major tasks and measures for Shanghai to build an international financial center, including expanding the financial market's breadth and depth, attracting and cultivating internationally competitive and influential financial institutions, building a cross-border Renminbi payment and clearing center, accelerating reform and innovation of the financial market, establishing a Renminbi cross-border investment and financing center, and working to create an internationally competitive financial development environment.

Today, as China's financial center, Shanghai encompasses almost all of China's financial market elements, and is home to China's financial institutions and financial resources.

3. *Analyzing Financial Agglomeration Effects of Shanghai FTZ*

3.1 *Demonstration Effect*

Since Shanghai FTZ was established, several new achievements and bold attempts have been made in positive exploration of financial reforms, engendering a lot of experience that can be replicated and popularized, which has created an obvious demonstration effect (Li, 2015).

3.1.1 FTZ model demonstration effect

As a pilot city to implement the FTZ model, Shanghai has special advantages in financial agglomeration. Other cities can combine their respective regional positioning and development characteristics when setting up an FTZ. In 2014, 12 provinces such as Henan, Tianjin and Liaoning applied to establish an FTZ. On March 24, 2015, the Central Politburo of the Communist Party of China deliberated and adopted overall FTZ programs, to be established in Guangdong, Fujian, and Tianjin.

3.1.2 Reform experience demonstration effect

On establishing Shanghai FTZ, it was agreed at the outset that reform experiences will be popularized batch-wise once they attain maturity. Presently enterprise registration system reformation is being popularized across China. In addition, cross-board bilateral Renminbi cash pools, centralized foreign exchange collection and payment, and other foreign exchange management policies not only support facilitation of foreign trade, investment, and financing, but also reduce financial costs of multinational corporations, making FTZ more attractive to multinational companies. These reform experiences are mature enough to be replicated and popularized on a larger scale, provided the risks are controllable.

3.1.3 Financial center demonstration effect

Shanghai FTZ is China's first national free trade zone and a pilot site for China's financial reforms and opening up. From the perspective of financial services, financial institutions in Shanghai FTZ provide a range of financial services including banking, securities investment and trading, insurance bonds trading, brokerage and exchanges. The financial market in the zone produces, captures, describes, and publishes all kinds of financial information. In addition, Shanghai FTZ can adjust and optimize global resource allocation through a package of financial activities such as capital financing, capital operation, and foreign investment, thereby exerting the financial center's demonstration effect.

3.2 *Innovation Effect*

The innovation effect of Shanghai FTZ's financial agglomeration is mainly embodied in the innovation effect of the financial system and functions. Innovations made by financial institutions in the zone promote financial center's development and further agglomeration of the financial industry. Financial institutions are concentrated in this zone, and thanks to the competition, the financial industry is bound to launch a variety of innovative activities (Li, 2015).

3.2.1 Innovation in payment and settlement

Shanghai FTZ not only simplifies payment and settlement procedures handled by FTZ enterprises that are engaged in cross-border import and export of goods and trade in services, but also provides foreign exchange settlement and sales services to FTZ enterprises to trade in commodities and financial derivatives. The development of new international market risk management channels has greatly facilitated commodity enterprises.

3.2.2 Innovation in investment and financing

To strengthen funds management and promote rational funds flow, Shanghai FTZ has carried out reforms on cross-border use of Renminbi, and investment and financing. These reforms have not only widened overseas investment and financing channels for enterprises, but also reduced enterprises' investment and financing costs. Shanghai is accelerating its pace to become a Renminbi product pricing and clearing center for cross-border Renminbi settlement business. As of April 2014, a total of 26 cross-border Renminbi offshore borrowing transactions had occurred, totaling RMB 4.5 billion, with cross-border Renminbi settlement amounting to RMB 42.6 billion, a more than 90% increase over the same period in the previous year, accounting for more than 10% of Shanghai's total amount (Li, 2015).

3.2.3 Innovation in interest rate marketization

Shanghai FTZ set an example by removing ceiling interest rates for small foreign currency deposits, taking the lead in realizing complete marketization of foreign currency deposit interest rates. This measure is mainly targeted at Shanghai FTZ residents, as Shanghai-based financial institutions can now implement independent pricing for small foreign currency deposits and loans to these residents. Shanghai FTZ's residents include Chinese-funded and foreign-funded enterprise legal persons (legal entity) and public institutions (including financial institutions) established legally in accordance with the zone's laws, organizations that are registered in the zone but do not have corporate capacity, other organizations, foreign legal person institutions' offices in the zone, and local individuals who have worked in the zone for more than one year.

3.3 *Linkage Effect*

Since Shanghai FTZ was established, Shanghai's financial development environment has been changing, providing new opportunities for constructing Shanghai International Financial Center. Financial reforms in Shanghai FTZ will promote financial agglomeration in this zone, and help create a platform that helps FTZ financial institutions go global, creating a linkage effect with construction of Shanghai Financial Center to a certain extent.

At present, Shanghai has developed a program to link Shanghai FTZ and Shanghai International Financial Center. The program proposes five initiatives, including accelerating pilot convertibility of Renminbi capital accounts, expanding cross-border Renminbi use, expanding opening of financial industry to both domestic and overseas markets, building an international-oriented financial market, and improving financial supervision. These initiatives will further promote development and deepening of Shanghai's finance, and speed up construction of Shanghai International Financial Center.

4. *Financial Impact of Financial Agglomeration in Shanghai FTZ*

The financial impact of financial agglomeration in Shanghai FTZ is represented by the process and state in which Shanghai — using financial impact sources arising from huge financial resources inside and outside Shanghai FTZ and its strong economic power — extends its reach to and guides the economy and finance of the FTZ itself, surrounding cities and even the world, by transmitting economic energy to regions inside and outside of the FTZ via financial impact media. Financial impact media include all kinds of financial instruments, information and services that can transmit economic energy. Financial agglomeration and financial impact complement each other (Li, 2015).

Shanghai FTZ's financial impact includes the effect inside and outside the FTZ, depending on the reach of financial impact.

4.1 *Financial Impact inside the Shanghai FTZ*

Financial agglomeration in Shanghai FTZ features advanced financial facilities, developed financial markets, and sensitive financial information. Funds come from larger geographic areas than the area where Shanghai is located, and pool in the FTZ. The FTZ's own financial development drives emergence and development of related industry financial services in the FTZ. All these phenomena give rise to financial impact to a certain extent. For example, shipping-related financial services need to be supported by financial institutions. The concentration of financial institutions in Shanghai FTZ will facilitate shipping business and fuel shipping services development in the FTZ, and attract more enterprises engaged in shipping business to the FTZ. Concentration of financial institutions in the

FTZ, and its more open and innovative financial system can solve the problem of capital control targeting multinationals, and play a certain role in promoting FTZ trade development.

4.2 *Financial Impact outside Shanghai FTZ*

4.2.1 Drive economic development of Shanghai's surrounding areas

Establishment of numerous financial resource trading platforms in Shanghai FTZ will attract more financial institutions to the FTZ. This will not only expand financial services and accelerate flow of financial resources in the FTZ, but also provide surrounding areas global channels for their financial development.

4.2.2 Boost technological progress in Shanghai's surrounding areas

A large number of financial institutions have entered the FTZ, creating a technology spillover effect on Shanghai and its surrounding areas, thereby affecting Shanghai and its surrounding areas' financial industry structure and promoting their financial industry development. With Shanghai at its core, Yangtze River Delta region has a comparatively well-developed economy and capability to undertake diffusion of financial technologies.

4.2.3 Promote international direct investment and corporate M&As

China's individual investors now have access to more larger overseas investment channels. Chinese asset management companies are authorized to sell mutual funds, including overseas stocks and bonds, to local investors; large-scale investment activities will also directly impact global financial market.

4.2.4 Build an international-oriented financial market

As clearly stated in the *Program for Further Promoting the Pilot Implementation of Financial Opening and Innovation in China (Shanghai)*

Pilot Free Trade Zone and Accelerating the Construction of Shanghai International Financial Center, stipulated in October 2015, it is necessary to support Shanghai Futures Exchange to speed up construction of Shanghai International Energy Exchange Limited, launch crude oil futures as soon as possible, and promote research on natural gas, marine fuel oil, refined oil and other futures products. Therefore, in future, Shanghai FTZ is expected to exert financial impact on the international financial market and commodity market, by acquiring pricing power for crude oil futures and other energy commodities.

5. *Impact of Financial Reforms in Shanghai FTZ on its Surrounding Provinces: A Case Study of Zhejiang*

Construction of a financial innovation pilot area in Shanghai FTZ provides both opportunities and challenges for Zhejiang. Opportunities are brought by financial impact arising from interest rate marketization, allowing private capital access to the financial sector and other financial reforms, while challenges mainly lie in the fact that Shanghai can leverage its pilot policy advantages to siphon off Zhejiang's financial capital, private capital, financial talents, and other elements (Zhan, 2013).

5.1 *Opportunities: Shanghai FTZ Financial Reforms' "Spillover Effect" on Zhejiang*

5.1.1 Utilizing interest rate marketization, foreign capital from foreign-funded banks will open up new financing channels and space for private enterprises in Zhejiang

European and American banks' interest rates on loans are generally lower than that of domestic ones. The policy to allow establishment of foreign-funded banks in Shanghai FTZ not only creates opportunities for international capital to gain interest arbitrage in China, but also provides new channels for low-interest loans to private enterprises, including those in Zhejiang.

5.1.2 Zhejiang's private capital will have a broader reach to the financial sector and at a faster pace, by holding shares in Chinese-foreign joint venture banks

For a long time, Zhejiang's private capital has been working to find ways to enter the financial sector, and financial reforms in Shanghai FTZ have opened a door for private capital to be invested in establishing Chinese-Foreign Joint Venture banks.

5.1.3 More foreign investment will be directed to Zhejiang-based innovative or high-tech small- and medium-sized enterprises (SMEs) through foreign private equity (PE) and venture capital (VC) funds

The new policies adopted in Shanghai FTZ are very attractive to foreign PE and VC funds, playing a positive role in incubating innovative or high-tech SMEs. PE and VC investment will provide financial support to Zhejiang's SMEs, and boost their transformation and upgrade.

5.1.4 Some foreign trade enterprises of Zhejiang will be "diverted" from Hong Kong to Shanghai, to handle re-export trade business, considering Shanghai's offshore financial policy

Shanghai FTZ's offshore financial policy will bring greater convenience to several international trade enterprises in Zhejiang, and significantly change the pattern of some foreign trade enterprises doing business via Hong Kong's free trade zone, in recent years.

5.2 *Challenges: Shanghai FTZ Financial Reforms' "Siphoning Effect" on Zhejiang*

5.2.1 "Siphoning off" of Zhejiang's private capital adversely affects Wenzhou's financial reforms

Shanghai FTZ permits private and foreign capital to be used to set up joint venture banks, which means that substantial amount of private capital can now enter Shanghai's financial sector, thus resulting in a lot of private capital accumulating in Shanghai. This will directly affect one of Wenzhou's financial reforms to transform small and medium-sized lending companies into rural banks or private banks (Zhan, 2013).

5.2.2 "Siphoning off" of Zhejiang's financial capital

Zhejiang's private capital investment is active. Shanghai's financial innovation pilot area permits private capital investors and foreign-funded financial institutions to jointly set up joint venture banks. This policy will "siphon off" Zhejiang's financial resources.

5.2.3 "Siphoning off" of Zhejiang's financial headquarters economy

Zhejiang's enterprises must establish enterprises in Shanghai FTZ in order to enjoy policy dividends. Alibaba's AliPay has taken the lead in having its Shanghai headquarters registered in Shanghai FTZ, with more than 700 employees having moved in there.

5.2.4 "Siphoning off" of Zhejiang's financial talents

As financial institutions both within and outside Zhejiang are establishing headquarters and branches in Shanghai FTZ, a considerable number of modern financial professionals from Zhejiang will also shift to Shanghai. As Sino-foreign joint venture talent intermediary agencies are permitted to be established in Shanghai FTZ, and Hong Kong and Macao service providers are permitted to set up wholly-owned talent intermediary agencies, these foreign-funded talent intermediary agencies will help Shanghai FTZ "siphon off" Zhejiang's financial talents.

In summary, Shanghai FTZ will have direct and indirect "spillover" and "siphoning" effects on Zhejiang. From the perspective of degree of effect, the opportunities outweigh the challenges, and the benefits outweigh the negative impact. In accordance with the State Council's positioning of the Yangtze River Delta cities, Shanghai is an international financial center, and Hangzhou, Ningbo and other places are regional and sub regional financial service centers. Zhejiang needs to clearly demarcate its position as a regional financial service center, and make active efforts to create new competitive advantages such as Zhejiang Internet Finance, thus ensuring overall staggered development (Zhan, 2013).

References

Dong Fangjun and Wang Jun. Reason for and solution to the lack of international pricing power for commodities. *China Economic & Trade Herald*, 2008 (4).

Hua Renhai and Chen Baizhu. Research on the correlation between futures price in domestic and international futures markets. *China Economic Quarterly*, 2004 (3).

Hu Yuyue and Liu Zhichao. The "Belt and Road" strategy and pricing power of commodities, *Futures Daily*, 2015, p. 03.

Li Xiaoning. *Research on the Effect of Financial Agglomeration in China (Shanghai) Pilot Free Trade Zone*, Master's Dissertation, Jilin University, 2015.

Pan Yingli. International financial center: Historical experience and future China. *Truth & Wisdom Press*, 2010.

Tang Yanwei, Wang Fengbao and Zhang Chenhong. China's lack of international pricing power for commodities and its countermeasures. *Statistics & Decision*, 2006 (9).

Yan Qingmin. International comparative study on the construction of Shanghai international financial center. *China Finance 40 Forum*, October 9, 2010. Available at: http://www.cf40.org.cn/plus/view.php?aid=3300.

Yang Likan and Xue Chaozhong. Silk Road gold fund intends to build a gold industry ecosystem. *Shaanxi Daily*, August 11, 2015, p. 14.

Zhan Minghua. The impact of financial reforms in China (Shanghai) pilot free trade zone on Zhejiang and suggestions. *Statistical Science and Practice*, 2013 (12).

Zhang Tianmiao. Global futures and options trading volume increased slightly last year. *Futures Daily*, April 20, 2015, p. 1.

Chapter 6

Building Shanghai into an International Trade Center — A Global Trading Network Hub

In the middle and later periods of the last century, information technology began to be applied in international trade. Since the 1990s, Internet technology has extended its reach to and been more widely applied in commercial industries where a large number of new e-commerce enterprises were emerging.

According to the 36th *Statistical Report on Internet Development in China* published by the China Internet Network Information Center, in June 2015, China had 668 million Internet users with an Internet penetration rate of 48.8%, up 0.9% by the end of 2014. Internet's contribution toward China's economic growth significantly improved and joined the leading ranks in the world. Internet economy's share in the GDP continued to rise and reached 7% in 2014, surpassing United States (Figure 6.1).

I. Internet and Trade

With development of information and communication technologies and the Internet, as well as emergence of virtual enterprises and vertical

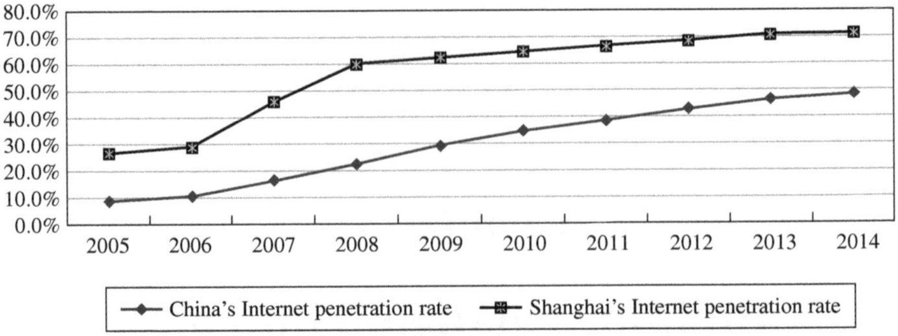

Figure 6.1 Internet Penetration Rates in China and Shanghai from 2005 to 2014

Source: http://www.cnnic.net.cn/hlwfzyj/hlwxzbg.

separation in the division of labor, enterprises are working to expand the scope of trade, reduce transaction costs, and deepen international division of labor through website construction, e-commerce, EDI, electronic clearing, and other applications, leading to profound changes in trading structure, mode and pattern, thus playing a role in promoting trade growth.

According to a survey by DHL e-Commerce, the global telemarketing industry is expected to grow by more than 10% annually over the next 5 years. Computers are the primary ordering channel, closely followed by mobile devices, and high-speed and efficient Internet connectivity is increasing the number of cross-border online shopping consumers. However, Figure 6.2 shows that the proportion of Chinese Internet users involved in cross-border e-commerce orders is still quite low, but the proportion of users interested in it, is quite high. Cross-border e-commerce is expected to see good development opportunities and prospects.

Development of Mobile Internet technology and popularity of smart phones have led Internet users to gradually shift to mobile terminals as a means to fulfill their consumption needs. As mobile terminals better satisfy Internet users' commercial consumption demand thanks to their immediacy and convenience, mobile commerce applications have become a new engine of growth for the Internet economy, with rapid growth in mobile Internet users. In the first half of 2015, China's mobile payment, mobile shopping, and mobile travel reservation users in China reached

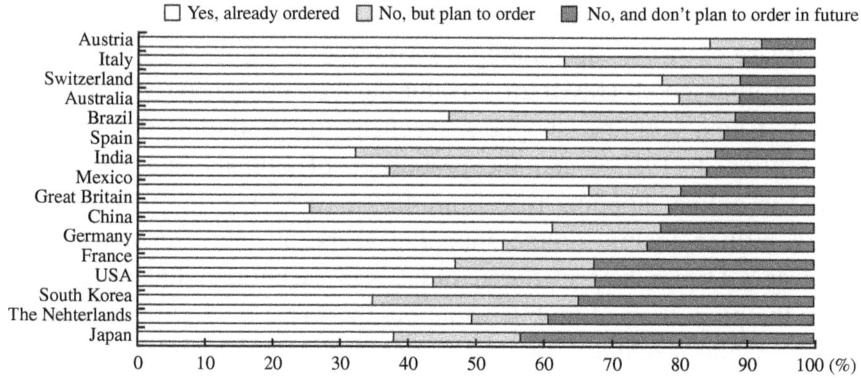

Figure 6.2 Proportion of Internet Users Involved in Cross-border E-commerce Orders in the World's Major Countries

Source: DHL's survey report — Shop the World.

276 million, 270 million, and 168 million with semi-annual growth rates of 26.9%, 14.5%, and 25%, respectively.[1]

During the "12th Five-Year Plan" period, China ranked first in the world in terms of e-retailing turnover. China had 361 million online shoppers, which was 55.7% of all Internet users. The e-retailing turnover totaled RMB 2.7898 trillion, a year-on-year increase of 2.6 times, meaning that China surpassed the United States and became the world's largest e-retail market. It is clear that the Internet has played an active role in expanding domestic consumer demand. According to data in the *Survey Report on China's Online Shopping 2015* published by the National Bureau of Statistics, 22% of new demand came from online shopping, 53.7% of online shoppers increased their consumer spending, and 48.4% of them will further enhance their proportion of online shopping.[2]

[1]China Internet Network Information Center: The 36th Statistical Report on Internet Development in China, July 22, 2015. Available at: http://www.cnnic.net.cn/hlwfzyj/hlwxzbg/.

[2]China Internet Network Information Center: Ten Highlights of the Internet Development in the "12th Five-Year Plan" Period, October 29, 2015. Available at: http://tech.163.com/15/1029/15/B73R0Q89000915BF.html.

In 2014, e-retailing turnover reached RMB 2.79 trillion, a year-on-year increase of 49.7%, accounting for 10.6% of the gross retail sales of social consumer goods (RMB 26.2 trillion) in the same period. By the end of 2013, China's online shoppers reached 361 million, growing by 59.53 million or 19.7%; and the proportion of China's Internet users involved in online shopping rose from 48.9% to 55.7%. In 2014, China had 236 million mobile online shopping users, an increase of 63.5%, which was 3.2 times the growth rate of users in the entire online shopping market; the proportion of mobile shopping increased by 13.5%, standing at 42.4%. China's online shopping market maintained a high degree of activity. 2014 saw 17.3 billion transactions, with 48 transactions completed per capita in that year. 76.1% of the user groups spent 20% or less of their daily consumer spending in online shopping. The spending on online shopping accounted for 14.2% of daily consumer spending on average. In 2014, only a small part or 4.8% of online shoppers used cross-border shopping. As major domestic e-commerce platforms are launching cross-border e-commerce channels, this proportion is set to increase significantly.[3] At present, multiple cities such as Shanghai, Chongqing, Hangzhou, Ningbo, Zhengzhou and Guangzhou have launched pilot integrated cross-border e-commerce import and export businesses. Relevant departments are stepping up to improve policy measures that support cross-border online trading platforms, logistics, payment and settlement, and promote continuous innovation in cross-border e-commerce models, including one-stop promotion, platform operation, and combination of online shopping business and exhibition. In future, domestic cross-border e-commerce and other new types of trade will become new growth points for China's foreign trade.

Relevant national departments have promulgated an array of policies and regulations to promote China's information consumption, consumer rights protection, cross-border e-retailing, innovative services, e-retailing market supervision, and other aspects. These policies and regulations have been boosting cross-border e-commerce development and innovation in

[3]China Internet Network Information Center: Research Report on China's Online Shopping Market in 2014, September 19, 2015. Available at: http://www.cnnic.net.cn/hlwfzyj/hlwxzbg/.

logistics, payment and other aspects that support enterprises, as well as the synergetic development of the industry chain. They also safeguard legitimate consumer interests and third-party operating platforms, and are conducive to standardized development and rapid growth of the entire e-retailing industry. On May 7, 2015, the State Council issued the *Opinions of the State Council on the Development of E-Commerce and the Acceleration of Fostering of New Economic Drivers.* On June 20, 2015, the State Council issued the *Guiding Opinions on Promoting the Healthy and Rapid Development of Cross-border E-commerce*, making important arrangements for cross-border e-commerce development, in a bid to promote standardized management, intensive services, and synergetic industrial chain development for China's cross-border e-commerce.

Technological development has had a great impact on the e-retailing industry. With rapid development of mobile payment technologies, smart phones may soon replace traditional wallets. In addition, as virtual fitting technology, UAV delivery and 3D printing are being developed and improved, they are expected to greatly enhance users' shopping experience in future.

According to a report submitted by the Ministry of Industry and Information Technology to the state, the new industrial revolution involves production means, mode and organization method, and is driving comprehensive changes in design, R&D, manufacturing, supply chain and marketing systems. It is symbolized by changes in the objects connected by Internet, from "people and people", to "people and things" and "things and things". Information tools represented by Internet Plus and the way of thinking it advocates will reshape the supply chain and value chain, and foster new business types featuring integration of the Internet and trade, thus realizing innovative development. Internet trade is expected to experience tremendous growth in future.

During the "12th Five-Year Plan" period, Shanghai's e-commerce transactions grew significantly, with an average increase of 35%. In 2014, Shanghai completed e-commerce transactions worth RMB 1.3549 trillion, up 28.3% over the previous year, accounting for about 10% of the e-commerce transactions nationwide. B2B transactions amounted to RMB 1.0645 trillion, up 23.3%, accounting for 78.6% of e-commerce transactions. Online shopping transactions amounted to RMB 290.4

billion, up 50.6%, accounting for 21.4%; wherein product transactions amounted to RMB 165.5 billion, up 52.8%, and service transactions amounted to RMB 124.9 billion, up 47.8%. A total of 55,000 enterprises were included in the port taxes e-payment system. The total amount of annual electronic document transmissions was 229 million, and electronic payments reached RMB 1.283 trillion, an increase of 12%.[4] In 2015, the China (Shanghai) Pilot Free Trade Zone was expanded and became a fertile ground for rapid development of cross-border e-commerce, as pilot policies such as Renminbi internationalization, trade facilitation, and seamless integration of regulatory platforms to be implemented in the field of cross-border e-commerce were introduced by Shanghai FTZ. Shanghai is committed to building an important hub and node for global trade networks, and therefore the construction of an online international trade center has become a major goal for Shanghai's development. This section will analyze Internet's impact on trade, and explore how Shanghai is building an international trade center in the Internet Plus era.

1. *How the Internet Influences Trade*

Continuous advancement of the information revolution has helped people break through time and space restrictions in the exchange of information, products and services, and has allowed smoother communications between manufacturers and consumers, thereby mitigating information asymmetry between production and marketing, reducing transaction uncertainty and blindness to market development, accelerating the close connection between the production side and the demand side, shortening trading time, flattening trade supply chain, and saving information and transaction costs. In addition, extensive information exchange has also weakened market monopoly caused by incomplete information or information asymmetry, and has promoted more effective resource allocation. Opening up marketing channels gives birth to new business models, bringing about changes in trade subjects, products, and processes. Figure 6.3 shows the path of how the Internet influences trade.

[4] Shanghai Municipal Commission of Commerce: The Development of E-Commerce in Shanghai in 2014, February 16, 2015. Available at: http://www.scofcom.gov.cn/swdt/237586.htm.

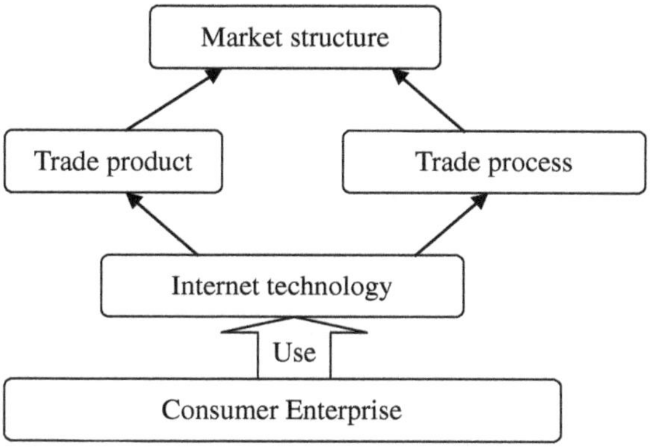

Figure 6.3 How the Internet Influences Trade

2. *Changes in Trade Due to the Internet*

2.1 *Changes in Trade Subjects*

Modern information and communication technology weave an interconnected network that includes a number of enterprises. Consumption flow, information flow, technology flow, and infrastructure can be shared in the network, resulting in huge network externalities which can enable participating enterprises to work in cooperation through division of labor, complement each other's advantages, use each other's resources, and share benefits. As a result, more diversified trade subjects are involved to promptly respond to the trend of individualized and diversified consumer demand, and to supply goods and services to the market more effectively. In the age of the Internet, the entry threshold into the international trade market for medium, small and micro-sized enterprises, as well as import and export costs have greatly reduced, offering a larger space for these enterprises to survive and grow. A large number of virtual enterprises have also emerged and flourished.

2.2 *Changes in Trade Model*

Digitization and web-based services have accelerated transaction processes, with more frequent trade marketing activities. A new marketing model is taking shape leading to great changes in sales channels. More interaction in information collection has enabled customers to directly participate in the marketing process, eliminating time and space obstacles in the marketing process. More advanced research techniques and various promotion means have brought about significant changes in marketing approaches. On the one hand, Internet interactivity has promoted all-round marketing process, and the Internet has made transaction links between two trading parties clearer. Timely and interactive communication on Internet platforms has helped reduce transaction, coordination and communication costs, and strengthen the initiative power of supply and selection. A seller and a buyer can have two-way interactive communication via the Internet anytime and anywhere. The marketing process has the effect of two-way linkage, and Internet's role in changing the spatial layout to a plane layout is fully embodied in this process. On the other hand, a flat Internet makes one-to-one information transmission possible. Enterprises and customers communicate more smoothly via the Internet, and more information is transmitted to potential consumers. On-demand consumption becomes possible, leading to a shift from mass sales to targeted sales.

2.3 *Changes in Trade Operations and Management*

Internet has greatly improved the efficiency of import and export agencies, customs clearance, inspection applications, ship chartering and space booking, shipment, foreign exchange settlement, foreign exchange offset, trade financing, factoring, and transaction review. Professional service providers are emerging, providing differentiated, all-round, multi-level, interactive commerce, and trade services for manufacturers and traders around the world. Thus, customers can focus on expanding overseas purchase channels, enlarging the scale of domestic sales, reducing overall foreign trade costs, and putting their limited time and efforts on their core business. Internet has also provided trade with a market environment with complete information and higher transactional efficiency, allowing optimal resource allocation and production factors, and has promoted in-depth trade development.

2.4 *Changes in Trade Operation Models and Environment*

Extensive application of information technology has extended trading space for products and services, and within a certain period of time, basically eliminated the influence of distance on information transmission between communication sites, thus effectively reducing the impact of traditional barriers to trade, changing traditional circulation model, reducing intermediate links, and allowing enterprises to greatly improve labor productivity, reduce costs and increase profits. It has completely changed traditional business patterns and trade operation models, engendering a unified global market. The accelerated global flow of goods, capital, technology, personnel, and other production factors brought about by information flow, as well as continuous improvement in tradability of services have led to the rise of global Internet economy, resulting in stronger economic and trade ties, and cooperation between countries.

2.5 *Changes in Trade's Intermediate Organization Structure*

With continuous improvement in Internet technology and its application, manufacturers and consumers can get in touch in a more direct and efficient manner via the Internet, and the flow of goods is smoother. A prompt delivery system with "zero inventory" production has been realized, and the principal–agent relationship and model formed due to information asymmetry has been disrupted. This has changed the position of trade intermediary from intermediate-type intermediary to platform-type intermediary, allowing business transformation from matching traders, to creating a trading environment that facilitates transactions. Trade intermediaries, agents and professional import and export companies have lower positions than before, and some professional information service companies have emerged such as advisory services, trade information services, financial information services, and international expert services, triggering changes in intermediate organization structure in international trade.

2.6 *Changes in Trade Costs*

Development of information and communication technology has greatly changed traditional business management practices in a way that allows foreign trade enterprises to get rid of conventional trading models and market constraints, thereby greatly reducing enterprises' information, communication and marketing costs. It has also improved the transmission speed of trade documents, shortened the document processing cycle, reduced data and file processing costs, and simplified business processes, making transactions more convenient and efficient. Intermediate costs for traders, wholesalers and other foreign importers in the intermediate links are squeezed or have even completely disappeared. Internet has enhanced competition and reduced prices and procurement costs. It has also improved inventory turnover rate, reduced enterprise inventory levels, and saved operating costs. Internet has enabled the production mode to shift from concentrated large-scale production to decentralized social production. This form of collaborative production is built on interconnected networks and allows more reasonable division of labor and cheaper costs, thus leading to lower trade costs.

2.7 *Changes in Trade Security*

Internet trade mainly involves the following security threats:

i. **Information leakage**, which mainly refers to leakage of trade secrets in e-commerce, where transaction content between two trading parties is stolen by a third party, or any document provided by one party to the other party is illegally used by a third party.
ii. **Information tampering**, where electronic trading information may be illegally altered, deleted or used repeatedly during Internet transmission, thereby losing its authenticity and integrity.
iii. **Identity recognition**, which, if not in place, a trading party's identity is at risk of being counterfeited by a third party. A third party can also undermine transactions, destroy reputation of the trading party or steal transaction results. Both trading parties should be responsible for their own behaviors; the information sender and recipient cannot deny this,

and it is known as non-repudiation. Identity recognition aims to prevent counterfeiting behaviors and repudiation of transactions during e-commerce activities.

iv. **Information destruction**. Firstly, it is related to reliability of Internet transmission, as problems may occur with Internet hardware or software, leading to loss and misinterpretation of trade information. Secondly, malicious destruction, wherein the network itself is destroyed by some malicious programs such as a virus or through hacking.[5]

II. Innovation in "Internet Plus Trade" Development Model

1. *Innovation in "Internet Plus Trade" Development Model and Its Characteristics*

1.1 *Innovation in Trade Model in the "Internet Plus" Era*

In the Internet era, the combination of international trade and Internet has engendered a new international trade model — cross-border e-commerce. Cross-border e-commerce refers to a new international trade model that allows trading parties from different countries or regions, in whole or in part, to transact goods or services via the Internet.

Cross-border e-commerce is classified into three basic types: B2B (Business-to-Business), B2C (Business-to-Customer), and C2C (Customer-to-Customer) depending on involved parties. As e-commerce has developed, many new types have been emerging. For instance, there's B2B2C (Business-to-Business to-Customer), O2O (Online-to-Offline), B2Q (Enterprise online shopping introduce quality control), and so on.

Cross-border e-commerce can be classified into two types based on degree of combination of international trade and Internet: a cross-border e-commerce transaction is conducted either in whole or in part via the Internet.

---

[5]Wang Hongxu, He Qingrui, and Wang Dongmei. Discussion of network security technology in the e-commerce transaction process, *Market Modernization*, 2008 (25), p. 81.

China's cross-border e-commerce has been growing year by year since 2008, making an increasingly high contribution to total imports and exports, as shown in Table 6.1. At the end of 2014, China's cross-border e-commerce contributed 14.2% to total imports and exports, serving as an important model of China's international trade.

1.2 *Characteristics of Cross-border E-commerce*

1.2.1 Virtual trading places which are not restricted by location and time

The Internet enables free communication and trade regardless of race, religion, state, occupation and social status, significantly reducing people's dependence on space or time. Thanks to the Internet, cross-border e-commerce allows international trade to dispense with geographical and time constraints that are typical of traditional trade, and connects to a unified, virtual and real-time large "market" that is based on information networks worldwide.

1.2.2 Simplified transaction process, less transaction links and lower transaction costs

In traditional trade model, the international trade process generally involves over 20 links, while the cross-border e-commerce process

Table 6.1 Trade Scale of China's Cross-border E-commerce

Year	Trade scale (RMB 1 trillion)	Growth of trade scale (%)	Trade scale in total import and export (%)
2008	0.72		4.0
2009	0.84	16.5	5.6
2010	1.19	42.4	5.9
2011	1.74	45.7	7.4
2012	2.09	20.1	8.6
2013	2.70	29.2	10.5
2014	3.75	38.9	14.2

Source: Data processing published by National Bureau of Statistics, Ministry of Commerce, and iResearch

typically requires only eight links, with simplified transaction processes and reduced costs.[6]

1.2.3 Direct, convenient and efficient communication with customers

Customer problems or differences arising from online trade can be directly forwarded by an enterprise's general network administrator to relevant responsible department, and the customer can directly communicate with someone from the department online, saving time, and improving efficiency.

1.2.4 Declining role of traditional intermediaries and flourishing "e-intermediaries"

Internet allows buyers and sellers to contact each other directly, thereby greatly reducing the role of intermediaries. Now, there's a new type of international trade intermediary called "e-intermediary", mainly providing an Internet platform to display products and services of many manufacturers to consumers, allowing them to communicate directly with manufacturers. These kinds of platforms efficiently promote transactions between manufacturers and consumers, greatly reduce transaction costs, and improve transaction efficiency.

1.2.5 Establishment of internet Big Data, increasing trade operation opportunities

When consumers trade online, a huge amount of their information such as personal information and consumption preferences remain online. Such information keeps getting accumulated and eventually builds up into consumer-centric Big Data, allowing manufacturers to publish product information to potential consumers in a targeted manner via the Internet, changing non-targeted, extensive, passive marketing to targeted

---

[6]Yao Lixin, Research on international trade innovation in the context of e-commerce, *Journal of International Trade*, 2000 (3).

and active marketing. In addition, manufacturers can learn more about raw materials supply, changes in technology, talent flow, and partner information online, allowing them to find more trade cooperation opportunities.

2. *Innovation Problems in China's "Internet Plus Trade" Development Model*

The Internet has triggered innovations in international trade model, and this innovative model has several new features that have played a great role in promoting international trade. However, there are still many problems to contend with.

2.1 *Network Security*

In the Internet era, network security is important for trade. Although enterprises and e-intermediaries involved in trade as well as other involved parties are taking effective measures for network security, the Internet's rapid development has led to a variety of security vulnerabilities, which criminals may take advantage of.

2.2 *Logistics*

Contrary to flourishing cross-border e-commerce in China, cross-border logistics is relatively lagging behind. Firstly, air transportation is still the primary mode for cross-border logistics, which greatly increases costs. Secondly, cross-border logistics is mainly monopolized by large international logistics companies, which is also another important reason for high prices.

2.3 *Intellectual Property Protection*

Consumer goods are mainly exported and traded in China's B2C e-commerce market. Due to low entry barriers, easy counterfeiting and low enterprise awareness of intellectual property protection, intellectual property violations occur regularly. Intellectual property disputes are easily resolved in Europe, United States, and Japan where sound legal intellectual property systems are in place, but it is still not the case in China, and this has a negative impact on further development of China's cross-border e-commerce.

2.4 *Regulating Fragmented Orders*

Most buyers in cross-border e-commerce are small and medium-sized manufacturers or foreign trading companies. They tend to place several small orders many times, making it difficult to regulate a large number of small, fragmented orders.

3. *Development Status and Economic Impact of Cross-border E-commerce in Shanghai*

3.1 *Development Status of Cross-border E-commerce in Shanghai*

With rapid development of cross-border e-commerce, the National Development and Reform Commission and General Administration of Customs carried out pilot cross-border e-commerce services in six cities with good economic and foreign trade foundations, including Shanghai in 2012.[7] In 2014, total amount of e-commerce transactions conducted in Shanghai reached RMB 1.3549 trillion, more than 28.3% over the previous year, accounting for more than 10% of the total e-commerce transaction value nationwide.[8] Shanghai's cross-border trade e-commerce currently includes both FTZ model and Songjiang model.

---

[7] Clear Direction is Necessary to Promote Cross-border E-commerce Development, *China Economic News Network* (www.cet.com.cn), June 9, 2014. Available at: http://www.cet.com.cn/ycpd/sdyd/1215607.shtml.

[8] Shanghai Launches Local Standards for E-commerce First, *China Quality News Network* (www.cqn.com.cn), April 3, 2015. Available at: http://www.cqn.com.cn/news/zgzlb/diyi/1023390.html.

FTZ model is based on cross-border e-commerce launched by Shanghai FTZ's official cross-border e-commerce platform — kjt.com. Established on September 10, 2013, "kjt.com" supports services for cross-border trade e-commerce. It is committed to providing domestic consumers with one-stop shopping and trading services of high-quality foreign goods online, and providing Shanghai port-based integrated customs clearance services for cross-border e-commerce enterprises to import goods.[9] The main business models adopted by "kjt.com" include: (1) Self-import — Consumers order imported food, cosmetics, maternal and child supplies, and high-grade bags, suitcases and clothing at "kjt.com", where cross-border foreign exchange payment is available. Then, relevant agencies that have registered at "kjt.com" handle customs declaration and inspection, and customs levies personal postal articles tax. After that, these goods are subject to quick entry and are delivered by courier companies directly to consumers. (2) Third-party enterprises that register at "kjt.com" import and sell goods on the platform (similar to JD.COM and TMALL.COM). "kjt.com" allows enterprises to establish their own platforms, and they do not need to register in the FTZ or require warehouse space. "kjt.com"[10] also handles backend services. In 2014, US based Amazon partnered with "kjt.com."

The Songjiang model, which relies on preferential conditions provided by the government, is an international expansion model based on domestic e-commerce platforms. "In 2014, TMALL.HK carried out bonded and direct mail cross-border e-commerce business in Songjiang Export Processing Zone; Giessen, an enterprise in Songjiang Export Processing Zone undertook warehousing management, import customs clearance, allocation and distribution, and other related services; and Songjiang District Government provided strong policy support and business development environment. Leveraging their respective advantages, the three parties actively explored innovation in the cross-border

---

[9] Introduction to "kjt.com", published on http://www.kjt.com/helpcontent/196.

[10] *An Investigation on the Progress of Cross-border E-commerce at "kjt.com" in China (Shanghai) Pilot Free Trade Zone*, Strategy, April 23, 2015. Available at: http://www.ishiju.com/2015/04.

model, and created a unique matching model for cross-border trade e-commerce."[11]

3.2 *How to Further develop Cross-Border E-commerce in Shanghai and Deploy its Economic Impact*

On July 28, 2015, the Shanghai Municipal Government General Office issued *Several Opinions on Promoting Development of Cross-border E-commerce in Shanghai* (hereinafter referred to as "12 Opinions"). These "12 Opinions", based on principle of "pilot application, setting priorities and gradual improvement", are intended to vigorously promote cross-border e-commerce system, management and service innovation, and guide large-scale, standardized, clustered and normalized development of Shanghai's cross-border e-commerce industry.[12]

Combined with actual development of Shanghai's cross-border e-commerce as well as "12 Opinions", Shanghai has to proactively make an effort in the following areas to further develop its cross-border e-commerce and capitalize on its economic impact on the Yangtze River Delta and across the country:

Shanghai should capitalize on its own advantages and make bold and pioneering endeavors to create a good business environment, and attract large domestic and foreign cross-border e-commerce operators. Based on complementary advantages, Shanghai should cooperate with Ningbo, Hangzhou and other pilot cities on cross-border e-commerce operation and regulation model, and promote public platform construction. Shanghai should also strengthen cooperation with and mutual learning from other pilot cities, and enhance its economic impact on other provinces and cities.

---

[11] Zhou Yangbo, Chen Yan, *TMALL.HK E-commerce Platform Settled in Shanghai Songjiang Export Processing Zone*, Songjiang News, October 31, 2014. Available at: http://www.huoyuanzhijia.com/news/show-556.html.

[12] The General Office of Shanghai Municipal Government, *Several Opinions on Promoting the Development of Cross-border E-commerce in Shanghai*, July 20, 2015. Available at: http://www.shanghai.gov.cn/nw2/nw2314/nw2319/nw12344/u26aw44405.html.

At present, Shanghai's main cross-border e-commerce operators focus on a limited range of products, and in future, Shanghai should actively encourage expansion of product categories.

Irrespective of the FTZ model or Songjiang model, Shanghai-based cross-border e-commerce operators are mainly large traders and well-known e-commerce operators. To attract small and medium-sized e-commerce operators, Shanghai should foster clustered development in industrial parks, to help and support growth of small and medium-sized e-commerce operators, especially those in subdivided sectors. Small and medium-sized enterprises are now facing higher trade costs, and they lag behind in use of information resources, low operating efficiency, etc. The Shanghai Government should integrate resources and establish SME e-commerce clusters in industrial parks, where products, logistics solutions, and mentor services are provided to small and medium-sized start-ups. Special training sessions need to be launched on a regular basis to raise awareness on the importance of product quality and intellectual property protection in cross-border e-commerce industry, and there need to be more preferential policies for small and medium-sized e-commerce operators.

Songjiang Export Processing Zone is a pilot area for Customs and Inspection and Quarantine Department to implement their supervision policies. Through pilot applications of "quick inspection and clearance", "paperless customs clearance" and "three ones" (one declaration, one inspection, one clearance), the Zone's customs clearance efficiency is the best in the country. These favorable conditions should be fully leveraged to create a sound environment for development thereby improving efficiency. Pre-event supervision should be changed to interim and post-event supervision, and in terms of export supervision, in particular, it is important to strengthen enterprise self-discipline, risk education, and early warning systems.

It is imperative to promote construction of cross-border e-commerce O2O display and experience flagship stores, support taxation and usage of such stores, and facilitate offline coordination through bonded display and trading, to connect offline experience stores and online e-commerce operators. A cross-border e-commerce center and bonded display and trading center needs to be established to promote development of

Shanghai's modern service industry, expedite construction of an imported goods display and trading base, and boost construction of an international trade center in Shanghai.

III. Construction of an International Trade Center in Shanghai in the "Internet Plus" Era

1. *Internet and its Impact on Change in a Core City's Trade Model*

The Internet is a large organization of connected local area networks. The biggest advantage of the Internet is that it can disseminate information across the widest range in the shortest possible time, thereby hugely impacting economy. The Internet expands the scope of business to every corner of the world using information technology, resulting in many game-changing effects on traditional businesses. International trade lies at the core of economic exchanges among countries, and is an important means to regulate supply and demand. In the Internet era, international trade has extended its reach to newer business areas with the help of communication technology.

Online platforms such as Alibaba Group, eBay and Amazon have brought Internet technology to international trade, greatly reducing trading costs for countries. Chinese Internet enterprises such as Alibaba Group have created B2B, B2C and C2C businesses, and further developed O2O and other Internet trading models, which provide greater convenience to consumers from all over the world. In addition, Internet enables global sellers to identify more opportunities and promotes the circulation of goods, making the shift from regional trade to global trade possible. Amid this trend, core cities' trade models have also undergone fundamental changes.

A core city is usually a regional or local center for transportation, commerce, circulation, marketing and trade, and has an economic impact on surrounding cities. Commercial circulation is the most important link. Most international trade centers have utilized foreign trade to evolve into financial, shipping and economic centers. Will the tide of Internet have an impact on a core city's trade?

2. *Study of Internet Development in Shanghai*

2.1 *Indicator 1: Comparison of Information Service Industry's Operations*

According to the data in the Shanghai Statistical Yearbooks, three indicators are used to conduct statistical analysis of Internet's development in Shanghai (see Table 6.2).

The operations of Shanghai's information service industry from 2004 to 2013 represented rapid development of Internet businesses, in which the computer service and software industry has played an increasingly important role. Not only has their operating income increased significantly, but so has the number of employees. Internet and related industries have been growing rapidly, as have the number of relevant employees (Table 6.3).

The operating income of Shanghai's information service industry exhibited growing momentum with more than 20% growth, indicating that Shanghai's Internet industry has not only gained quantitative growth, but also achieved great improvement in quality and efficiency.

Shanghai's computer service and software industry has been making an increasingly higher contribution to the information service industry in terms of operating income, from 46.184% in 2004 to 65.719% in 2013, marking the importance of Shanghai's Internet industry (Table 6.4).

2.2 *Indicator 2: Information Infrastructure*

Between 2004 and 2013, Shanghai's information infrastructure improved significantly in terms of the level of informatization development. The length of information communication pipelines has been increasing for many years, and the number of Internet users and the Internet penetration rate have been rising significantly (Table 6.5).

2.3 *Indicator 3: Information Technology Application*

From the perspective of application of Internet information technology in Shanghai, the number of transactions (unit: 10,000) handled on the EBPP platform (Fu Fei Tong) — an example of information technology

Table 6.2 Operations of Shanghai's Information Service Industry from 2004 to 2013

Information service industry	2004	2005	2006	2007	2008	2009	2010	2011	2012	2013
Operating income of the information service industry (unit: RMB 100 million)	655.6	916.8	1221.45	1294.44	1634.91	1642.12	1978.51	2251.63	2593.95	3285.17
Computer service and software industry	302.78	455.17	616.7	655.19	889.11	925.08	1145.1	1302.89	1571.46	2158.99
Employees in the information service industry (unit: 10,000 people)	9.9	14.46	18.03	24.45	24.7	30.48	31.2	33.51	39.36	48.15
Computer service and software industry	7.1	11.83	14.12	17.34	17.6	22.88	23.25	25.31	30.18	37.69

Source: Shanghai Bureau of Statistics (2003–2014 Statistical Yearbooks).

Table 6.3 Comparison of Shanghai's Information Service Industry's Operations from 2004 to 2013

Information service industry	**2005/ 2004**	**2006/ 2005**	**2007/ 2006**	**2008/ 2007**	**2009/ 2008**	**2010/ 2009**	**2011/ 2010**	**2012/ 2011**	**2013/ 2012**	**Average growth rate**
Operating income of the information service industry (unit: RMB 100 million)	0.39841	0.33230	0.05976	0.26302	0.00441	0.20485	0.13804	0.15203	0.26647	0.20214
Computer service and software industry	0.50330	0.35488	0.06241	0.35703	0.04046	0.23784	0.13780	0.20613	0.37388	0.25264
Employees in the information service industry (unit: 10,000 people)	0.46061	0.24689	0.35607	0.01022	0.23401	0.02362	0.07404	0.17457	0.22332	0.20037
Computer service and software industry	0.66620	0.19358	0.22805	0.01499	0.30000	0.01617	0.08860	0.19241	0.24884	0.21654

Source: Shanghai Bureau of Statistics (2003–2014 Statistical Yearbooks).

Table 6.4 Percentage of Income and Employees of the Computer Service and Software Industry in Shanghai's Information Service Industry from 2004 to 2013

Percentage of income of the computer service and software industry	0.46184	0.49648	0.50489	0.50616	0.54383	0.56334	0.57877	0.57864	0.60582	0.65719
Percentage of employees of the computer service and software industry	0.71717	0.81812	0.78314	0.70920	0.71255	0.75066	0.74519	0.75530	0.76677	0.78276

Source: Shanghai Bureau of Statistics (2003–2014 Statistical Yearbooks).

Table 6.5 Shanghai's Information Infrastructure from 2004 to 2013

Indicator	**2004**	**2005**	**2006**	**2007**	**2008**	**2009**	**2010**	**2011**	**2012**	**2013**
Length of information communication pipelines (unit: km)	1255	1621	2451	3131	4007.14	5354.13	5 821	6 258	7003	7866
Satellite site	917	925	831	805	781	772	770	817	479	—
Internet users (unit: 10,000 people)	633	803	957	1080	1160	1250	1560	1691	1750	—
Internet user penetration (%)	37.0	45.2	52.7	58.1	61.4	65.1	68.1	72	73.5	75.7
Home broadband access users (unit: 10,000 households)	142.9	222.7	301.7	327.6	376.7	470.32	517.4	530.7	626.82	494.03
Home broadband access user penetration (%)	23.4	33.8	44.9	47.6	53.9	60.6	51.59	52.3	54.1	55.2

Source: Shanghai Bureau of Statistics (2003–2014 Statistical Yearbooks).

application — increased by 20.47 times from 2005 to 2013, and the amount increased by 9.77 times. The use of bank cards, transit cards, and social security cards has also increased, marking extensive application of information technology in people's daily lives (Table 6.6).

3. *Study of Trade Flow Changes in Shanghai*

In the Internet era, Shanghai's trade model has undergone great changes particularly due to establishment of the Shanghai FTZ.

Internet enables effective electronic delivery. EDI (Electronic Data Interchange) is an electronic system that allows automatic transmission and processing of purchase orders, shipping notices, invoices, and other business documents among enterprises via the Internet.[13] EDI can minimize human intervention and takes only a few seconds to send data, greatly improving trade facilitation and reducing transaction costs. The rapid development of EDI has promoted development of paperless international trade. This change in the trade model has enabled more small and medium-sized enterprises to participate in international trade. As a new business management model, EDI allows integration of information flow, business flow, capital flow and logistics, substantially reducing transaction costs of foreign trade enterprises. In addition, the emergence of EDI technology is more conducive to applying the advantage of paperless trade-in goods, to trade-in services. This is one aspect of how Internet influences Shanghai's trade-in goods.

Shanghai FTZ was formally established on September 29, 2013. EDI technology significantly improves the speed of customs clearance and helps create a new convenient customs clearance model featuring a hands-off policy in ports, safe and efficient control of channels, and free operation within the FTZ. Entry followed by declaration is adopted in ports; batch entry/exit and centralized declaration are adopted in channels; self-transportation is allowed in Shanghai FTZ. This customs clearance model is also adopted in the international free trade zone. At present, average customs clearance time required for entry/exit within Shanghai FTZ is reduced by 41.3% and 36.8%, respectively, as opposed to the time

[13]Retrieved from Baidu Baike.

Table 6.6 Information Technology Application in Shanghai from 2005 to 2013

Indicator	**2005**	**2006**	**2007**	**2008**	**2009**	**2010**	**2011**	**2012**	**2013**
Registered users of "Citizen Mail" (unit: 10,000)	33.98	124.26	332.93	361.20	385.46	399.00	409.00	416.76	427.00
Transactions handled on the EBPP platform (Fu Fei Tong) (unit: 10,000)	733.75	1976.48	2907.00	3801.50	4649.81	7483.10	9555.90	10947.14	15755.00
Amount of transactions handled on the EBPP platform (Fu Fei Tong) (unit: RMB 100 million)	9.27	16.23	24.69	35.48	46.53	62.40	70.90	72.75	99.91
Social security cards issued (unit: 10,000)	72.68	1004.32	1112.23	1425.57	—	—	—	—	—
Transit cards sold (unit: 10,000)	504.73	2568.06	3240.64	4161.49	4944.28	6486.28	—	—	—
Amount of sales of traffic cards (unit: RMB 100 million)	8.28	10.06	11.66	13.41	11.94	26.00	13.60	14.39	13.09
Bank cards issued (unit: 10,000)	5729.80	5610.89	6781.64	7915.22	10009.93	11427.54	13098.00	14207.38	16556.26
Amount of bank card transactions (unit: RMB 100 million)	2761.18	3666.19	5996.81	6918.92	9517.10	11306.30	13887.70	16608.12	21403.08
Amount of card consumption	1233.15	1793.70	2852.56	2486.72	4200.08	4963.76	6425.12	8843.11	12072.26

Source: Shanghai Bureau of Statistics (2003–2014 Statistical Yearbooks).

required outside the FTZ. This convenient customs clearance model greatly reduces the entire port's customs clearance logistics time, from the arrival of goods at Yangshan Port to delivery to warehouses. For example, it costs only 5 hours to complete the customs clearance process for clothing declared by COSCO Logistics (Shanghai), as opposed to the 2–3 days required before. According to the *Trade Environment Satisfaction Survey* conducted by the American Chamber of Commerce in Shanghai (AmCham Shanghai), the customs clearance reform launched in Shanghai FTZ has been fully accepted by interviewed enterprises, and the FTZ's paperless customs clearance rate has increased from 8.4% at the time of its establishment, to over 80%. At present, more than 70% of the customs declaration forms are automatically inspected and released by computers, and the rate of intelligent inspection and release at a checkpost exceeds 50%, reducing an enterprise's logistics costs by 15% to 20% and improving the overall transportation capacity by 25% to 50%.[14]

It is EDI that has allowed Shanghai FTZ to set up a regular platform for cross-border online shopping — kjt.com. At present, kjt.com has two models, namely, direct mail to China and FTZ model. Goods ordered on kjt.com are directly delivered to customers after customs declaration and inspection via EDI and payment of personal postal articles tax. In addition, driven by kjt.com, corporate electronic invoices have been widely used within the Shanghai FTZ.[15] The implementation of these measures is possible because the Internet economy has facilitated Shanghai's trade-in goods whose growth during the period 1990–2013 is explained in Table 6.7.

3.1 *Study of Changes in the Flow of Shanghai's Trade-in Goods in the Internet Era*

Imports and exports of Shanghai's trade-in goods from 1990 to 2012 showed an obvious growth trend, which was particularly evidenced after China joined the WTO in 2002 (Figure 6.4). According to the growth of

[14]The General Administration of Customs: *New Convenient Customs Clearance Model Created in China (Shanghai) Pilot Free Trade Zone*, October 8, 2015.

[15]*30 E-commerce Operators including Amazon will Enter the kjt.com Platform of China (Shanghai) Pilot Free Trade Zone*, *Pudong Times*, July 10, 2014.

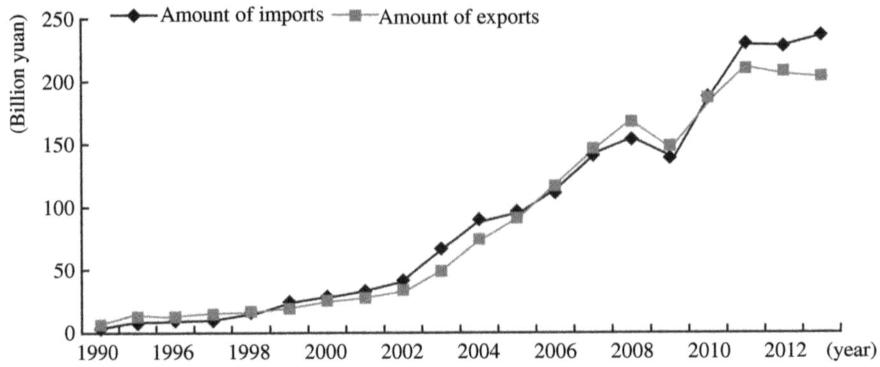

Figure 6.4 Growth Trend of Shanghai's Trade-in Goods from 1990 to 2012

Source: Shanghai Statistical Yearbook (2014).

Table 6.7 Growth in Shanghai's Trade-in Goods from 1990 to 2013

Year	Growth of imports	Growth of exports	Year	Growth of imports	Growth of exports
1995/1990	2.52986	1.17572	2005/2004	0.10539	0.23425
1996/1995	0.21173	0.14347	2006/2005	0.19130	0.25160
1997/1996	0.11247	0.11225	2007/2006	0.22059	0.26727
1998/1997	0.53267	0.08367	2008/2007	0.09884	0.17663
1999/1998	0.28795	0.17730	2009/2008	−0.11108	−0.16201
2000/1999	0.48120	0.34969	2010/2009	0.38484	0.27390
2001/2000	0.13333	0.08969	2011/2010	0.21034	0.16044
2002/2001	0.22059	0.16024	2012/2011	0.01012	−0.01421
2003/2002	0.57391	0.51246	2013/2012	0.03132	−0.01239
2004/2003	0.35345	0.51644	Average	0.28617	0.17479

Source: Shanghai Statistical Yearbook (2014).

imports and exports, the amount of Shanghai's import and export trade declined substantially in 2009 because of the US financial crisis, and climbed to the next high point in 2010. Exports of goods fell slightly from 2010 to 2012, but imports of goods rose rapidly. Trade-in goods exhibited a deficit trend from 2010 to 2012.

The establishment of China's first web portal in 1998 symbolized China's entry into the Internet era. Using 1998 as a demarcation point, Shanghai's existing trade data was divided into two stages: 1990–1998 and 1998–2013. The growth of imports and exports in Shanghai's trade-in goods was the highest during 2002–2003 when China just joined the WTO, reaching more than 50%. Due to the impact of the financial crisis, the deficit in Shanghai's trade became prominent since 2009.

There is a significant difference between the growth rates of imports and exports of Shanghai's trade-in goods in the Internet era. Between 1990 and 1998, the average annual growth rates of imports and exports of Shanghai's trade-in goods were 10.69% and 10.03% of the average annual growth rates between 1999 and 2013, respectively. In other words, according to changes in the growth of goods trade flow, the average annual growth rate of Shanghai's trade-in goods exhibited a clear upward trend in the Internet era, that is, the flow of Shanghai's trade-in goods increased significantly in the Internet era. Information technology greatly boosted the development of Shanghai's trade-in goods on the whole, as shown in Figure. 6.5.

The Internet played a positive role in promoting construction of a goods trade center in Shanghai. Paperless customs clearance that is

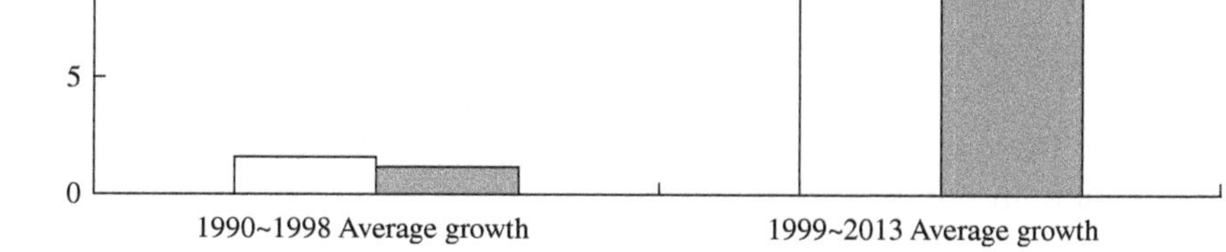

Figure 6.5 Changes in Average Annual Growth of Import and Export Flows of Shanghai's Trade-in Goods from 1990 to 2013

Source: Shanghai Statistical Yearbook (2014).

currently being implemented in Shanghai FTZ has reduced enterprises' costs by 15% to 20%. In future, if the Internet effect continues to be leveraged, enterprises' logistics and customs clearance costs can be effectively reduced, thereby stimulating the next wave of economic growth.

The Internet has played a significant role in increasing the flow of Shanghai's trade-in goods. Thus, the next step is to increase Internet-enabled customs clearance speed and efficiency. If conditions permit, it is recommended that Internet of Things technology be further introduced and the entire goods import and export process should implement electronic monitoring. These measures can not only greatly improve customs inspection efficiency and accuracy, but also stimulate the Internet's positive effect on imports and exports on Shanghai's trade-in goods, promote development of entry/exit and re-export services, and further consolidate and highlight advantages of Shanghai's Customs, thereby providing necessary informatization conditions for expanding the port throughput and fast customs clearance.

On the whole, Internet has played a significant role in promoting agglomeration of trade-in goods in the process of construction of an international trade center in Shanghai, and has given an important impetus to the improvement of trade flows and paperless customs clearance.

After 2011, the import and export flows of Shanghai's trade-in goods were characterized by a trend that imports accounted for a higher proportion than exports. In the Internet era, convenient information access has increasingly highlighted the importance of trade-in imported goods (Figure 6.6).

As to Shanghai's trade-in exported goods from 2000 to 2007, manufactured goods had no obvious comparative advantage over primary goods (Figure 6.7). This result was similar to the export classification structure of general trade and processing trade. According to the subdivided structure of trade-in goods:

The export volume of primary goods was slightly higher than that of manufactured goods. In other words, the structure of Shanghai's trade-in goods in the Internet era was not particularly optimized and still in the low-end development stage, dominated by primary goods.

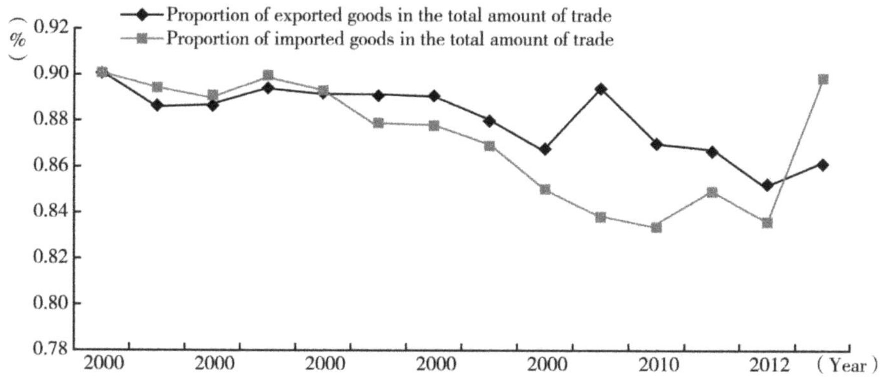

Figure 6.6 Changes in Growth of Import and Export Flows in Shanghai's Trade-in Goods from 2000 to 2012

Source: Shanghai Statistical Yearbooks (2000–2014).

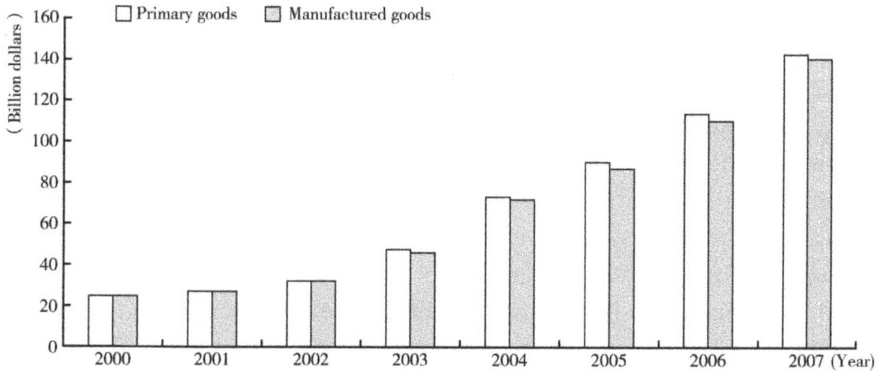

Figure 6.7 Analysis of the Structure of Shanghai's Trade-in Exported Goods from 2000 to 2007

Source: Shanghai Statistical Yearbooks (2000–2014).

3.2 *Study of Changes in the Flow of Shanghai's Trade-in Services*

Unlike trade-in goods, information technology does not have an incremental effect on Shanghai's trade-in services, in the Internet era. Especially due to the US financial crisis of 2009, the growth of Shanghai's

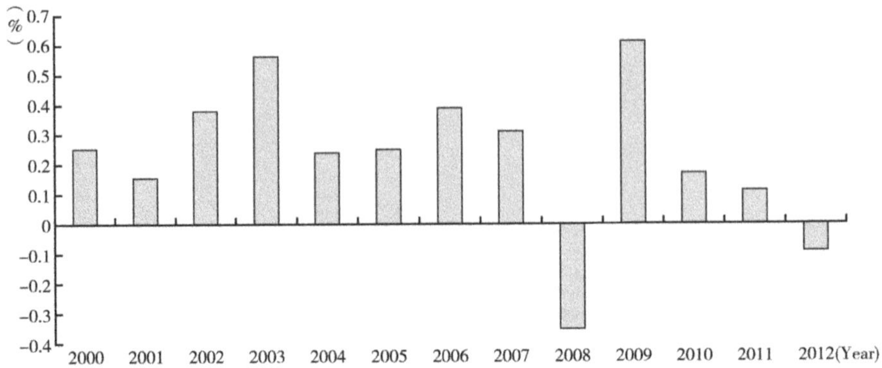

Figure 6.8 Changes in Annual Growth Rate of Shanghai's Trade-in Exported Services from 2000 to 2012

Source: Shanghai Statistical Yearbooks (2000–2014).

trade-in services fell sharply (Figure 6.8). Despite a substantial increase in 2010, it declined in 2011 and 2012.

According to Figure 6.9, imports of Shanghai's trade-in services had grown substantially since 2000. The overall annual growth of Shanghai's trade-in services exhibited a downward trend, except in 2009 which saw a severe impact of the US financial crisis and in 2010 when imports of trade-in services had a greater rebound. In other words, amid the in-depth development of the Internet, growth of Shanghai's trade-in imported or exported services fell significantly. 2009 represented a turning point when the volume of trade-in goods and services both declined sharply. Thus, we need to take note of the overall downward trend of Shanghai's trade-in goods and services in the wake of in-depth development of the Internet.

The average annual growth of Shanghai's trade-in services was far lower than that of trade-in goods from 2000 to 2013. From 1999 to 2013, the average annual growth rate of Shanghai's trade-in imported goods was 155.23%, while that of trade-in exported goods was 132.47%. In contrast, from 2000 to 2013, the average annual growth rate of Shanghai's trade-in imported services was only 18.29%, while that of trade-in exported services was 23.05% (Figure 6.10). The main reason for this big difference is the lack of international competitiveness of Shanghai's trade-in services. But it also shows that in-depth development of the Internet did not lead to

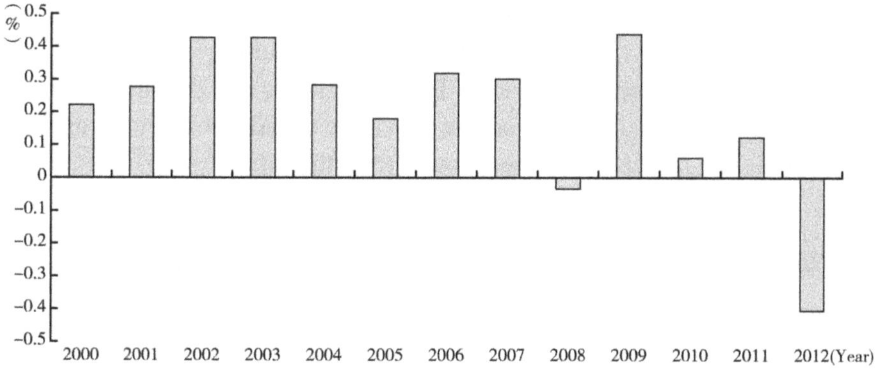

Figure 6.9 Changes in Annual Growth Rate of Shanghai's Trade-in Imported Services from 2000 to 2012

Source: Shanghai Statistical Yearbooks (2000–2014).

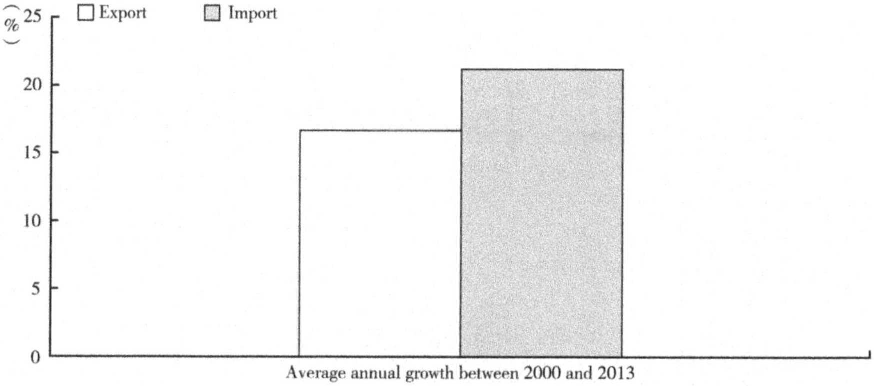

Figure 6.10 Changes in the Growth of Import and Export Flows of Shanghai's Trade-in Services from 2000 to 2013

Source: Shanghai Statistical Yearbooks (2000–2014).

significant improvement in Shanghai's trade-in services, and its real-life effect did not improve significantly.

Shanghai's entry into the Internet era played a positive role in sparking changes in total trade flows. However, given the difference between trade-in goods and trade-in services, trade-in goods which are tangible in the Internet era has stronger dependence on information technology than trade-in services, as evidenced by the fact that the average annual growth rate of import and export flows of Shanghai's trade-in goods was far greater than that of trade-in services. This also shows that the Internet had a larger impact on Shanghai's trade-in goods than trade-in services, as the former achieved larger trade flow growth than the latter.

4. *Study of Trade Structure Changes in Shanghai*

4.1 *Study of Changes in the Structure of Shanghai's Trade in Goods*

According to Figure 6.11, optimization of trade structure in exported goods was not as prominent as that of trade-in imported goods. This indicates that after 1990, especially after 1998 when the Internet era commenced, despite the Internet's rapid development, the structure of

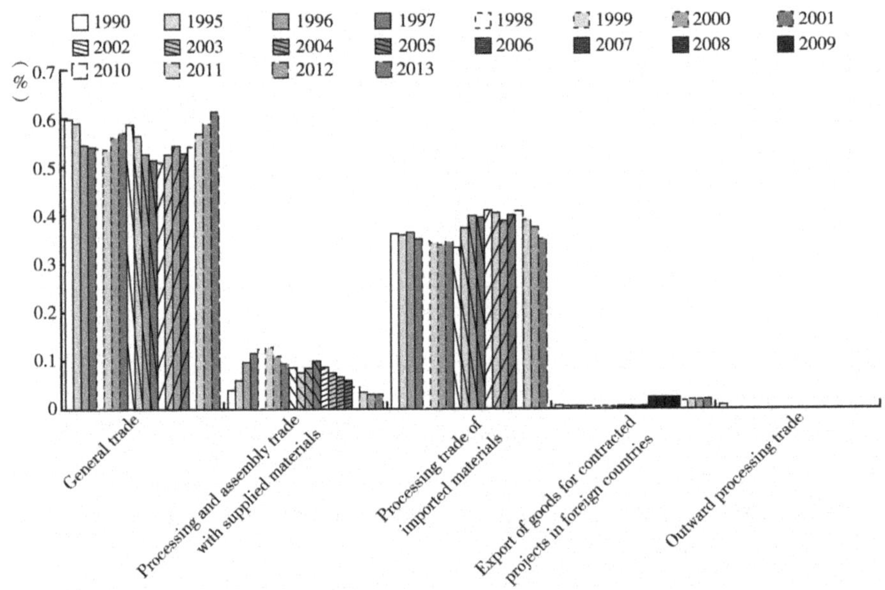

Figure 6.11 Characteristics of Changes in the Structure of Shanghai's Trade-in Exported Goods from 1990 to 2013

Source: Shanghai Statistical Yearbooks (2000–2014).

Shanghai's trade-in exported goods was not greatly optimized, and did not have significant optimization effect.

Figure 6.12 shows the comparison between 1990 to 1998, and 1999 to 2014.

The optimization degree of the structure of Shanghai's trade-in exported goods was slightly lower between 1990 and 1998 than between 1999 and 2014, which ushering in the Internet era. With the Internet's rapid development, changes in Shanghai's trade flow show that it increased rapidly, and export structure was optimized. On the whole, import trade flow grew faster than export trade flow, and the trade structure in imported goods was better optimized than the trade structure in exported goods.

Primary goods and manufactured goods grew concurrently as part of the structure of Shanghai's trade-in exported goods, from 1990 to 2013. The Internet's development enabled a consistent pace of progress in these two types of goods. To accelerate growth of Shanghai's trade-in exported goods, the Internet should impose equal facilitating effects.

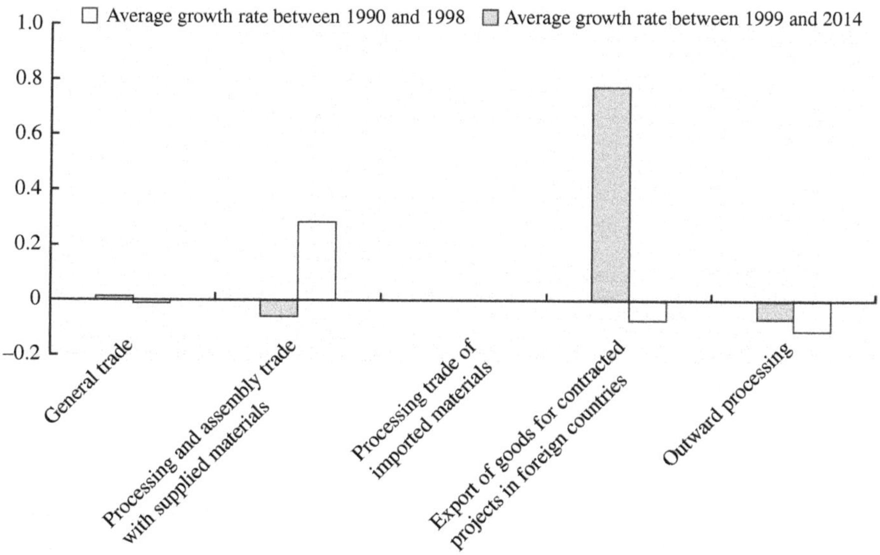

Figure 6.12 Characteristics of Changes in the Structure of Shanghai's Trade-in Exported Goods from 1990 to 2014

Source: Shanghai Statistical Yearbooks (2000–2014).

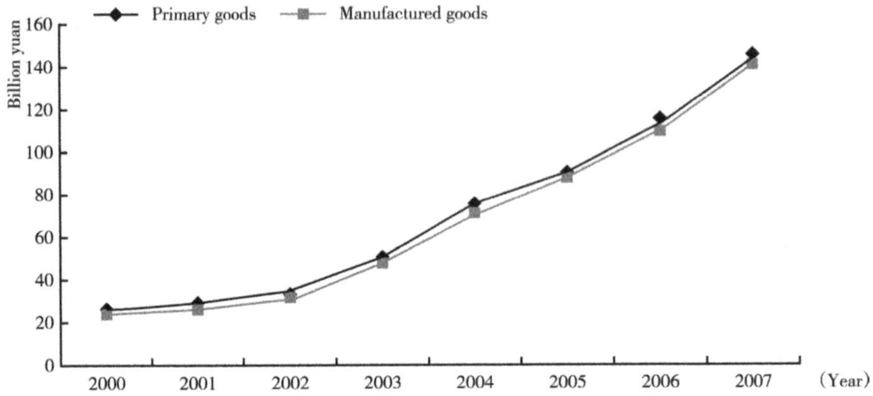

Figure 6.13 Characteristics of Changes in the Structure of Shanghai's Trade-in Exported Goods from 2000 to 2007

Source: Shanghai Statistical Yearbooks (2000–2014).

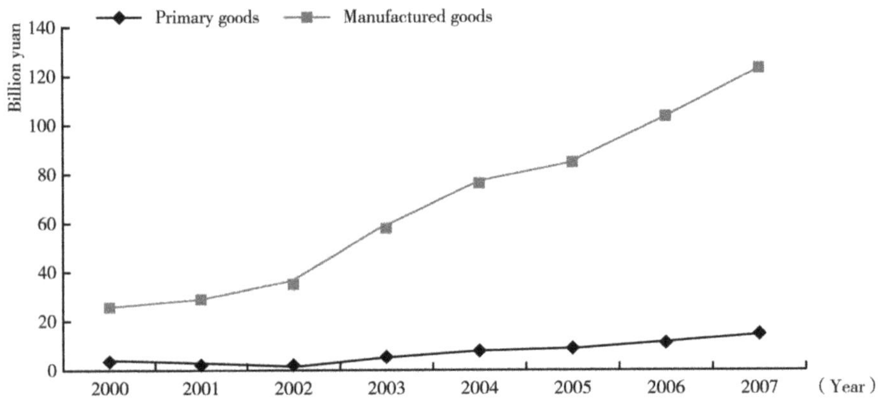

Figure 6.14 Characteristics of Changes in the Structure of Shanghai's Trade-in Imported Goods from 2000 to 2007

Source: Shanghai Statistical Yearbooks (2000–2014).

The changes in the structure of Shanghai's trade-in exported and imported goods during 2000–2007 are shown in Figures 6.13 and 6.14.

Obviously, import of manufactured goods was far greater than that of primary goods. In other words, with the Internet's development, not only did the overall flow of Shanghai's trade-in goods increase, but import of manufactured goods also grew significantly, as evidenced by demands for technology-intensive products, other than imported primary goods that grew relatively slowly during 1990–2013 (Figure 6.15). However, export of primary goods and manufactured goods both rose rapidly. This result highlights the characteristic that trade convenience speed up the development of Shanghai's trade-in imported goods in the Internet era. This characteristic is very helpful in analyzing why consumers have far greater demand for high-quality overseas products rather than primary goods, which can be attributed to a rise in people's living standards. But the development level and scale of Shanghai's local manufacturing industry and agriculture show that Shanghai is still in the initial development stage, with equal focus on primary goods and manufactured goods, and its advantages are not being particularly exhibited.

This result also shows that to some extent in the rapid development of economy today, the effect of wealth accumulated by processing trade lies in the reality that consumers having higher income have far greater

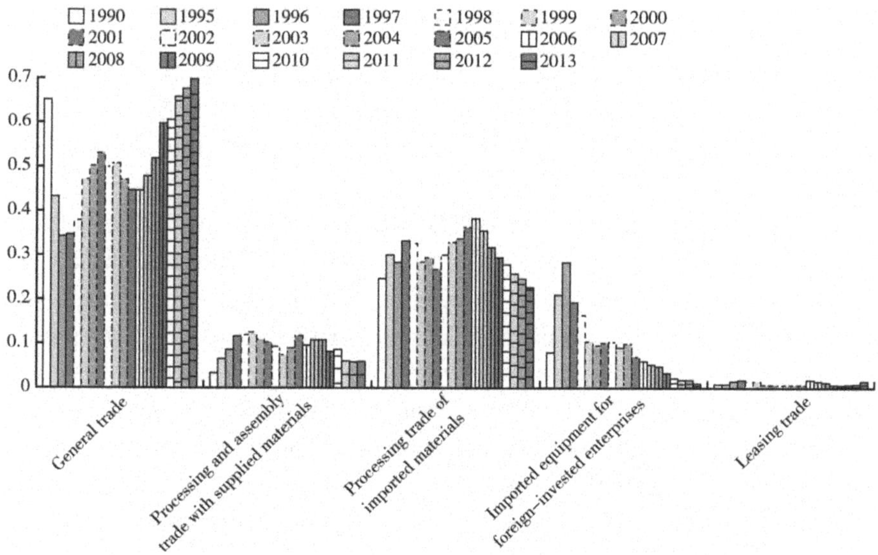

Figure 6.15 Characteristics of Changes in the Structure of Shanghai's Trade-in Imported Goods from 1990 to 2013

Source: Shanghai Statistical Yearbooks (2000–2014).

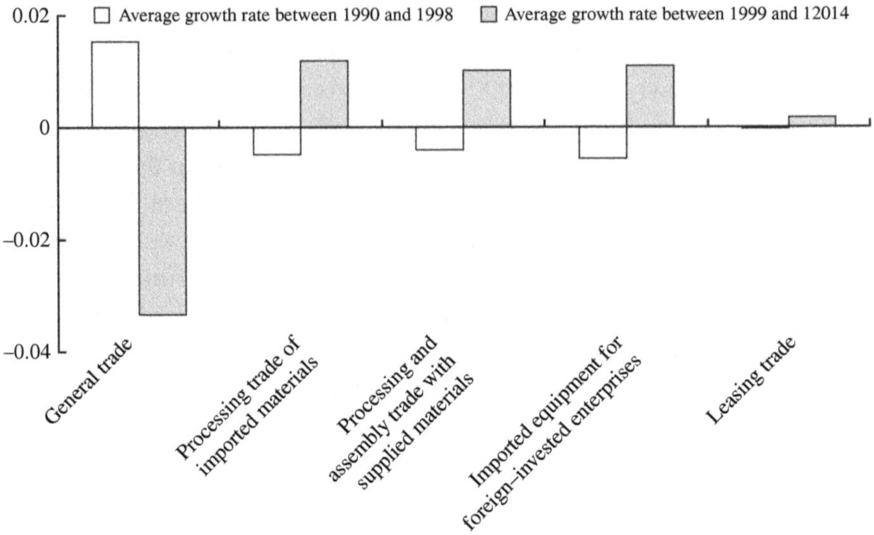

Figure 6.16 Characteristics of Changes in the Structure of Shanghai's Trade-in Imported Goods from 1990 to 1998 and 1999 to 2014

Source: Shanghai Statistical Yearbooks (2000–2014).

demands for manufactured goods and some high-grade goods than primary goods. When domestic industries cannot provide quality and efficient products, consumers tend to select imported goods to meet current demands.

Similar to trade-in exported goods, between 1990 and 1998, before Shanghai entered the Internet era, the structure of Shanghai's trade-in imported goods manifested as a trend indicating average annual negative growth in general trade, and average annual positive growth in processing trade (Figure 6.16). This structure was further optimized from 1999 to 2014, as evidenced by the trend of average annual positive growth in general trade and average annual negative growth in processing trade. Although positive growth in general trade was very small, the overall trend was positive. This is one aspect that reflected the optimization of the structure in Shanghai's trade-in exported goods.

Therefore, from the perspective of the overall trade flow in Shanghai in the Internet era, the flow of trade-in goods and trade-in services as well as the structure of import and export trade were optimized. From the perspective of the structure of Shanghai's trade-in imported goods from 1990 to 2013, as a result of Internet's development, trade-in imported goods was optimized in a way that resulted in an increase in the share of general trade and a decline in the share of processing trade. In case of processing trade, processing trade of imported materials grew much faster than processing and assembly trade with supplied materials.

4.2 *Study of Changes in the Structure of Shanghai's Trade-in Services*

Between 2000 and 2013, Shanghai's trade-in exported services increased significantly, with transportation, consulting, and computer and information services achieving the highest growth.

With the growth in total volume of Shanghai's trade-in services, Shanghai's trade-in imported services from 2000 to 2014 was mainly characterized by rapid growth in overall transportation services. In spite of lower technological levels as opposed to computer and information services, consulting, finance and other services, transportation services were mainly imported in Shanghai's trade-in services. The slight decline

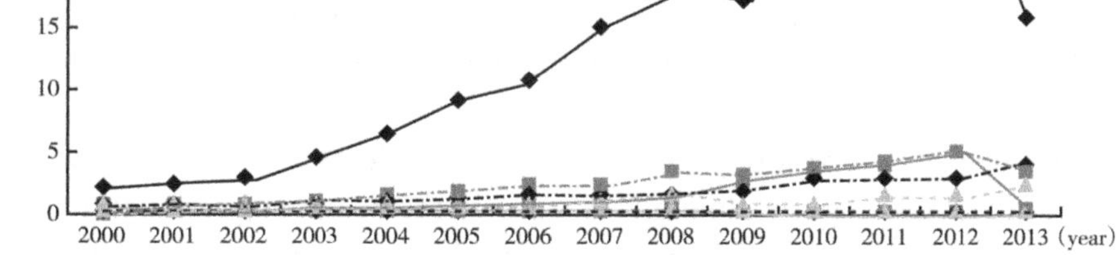

Figure 6.17 Analysis of Shanghai's Trade-in Imported Services from 2000 to 2013
Source: Development Report of Shanghai's Trade-in Services (2000–2014).

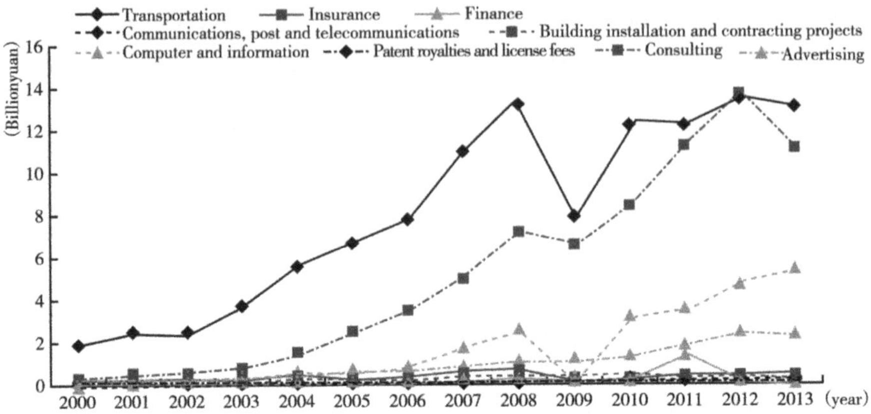

Figure 6.18 Analysis of Shanghai's Trade-in Exported Services from 2000 to 2013
Source: Development Report of Shanghai's Trade-in Services (2000–2013).

in the volume of trade-in transportation services exhibited an overall downward trend. In other words, although imports in Shanghai's trade-in services increased in the Internet era, the structure of trade-in services did not improve significantly, and medium and low-tech service products were mainly imported. The analysis of Shanghai's Trade-in Exported and Imported Services from 2000 to 2013 are shown in Figures 6.17 and 6.18.

A further study of Shanghai's trade-in exported services showed that export of medium and low-tech transportation services increased. Furthermore, the high-tech consulting industry played a vital role in Shanghai's trade-in exported services. Moreover, despite modest growth of trade-in computer and information services, the Internet era saw a substantial increase on the whole. Advertising also exhibited a slight increase.

Overall, the structure of Shanghai's trade-in services from 2000 to 2014 is characterized by higher optimization of the export structure than the import structure, as opposed to the characteristics of trade-in goods. In other words, as cross-border e-commerce accelerates the development of trade-in services today, Shanghai's trade-in services can go global more easily. Based on this finding, the focus should be on encouraging human capital-based trade-in services with small pre-investment costs, to enable Shanghai's enterprises to go global at a faster pace.

4.3 *Study of Structural Changes in the Commercial Presence of Shanghai's Trade-in Services*

Three indicators are used to measure commercial presence in trade-in services.

Indicator 1: Number of investment projects

According to Figure 6.19, there were few opportunities in the primary industry to attract further investment projects after 2000. The number of investment projects in the secondary industry decreased significantly. In contrast, the number of investment projects in the tertiary industry increased sharply. This shows that the tertiary industry, i.e. commercial presence, is the focus of not only trade-in services but also entire industrial investment in Shanghai.

Indicator 2: Amount of contracted investment

According to Figure 6.20, the amount of contracted investment decreased constantly in the primary industry, declined significantly in the secondary industry, and rose sharply in the tertiary industry. This trend shows that commercial presence plays an increasingly important role in Shanghai's

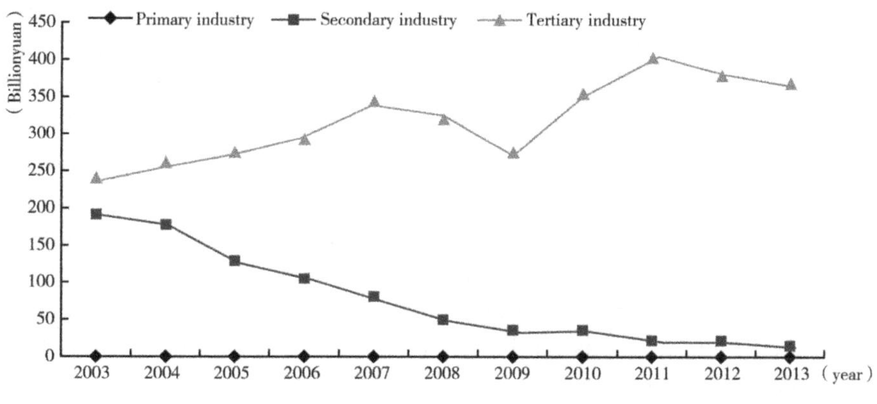

Figure 6.19 Analysis of the Number of Investment Projects in Commercial Presence in Shanghai's Trade-in Services from 2003 to 2013

Source: Shanghai Statistical Yearbooks (2000–2014).

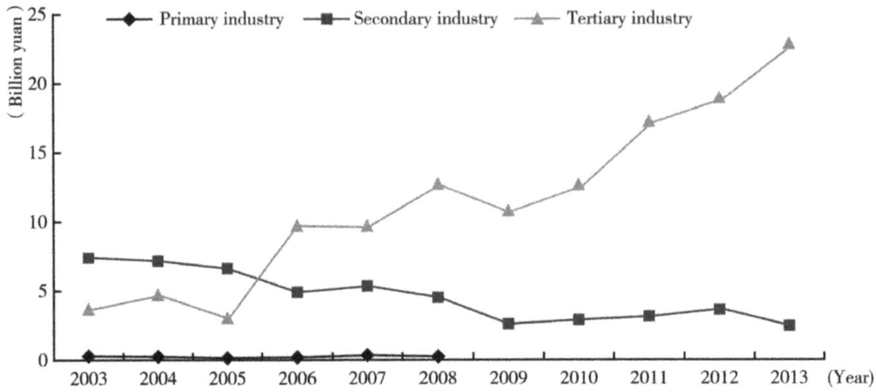

Figure 6.20 Analysis of the Amount of Contracted Investment in Commercial Presence in Shanghai's Trade-in Services from 2003 to 2013

Source: Shanghai Statistical Yearbooks (2000–2014).

trade-in services, and has become the main industrial direction for Shanghai to attract foreign investment.

Indicator 3: Actual number of attracted foreign investments

The number of attracted foreign investments in Shanghai's trade-in services rose far more than that in the primary and secondary industries (Figure 6.21), thus the tertiary industry became a major industry for investment in Shanghai. A faster rise was seen in the tertiary industry after 2008. In the face of the 2008 US financial crisis, China's relatively stable situation and economic development environment attracted more foreign direct investment from developed countries to the Chinese market. As China's economic, financial, trade and shipping center, Shanghai is home to more and more service industries. In other words, thanks to the Internet economy's development, although Shanghai's trade-in services grew slower than trade-in goods on the whole, Shanghai is exerting a strengthened central agglomeration effect in terms of commercial presence, especially as is evident by the clustering of foreign investment.

Therefore, from an overall point of view, as a core city and an international trade center under construction, Shanghai has a prominent agglomeration effect on trade-in goods, and plays a key role in increasing

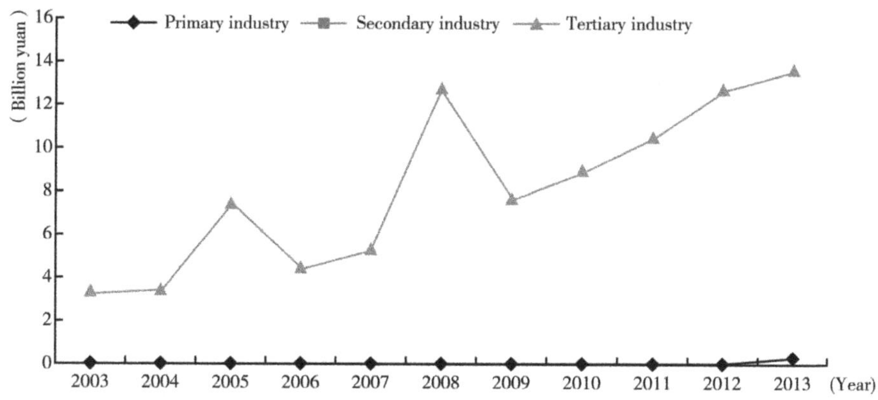

Figure 6.21 Analysis of Actual Number of Attracted Foreign Investments in Commercial Presence in Shanghai's Trade-in Services from 2003 to 2013

Source: Shanghai Statistical Yearbooks (2000–2014).

trade flow with the help of information technology in the Internet era. Therefore, further accelerating construction of the Internet is conducive to the growth in the flow of Shanghai's trade-in goods. Given the Internet's central agglomeration effect on trade-in services, this effect is very weak and makes no difference. In other words, facing the Internet's rapid development in future, Shanghai can accelerate the construction of Internet infrastructure by applying paperless customs clearance, to further speed up substantial increase in the volume of trade-in goods. However, the potential crisis mainly lies in trade-in services, that is, further development of the Internet may have a more obvious dispersion effect on cross-border trade-in services. It is imperative to focus on fostering Shanghai's special service industry and promoting development of trade-in services, particularly with a focus on the agglomeration effect of commercial presence in trade-in services. At present, Shanghai is working to rapidly develop the "headquarters economy" as one measure to realize this goal. The next step is to further increase the spatial agglomeration effect of trade-in services with Shanghai's "headquarters economy" as the center, which may have a greater impact on the service industry's commercial presence. This, to a certain extent, can ease and offset the dispersion effect of cross-border trade-in services.

Strengthening the construction of information networks is very important in the Internet era. Shanghai FTZ is building and popularizing an e-commerce system in order to enhance rapid customs clearance for trade-in goods. In future, to leverage Shanghai FTZ's pioneering role in trade-in goods, an e-commerce exchange system needs to be established first, to enhance the effect of convenient Internet-enabled information dissemination on expanding traditional trade flow. This effect will be highly significant.

In the Internet era, increasing trade flow in Shanghai is an inevitable trend. Effective EDI application in customs clearance for goods, promoting removal of non-tariff barriers to trade-in services, and creating a more fair, transparent and efficient market mechanism are highly conducive to offsetting the Internet's negative decentralized effect on trade-in services.

Chapter 7

Construction of Shanghai International Shipping Center to Enhance Industrial Value Chain

After the golden growth for more than 30 years, China's economic development has entered a new normal state. Drivers of economic growth have gradually shifted from being factor-based to innovation-based. The economic growth model also needs to shift from extensive, denotative development to intensive, connotative development, with scientific and technological innovation as a key factor in this shift. Shanghai will continue to play a leading and demonstrative role in the national economy. Its "4 + 1 + 1" construction (four centers, one center for scientific and technological innovation, and Shanghai FTZ) is based on national strategy and will support its own development. In the context of the current world economic landscape and regional development, the success or failure in constructing an International Economic Center, International Shipping Center, International Trade Center, and International Financial Center reflects a city's and a country's competitiveness, core position, and standing in the international community. Scientific and technological innovation surely gives a fundamental impetus for completing, upgrading, and organically integrating construction of the four centers.

With the rise of the information era and Internet Plus, coordinating the construction of an International Shipping Center in Shanghai with the construction of the Center for Scientific and Technological Innovation, provides important support for constructing and upgrading the four centers in Shanghai. This coordination further stimulates and deepens Shanghai's agglomeration and economic impact as an international shipping center, so as to effectively absorb and configure global shipping and industrial resources, and serves to boost the hinterland's economic development, which helps establish Shanghai's core position as a world-class central and global city. Specifically, to realize this coordination, electronic-enabled and Internet Plus based scientific and technological innovation need to be applied widely in shipping products and services. Also, strategic emerging technologies such as Big Data, Cloud Computing, trading platforms, and mobile payments should be used to promote the construction of a smart port and a smart International Shipping Center in Shanghai (Huang Yejing, 2005). This chapter proves through analysis that leveraging the International Shipping Center's agglomeration function and economic impact requires sound coordination with the Center for Scientific and Technological innovation, as well as the use of technology to drive the International Shipping Center's construction and advancement.

I. Basic Status of the Construction of Shanghai International Shipping Center

1. *Basic Background and Main Objective of Shanghai International Shipping Center's Coordinated Construction along with the Center for Scientific and Technological Innovation*

Shanghai International Shipping Center's construction is not only necessary for the city and country's development strategies, but also inevitable amid the trend of global economic and trade development. Shanghai International Shipping Center's coordinated construction along with the

Center for Scientific and Technological Innovation, is taking place against the backdrop of global economy. As the global economic center shifts from west to east and from the Atlantic to the Pacific, East Asian economic and trade development is slated to become an important pivot of the world economy due to its fast growth. In addition, international shipping resources, elements and industries will shift and aggregate eastward at a faster pace resulting in the redistribution and division of labor in global international shipping centers, which will have an economic impact on the development of hinterland and surrounding areas. Singapore, Hong Kong, and Tokyo are rising as competitive representatives of international shipping centers, and complement each other's advantages, like London and New York. In this process, as a core contributor in constructing an international shipping center in China, Shanghai needs to seize a key position in the international shipping industrial chain. Hinterland economic situations and a port city's service functions determine whether the city can become a hub in the international shipping network. In the current Internet Plus era, scientific and technological innovation is a key driver for a port city to enhance its service functions.

In addition, it should be noted that under the framework of multilateral and bilateral trade agreements such as TPP, TIPP, and PSA, the rapid development of regional economic collaboration may lead to negative impacts on ports and shipping centers not covered by these agreements, however, small and medium-sized ports will directly benefit from these agreements.

Global international shipping centers experience functional evolution and differentiation. According to the evolution of port functions summarized in *Port Marketing and the Challenge of the Third Generation Port* published by the United Nations Conference on Trade and Development (UNCTAD) in 1992, international shipping centers have evolved with three models (Figure 7.1). In 1999, the UNCTAD further proposed fourth generation ports. Combined with the characteristics of an international shipping center, the fourth-generation international shipping centers are a combination of big ports, digital and information-based smart ports, low-carbon and smart green ports, and networked and agile smart ports, and include forms such as joint venture parent–child ports, port-shipping alliance, inter-port alliance, port-city combination,

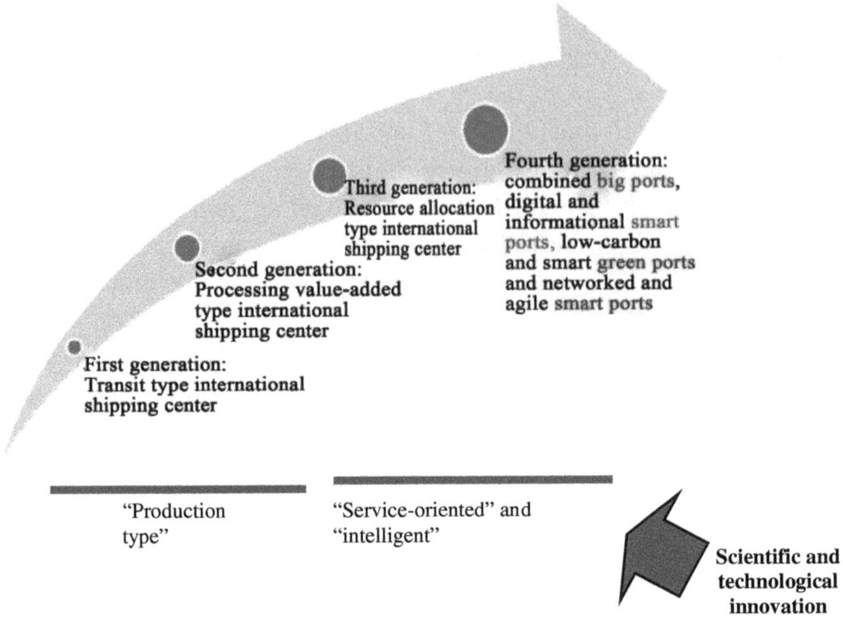

Figure 7.1 Global International Shipping Centers' Functional Evolution

and port-town combination. This aims to realize a port shipping and seamless inter-port supply chain. In the current information age, information, innovation, intelligence, and logistics have gradually entered shipping activities, and have become important production factors, thus contributing to the development of third-generation and fourth-generation international shipping centers. The third-generation and fourth-generation ports, which are represented by international, large-scale, systematic logistics and value-added logistics, as well as technology-intensive smart ports, combined ports and virtual logistics chain control centers, not only represent the global international shipping center development trend, but also provide an objective for Shanghai International Shipping Center's construction (Li Hehua and Tang Guochun, 2006; Han Hanjun, 2006; Xie Qi, 2012; Yu Dongyun and Zheng Lifeng, 2013).

Shanghai is still a production-type international shipping center. With the rise and development of information technology, the Internet Plus and logistics technology, Shanghai International Shipping Center's construction is expected to face new opportunities and challenges. These advanced technologies, and information and logistical factors are the opportunities for Shanghai to build an International Shipping Center that will be better than London, New York, Singapore and Rotterdam's shipping centers, but they also pose challenges. Only effective, timely and fast integration and leveraging of information technology development will contribute to Shanghai International Shipping Center's successful construction, failing which its construction would be impeded.

From a relationship perspective, among the four centers, the International Shipping Center is the foundation for the International Trade Center. The International Shipping Center's development not only directly promotes International Financial Center's development but also propagates the International Financial Center's influence to the whole world. At the same time, the International Financial Center expands the reach of the International Shipping Center's economic impact, and the three centers jointly serve the International Economic Center's construction.

Therefore, given the aforementioned background, Shanghai International Shipping Center's construction needs to leverage the Center for Scientific and Technological Innovation's construction, in order to improve production functions as a production-type international shipping center, and upgrade to a service-oriented and smart international shipping center. Shanghai International Shipping Center should exert its factor agglomeration and economic impact through constantly upgrading the international shipping value chain.

2. *Construction of Shanghai International Shipping Center's Overall Status*

2.1 *Shanghai International Shipping Center's Global Status*

Shanghai International Shipping Center's construction has begun to bear fruit, garnering a certain international status. The Global International Shipping Center Index (GSCI)[1] shows that London, Tokyo, Hong Kong,

[1]The GSCI was developed by the Shanghai Pudong New Area Management Consulting Industry Association and the Research Center for Shanghai Pudong International Financial

New York, and Shanghai ranked top five among the 50 international shipping centers selected. In addition, Tianjin ranked 14th and Dalian ranked 18th. Considering the changes in the global international shipping center model, the GSCI is focused on a port's performance in carbon emissions and global resource allocation capacity. In the case of Xinhua–Baltic International Shipping Centre Development Index that is focused on port conditions, shipping services and integrated environment, Shanghai ranked sixth among the top 10 international shipping centers in the world, which included four Asian cities (Singapore, Hong Kong, Shanghai, and Busan).[2]

In addition, according to the concentration indices obtained by Lv Kangjuan and Zhang Rongrong (2012), the core layer of global international shipping centers consist of five node cities, namely, London, New York, Singapore, Hong Kong, and Tokyo. Other cities including Hong Kong and Shanghai are at the second layer, i.e. periphery layer. Zhang Rongrong (2012) built a complex worldwide shipping network using data from international multinational shipping companies, and estimated the shipping value and other indicators of each node (shipping center city) in the network. Shanghai ranked second nationwide, only second to Hong Kong in terms of degree, centrality and core (concentration), and ranked eighth worldwide.

Based on the historical evolution of global international shipping centers and the shipping industrial chain, international shipping centers can be divided into four levels: (i) basic shipping, with goods transshipment to meet basic shipping needs; (ii) goods transshipment and processing; (iii) goods transshipment, processing and service; and (iv) smart shipping. The first two types are production-type international shipping centers; the third is service-oriented international shipping center; the fourth is knowledge/technology intensive international shipping center.

---

and Shipping Centers, and was first released on March 8, 2010 in Pudong, Shanghai. It takes into account 58 indicators for shipping level, shipping services and shipping ecology.

[2]*Source*: *Xinhua–Baltic International Shipping Center Development Index Report (2015).*

2.2 *Construction of Shanghai International Shipping Center and Its Agglomeration and Economic Impact*

The main driver of industrial agglomeration is derived from reducing trade costs and agglomeration effect of economies of scale, which can significantly increase labor productivity and lead to economic growth (Martin and Ottaviano, 2001). According to the new economic growth theory, agglomeration and innovation are the sources of economic growth drivers. Yu Dongyun and Zheng Lifeng (2013) pointed out that the impact of innovative ideas and new knowledge agglomeration on regional economy often surpasses production agglomeration. They also stated that industrial agglomeration also has an impact on innovative behaviors through external effect characterized by technology spillover and scale effect, featuring enterprise learning and upstream and downstream interaction.

At present, the construction of Shanghai International Shipping Center is still in the primary stage of production-type international shipping center, i.e. goods distribution stage. This stage is mainly characterized by labor-intensive industries, that is, main agglomeration factors and their production-type functions are closely linked in the extensive development stage when the agglomeration function is not sufficiently exerted. As international shipping centers are developing toward the mid-segment of the shipping industrial chain, they have become capital-intensive, and a higher degree of intensification has led to sufficient exertion of the agglomeration effect. When international shipping centers turn knowledge-intensive, shipping center construction will break through the agglomeration in the physical sense of industries and enterprises, creating a shipping industry model combining virtual industrial parks and improved shipping service industrial clusters. In this model, information technology serves as an adhesive to organically combine basic shipping industries and shipping service industries. The Internet Plus era provides infinite possibilities for this combination.

The main role of Internet Plus is to accelerate the integration of industrial value chains on a global scale, expand and deepen the division of labor, speed up industrial integration and global integration, and generate new business models (Jiang, 2011). Therefore, if we say that capital-intensive agglomeration effect results from economies of scale and the reduction in logistics costs in the middle and later stages of a production-type international shipping center, then the agglomeration effect of a service-oriented and smart international shipping center is mainly reflected by the role of agglomeration in stimulating and promoting innovation activities; and the shipping industrial chain's extension from within a region or a city to the world, to form a global virtual connection, also sparks the international shipping center's economic impact. Thus, the Internet Plus breaks through the traditional process of factor agglomeration, i.e. the process of industrial agglomeration, so as to leverage the agglomeration effect beyond physical boundaries. Specifically, the combination of the Internet Plus with an international shipping center also plays a different role in the different development stages of the shipping center. In the production-type stage, it is essential to facilitate the basic functions of shipping and build a knowledge and technology information sharing platform for shipping enterprises via Internet Plus. Further, to promote a service-oriented international shipping center and ensure its smart development, it is necessary to build a tight network of advanced shipping services, and accelerate the agglomeration and development of advanced shipping services.

3. *Construction and Agglomeration Function of Shanghai International Shipping Center*

3.1 *Agglomeration Function of Shanghai as a Production-type International Shipping Center*

The flow of goods is the basis and support enabling a port city to become an international shipping center. The throughput measures the international shipping center's agglomeration effect of goods and the city's capacity to handle goods and logistics. Agglomeration is the basic function of the international shipping center. At present, construction of Shanghai International Shipping Center as a production-type international shipping center is still in its early stage. Thanks to China's rise and expansion of global industrial chains, Shanghai has become an important hub in the global international shipping system and the shipping market is booming. According to the *China Port Yearbook 2014*, Shanghai replaced Singapore to become the world's first in terms of container throughput in 2010; Shanghai Port's container throughput reached 33.617 million TEU by 2013, 1.038 million TEU more than Singapore Port.

The city also plays a crucial role in the cruise economy. The Shanghai Port has hosted a large number of international cruises and inbound/outbound tourists. The *China Port Yearbook 2014* shows that a total of 197 cruise ships arrived and docked at the Shanghai Port received by 2013, far more than for the other three ports. Shanghai Port also hosted the main inbound/outbound tourists, and received 756,600 inbound/outbound tourists from international cruise ships in 2013, much higher than the second-ranking Tianjin Port (250,000). In terms of goods throughput, Shanghai Port's goods throughput reached 682.73 million tons in 2013, an increase of 7.11% over 2012. It accounted for 9.38% of total port goods throughput in China, second only to Ningbo–Zhoushan Port. This further verifies Shanghai's strength as an international shipping hub with Shanghai as the center, Jiangsu and Zhejiang as its two wings, and Yangtze River Basin as the hinterland.

In addition, Shanghai has established an orderly and effective system of division of labor within its urban port areas. Wusong Port transports containers for domestic trade; Waigaoqiao port handles containers from the hinterland as well as containers for transshipment; Yangshan Port is engaged in transshipment of international containers (Jiang, 2010). To sum up, from the perspective of throughput, as a production-type international shipping center, Shanghai plays a significant agglomeration effect globally, however, the rapid increase in goods and container throughput is not conducive to Shanghai's future development toward a low-carbon, green international shipping center. In addition, the high costs of logistics in Shanghai hinder its further agglomeration effect on products and production entities.

3.2 *Shanghai's Agglomeration Function as a Service-oriented International Shipping Center*

Throughout the development of the world's major shipping centers represented by ports such as those in London, Singapore, Hong Kong, Rotterdam, and New York, the physical functions of shipping centers have gradually weakened and the "port of value" has become a benchmark for international shipping centers (Zhang, 2008). Although Shanghai ranks No. 1 in the world in terms of port throughput, Shanghai lags far behind London, Hong Kong, and other major international shipping centers in terms of shipping brokerage, maritime arbitration, shipping finance and insurance, and other high-end shipping services (Zhang and Zhou, 2012).

Based on the overall development of Shanghai's service industry, the proportion of Shanghai's tertiary industry was relatively low at 62.2%, lower than Beijing's 76.9% and much lower than Hong Kong's 93.22% (2011). As for the sector's distribution in the tertiary industry, despite improvement since 2001, Shanghai's tertiary industry still consists mainly of wholesale, retail and other traditional services, which bear relatively low-added value and stand at the low end of the industrial chain. The internal structure of Shanghai's tertiary industry needs to be further optimized and improved.

The shipping service industry occupies a small share in Shanghai's economy and is likely to become a weak spot in Shanghai International Shipping Center's construction. Modern shipping service industry is the core competitiveness of an international shipping center, and an important element that helps expand the international shipping center's factor agglomeration effect and enhance the shipping industry's added value. However, Shanghai's international shipping services are mainly confined to freight forwarding, transport, warehousing and other middle and low-end shipping services, and lack agglomeration of shipping finance, law and other high-end services (Jiang, 2011). In particular, development of shipping finance and consulting is seriously lagging behind, accounting for less than 1% of the global shipping loan market, with international water–water transfer only accounting for 10% (Xiao *et al.*, 2015). Effective agglomeration of high-end services has not yet taken shape in Shanghai, which may hinder the construction of a world-class international shipping center in future (Jin, 2010).

Despite being weaker than the world's major international shipping centers, Shanghai has established a number of important shipping services agglomeration areas, including the North Bund, Lujiazui, and Lingang, which are efficiently coordinating with each other to serve Shanghai International Shipping Center's construction. Shanghai Pudong Airport Comprehensive Free Trade Zone also serves as an agglomeration area that provides functions typical to a high-end service stage of a production-type international shipping center such as international transit, export processing, maintenance, commodity display, and other processing-based value-added services (Zhao and Shan, 2010).

3.3 *Agglomeration Function of Shanghai as a Knowledge-based International Shipping Center*

The way in which low-end shipping elements are embedded in the global shipping value chain inevitably inhibits the development and upgrade of Shanghai Shipping Center's service functions. Information, knowledge, and innovation are important drivers for enhancing Shanghai International Shipping Center's service functions, upgrading Shanghai's position in the global shipping industrial chain, and promoting the Shanghai Shipping Center's transformation to a third-generation or fourth-generation international shipping center (Zhuang and Che, 2010; Xie, 2012). The Internet Plus and Big Data era has provided Shanghai with different opportunities than the ones New York and Tokyo had when they built international shipping centers. The key to seizing these opportunities and effectively utilizing information technology lies in talents, especially talents in science and technology and management. The agglomeration of high-end local and international talents provides a continuous stream of motivation and intellectual support for these international shipping centers' development and growth. Attracting high-end shipping talents is necessary to effectively promote emerging high-end shipping industrial agglomerations in Shanghai, boost the industry's structural adjustment, and enhance the evolution and upgrade of Shanghai's shipping industry (Gao *et al.*, 2009).

Specifically, key shipping industry talents mainly include senior sailor and seamanship talents, senior management talents, ship management talents, senior ship repair & building and port machinery manufacturing professionals, international maritime education and training talents, ship inspection and survey talents, maritime safety and maritime transport technical service talents, international shipping brokers, international shipping financial professionals, international maritime law and arbitration talents, international shipping insurance talents, shipping consulting and research talents, etc. (Qu and Wang, 2012).

With regard to the current talent agglomeration in Shanghai International Shipping Center's construction process, Gao *et al.* (2009) built a comparison and evaluation system for talent agglomeration in international shipping centers, showing that Shanghai lags far behind Hong Kong, Singapore, and London in terms of talent size, quality, environment, and internationalization. This result objectively requires Shanghai to seek innovative cultivation models for shipping talents, while increasing the introduction of high-end shipping talents, in order to improve the overall quality of Shanghai's shipping talents. In addition, Shanghai should strive to further improve the social environment for development of talents, and increase efforts to open up and introduce talents with an international vision.

3.4 *Agglomeration Function of Shanghai as a Headquarters-type International Shipping Center*

Shanghai needs to comprehensively leverage the headquarters effect, including the agglomeration effect of micro-enterprises, in order to build and improve an international shipping center. Based on international experience, in addition to the fact that London is home to the world's largest international shipping services market, London International Shipping Center's leading position is related to London shipping industry's developed headquarters economy. By the end of 2011, the world's renowned container liner companies and classification societies had all set up headquarters, regional headquarters or branches in Shanghai. In addition, the Baltic and International Maritime Council (BIMCO) Shanghai Center was unveiled in 2013, becoming the first internationally-recognized international shipping organization to officially set up operations in Shanghai (Che *et al.*, 2013). In 2012, the number of shipping enterprises alone reached 3,530, in the shipping services agglomeration area on the North Bund.[3]

In addition to the positive introduction of domestic and foreign capital, Shanghai International Shipping Center is also working with the

---

[3] *Source*: Shipping Services Agglomeration Area on the North Bund. Website of Hongkou, Shanghai. Available at: http://hkq.sh.gov.cn/shhk/tzhk/20140610/003001_ef4914e2-d439-41cd-98bf-341ffcb2b24d.htm.

Belt and Road Initiative, especially the 21st Century Maritime Silk Road, to promote complementary operation and connection of land resource and energy channels, and to promote micro-enterprises' push to go global.

II. Economic Impact of Shanghai International Shipping Center's Functions

Historically, port cities that evolved into shipping centers eventually became centers of regional economy and became the breeding ground for innovative ideas. Due to the fact that such core cities have geographical advantages, they also tend to become the center for several types of manpower and material resources. New ideas, new technologies, and new cultures are exchanged and have an economic impact on local and surrounding areas during the process of exchange and transport of goods. In the following analysis, starting with international shipping center's "economic impact", we rethink its conceptualization and significance to Shanghai from the perspective of industrial value chain, region, and "Internet Plus".

1. *Shipping Industry Industrial Chain and its Economic Impact Mechanisms*

1.1 *Analysis of Shipping Industry's Industrial Chain*

So far, the academic community has not yet clearly defined the concept of shipping industrial chain. Here, we use Jin Jiachen and Zhen's definition (2013): Combining existing discussions on the concept of industrial chain as well as shipping industry's characteristics, the shipping industrial chain is a value-added network chain of relationships established among shipping and related enterprises based on specific technological and economic relations within certain time and space, with trade demand as its guide and trade facilitation as its purpose. Jin and Zhen (2013) also defined a shipping industrial chain to consist of a main chain and two auxiliary chains. The main chain is reflected by the traditional shipping industrial chain composed of traders, shipping companies, and port enterprises as main bodies, as well as freight forwarders and shipping agents as connection points, all of which provide a goods transport service chain. The other two auxiliary chains are more "complicated": the ship auxiliary chain mainly involves shipbuilding industry and service industry, covering ship design, manufacturing, repair, inspection, registration and management; the service auxiliary chain covers more industries such as finance, insurance, law, education, consulting, information, culture & media, and industrial management. We believe that shipping industry can connect to other industries through the main chain, thereby forming a complete industrial chain network in both breadth and width, as shown in Figure 7.2.

According to international shipping industry's current development status, the upgrade and innovation in shipping industry mainly comes from the two auxiliary chains. Shipbuilding and design involved in the ship auxiliary chain are closely related to advanced manufacturing, and serve as ways to upgrade manufacturing industry and increase added value. The service auxiliary chain covers a variety of high value-added services and represents an inevitable development direction for industrial upgrade. Although it is not considered as the shipping industry's

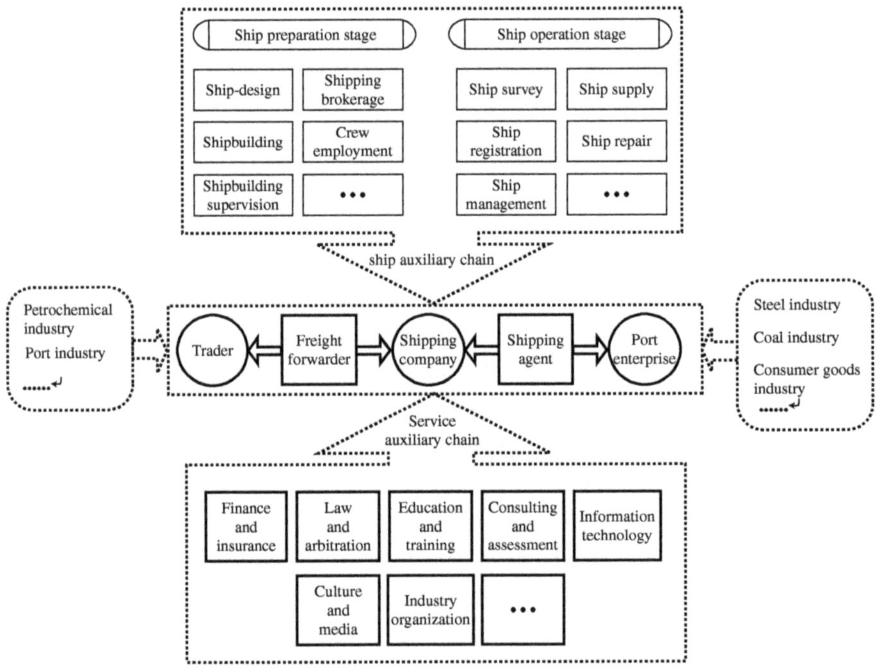

Figure 7.2 Shipping Industrial Chain

foundation, it is at the top of the industrial chain. Shipping industry's main chain is its foundation and is indispensable, but its role has been gradually weakened. The main reason is that the main chain's development prospect is largely related to the shipping center city's location and the city's natural conditions and infrastructure construction, as well as the country's status in international trade and international division of labor, which is subject to many objective factors.

1.2 *Relationship between Shipping Center's Development Model and Shipping Industrial Chain*

At present, an international shipping center is widely considered as a functional integrated concept, and refers to an international shipping hub that integrates developed shipping markets, abundant logistics resources and sufficient flight routes, and generally relies on international trade, financial and economic centers (Peng, 2015). Based on shipping industrial chain's analysis, the shipping industrial chain is long and wide enough to cover secondary and tertiary industries, hence, shipping industry's development has a wide economic impact on other industries and directly influences shipping center city's industrial layout. However, changes in shipping center's development model in turn influences shipping industrial chain's development, and even development of the shipping center city. Therefore, it is a highly suitable development strategy for a shipping center city to realize its economic impact and promote industrial upgrade, industrial innovation and urban development, by capitalizing on shipping industrial chain's development and the shipping center development model.

Along with some common geographical and natural conditions, international shipping centers have different characteristics. According to analysis described in the previous section, the international shipping centers' development model has undergone several generations of important transformation, and different shipping centers have varying kinds of industrial chain layout. Specifically, compared to the first-generation model, the second-generation model improves international shipping center's value in trade and production, and the international shipping center has higher requirements. The third-generation "resource allocation type" international shipping center may not have an absolute advantage in the main chain, but its auxiliary chains play an important role, especially the service auxiliary chain that bears high professionalism and added value. As industries involved in the service auxiliary chain are not directly related to shipping, this development model has higher requirements for the international shipping center's industrial development and urban development levels. Thus, such an international shipping center is always a regional and even an international economic and financial center.

At present, the fourth-generation international shipping centers are developing towards "low-carbon and smart-network" centers. This development model has the following important features: (i) low carbon; (ii) global sea and air port smart networks; (iii) virtual combined ports created based on function and space; (iv) increasingly strengthened "capabilities to optimize and allocate global resources"; and (v) intelligence-intensive emerging industries based on "international shipping" and "global shipping services" to be established, to achieve "win–win results".[4]

Beginning with the second-generation international shipping centers' development model, the shipping industry's main chain is no longer the focus of development, and the two auxiliary chains are important drivers for constant upgrade of international shipping centers. The latest fourth-generation model has broken through the "chain" form. Due to information technologies and Internet-enabled connectivity, the shipping industrial chain has become an industrial network, where every link involves a variety of industries among which there are no obvious upstream and downstream relationships. The entire international shipping center has transformed into an organic entity providing services.

2. *Analysis of Shanghai Shipping Center's Current Status in Domestic and Foreign Shipping Industrial Value Chains*

Shanghai's shipping industry has developed rapidly since 1990. According to data from Shanghai Bureau of Statistics, domestic goods

[4]Refer to the report of Shenzhen Logistics Network on May 26, 2010. Available at: http://wuliu.sz.bendibao.com/news/2010526/206639.shtm.

trade throughput steadily increased, along with international trade throughput, which rose from 1990 to 2013 at an average annual rate of 12.34%, while the international container throughput grew at an average annual rate of 20.77%. In 2014, Shanghai Port achieved goods throughput of 755 million tons; and container throughput reached 35.285 million TEU, a year-on-year increase of nearly 5%, ranking first in the world for 5 years in a row.

In addition, Shanghai's ship auxiliary chains (shipbuilding-related industries) and service auxiliary chains and Yangtze River Delta region have considerable national-level advantages and are now developing.

Inevitably, Shanghai now serves as a shipping hub in Yangtze River Delta as well as for the country, and is also one of China's important foreign trade "windows". Despite ranking No. 1 worldwide in terms of goods throughput, considering various indicators, Shanghai as a shipping center does not leverage its position in throughput, and only falls into second-tier ranks of international shipping centers. According to statistical data for the first half of 2015, although international container throughput and airport passenger throughput increased over the same period last year, port goods throughput decreased by 6.4% over the same period last year, total freight volume of goods fell by 0.6%, and railway freight volume declined substantially by 20%. Decrease in goods throughput could not indicate a decline in Shanghai International Shipping Center's status. London's historical experience is worth learning from. Although London faced a decline in throughput and there was migration of traditional shipping services, relevant industries in London successfully transformed into high-end shipping service industries, which in turn consolidated its status as an international shipping center. This makes it essential for Shanghai to foster new economic impact and competitive advantages in other areas for future development, in addition to the traditional throughput indicator. Next, from the "Internet Plus" perspective, this section will introduce policy recommendations on how Shanghai can develop the international shipping center, deploy industrial and regional economic impact, and coordinate with construction of a center for scientific and technological innovation.

3. *Analysis of Upgrade Path and Economic Impact Mechanisms of Shanghai International Shipping Center*

There are several different views on the definition of "Internet Plus". According to one of them, "'Internet Plus' represents a new mode of social activity enhancing the entire society's innovativeness and productivity. It does this by leveraging the Internet's strength in improving allocation efficiency of social resources and integrating them seamlessly, and in ensuring practical application of innovations in Internet development, across a broad range of economic and social fields. In this sense, 'Internet Plus' forms a part of the infrastructure of a new model of economic growth".[5] Therefore, as an innovative carrier, "Internet Plus" does not constitute a part of any industrial chain, but it is an important element for value chain upgrade. It acts as a platform and media of scientific and technological innovation. With the help of the new thinking and production modes, it is a fantastic opportunity to upgrade the shipping industrial chain, transform the international shipping center, and expand industrial and regional economic impact of innovations in a core city.

3.1 *Impact of "Internet Plus" Era on Shipping Industry: Coordination with Construction of the Center for Scientific and Technological Innovation*

Here, we analyze how shipping industry construction and the International Shipping Center can create a platform for construction of the Center for Scientific and Technological Innovation via "Internet Plus", from three aspects. Firstly, trade demand, the shipping industry's most basic function, is the foundation for international shipping center construction. The "Internet Plus" has changed original consumption and business ideas. Due to emergence of a large number of e-commerce providers, online shopping has become a popular way of consumption. Although the "Internet Plus" has changed how manufacturers and consumers choose each other

[5]China Network of Information Industry (CNII), November 2, 2015. Available at: http://www.cnii.com.cn/city/2015-11/02/content_1644673.htm.

and trade, bridging the physical gap between the two sides is no longer an obstacle, and it does not reduce transport needs. On the contrary, goods transport and circulation has become more frequent in the "Internet Plus" background. Compared to the earlier mass, centralized transport, e-commerce trade results in more scattered transportation needs. These transport activities are often undertaken by local logistics companies, most of which, do not have international logistics networks and often outsource transportation activities to large multinational logistics companies. However, these large multinational companies are always reluctant to accept scattered goods from e-commerce providers. As a major function of the shipping industry's main chain, the international shipping center needs to seek innovations to break through the combination of traditional trading companies and shipping companies, and work with more local logistics and transport enterprises to form a new industrial chain that can connect e-commerce providers, local logistics companies and multinational logistics enterprises, and the international shipping center can deploy its resource allocation role. Regarding warehouse and large logistics management, the international shipping center needs to extend original traditional industrial chain by fully leveraging "Internet Plus" and information technologies, thus involving e-commerce providers and local logistics companies in one end of the shipping industry's main chain.

Secondly, from the perspective of the two auxiliary chains, the "Internet Plus" can increase industrial chain value and promote industrial upgrade. In the case of shipbuilding industry, Shanghai has a solid foundation and its economic development level and status as an international shipping center has a very positive impact on the shipbuilding industry. Studies by Yang Dagang *et al.* (2014) showed that degree of synergy between shipbuilding industry and Shanghai shipping center's construction reached an average of 0.86. Therefore, "Internet Plus Traditional Shipbuilding Industry" will be a development direction for advanced manufacturing. Unlike other manufacturing (such as automobile, machinery and equipment, etc.), shipbuilding industry has high requirements for geographical location, and not all cities with developed manufacturing have conditions to develop shipbuilding industry. As an international shipping center, Shanghai not only boasts location and historical advantages, but it has also taken the opportunity of building the center for scientific and technological innovation to intensely develop the shipbuilding industry and achieve unique industrial upgrade. An insider contended that "Internet Plus Shipbuilding Industry" can further transform traditional shipbuilding equipment and processes, and enhance standardization and informatization level in shipbuilding process, by comprehensively leveraging Cloud Computing, Big Data, Internet of Things, and other technologies.[6] Ship design, ship equipment manufacturing, and other shipbuilding-related industries add higher value and high-tech links in shipbuilding industrial chain, and need special attention to form shipbuilding industrial clusters.

Thirdly, the service auxiliary chain is also a new growth point for shipping industry's development. High-end services deliver information and knowledge flows instead of external entities. For example, shipping finance no longer provides just ship and transport insurance, but insurance programs and contracts that are customized for transport routes and destinations. More importantly, shipping insurance, law, ship registration and other services can accomplish information integration using "Big Data", to provide customers with a full range of consulting programs and information services. This indicates a direction to upgrade shipping industry under the "Internet Plus" background.

3.2 *Shanghai's Economic Impact across Yangtze River Delta and the Country in the "Internet Plus" Era: Coordination with the "Belt and Road Initiative"*

In the "Internet Plus" context, as a core city, Shanghai's economic impact across the Yangtze River Delta and the country will change fundamentally. Especially driven by the "Belt and Road Initiative", Shanghai can become an economic impact center of the "21st Century Maritime Silk Road" (the "Road") and provide strong support for the "Silk Road Economic Belt" (the "Belt") through "Internet Plus", through Shanghai

---

[6]China Ship News, March 31, 2015. Available at: http://www.chinashipnews.com.cn/show.php?contentid=8804.

International Shipping Center's role as a window, and its resource allocation functions.

According to shipping indices published by Shanghai Shipping Exchange, the "Belt's" freight index has soared since March 2015, while the "Road's" freight index has had ups and downs. However, overall the "Belt and Road" freight index has continued to rise since March, revealing that the "Belt and Road Initiative" has played a positive role in boosting China's trade-in goods. As a coastal shipping center, Shanghai has played a vital role in the "Road", by radiating toward and serving the "Road's" strategic development, directly through trade-in goods. Thus, "Internet Plus" has changed the shipping industry and goods consumption patterns. Fundamentally speaking, it has changed goods allocation. In this case, the Shanghai Shipping Center needs to expand its shipping network and leverage its core city role, to bring freight transport resources from other cities to Shanghai and deliver these resources to the world, thereby forming a resource allocation center, featuring "centralization of resources and economic impact on surrounding areas".

This is a traditional shipping center model, but such direct economic impact is still required for development of the "Road". However, for development of the "Belt", as an eastern coastal city, Shanghai needs to have an innovative economic impact using "Internet Plus". Although Shanghai may not be able to play a role in the "Belt" because of its geographical position and the "Belt" trend, Shanghai is able to provide higher value through advanced manufacturing technologies and information services. While Shanghai Shipping Center is developing itself, accumulated innovative technologies, information, knowledge, and talents can spread more quickly to the western regions through the Internet. Advanced manufacturing driven by the shipping center can provide technical support for infrastructure construction and development for the "Belt". Information and knowledge related to finance, insurance, logistics and law accumulated in the shipping center can serve the northwestern region's trade to Central Asia and European continent through the Internet. Talent generation in the shipping center can also serve all aspects of the "Belt's" construction through the Internet. The value produced by talents and resources can flow in a broader range via the Internet without actual physical movement. This is a new economic impact mechanism and service function that the Shanghai International Shipping Center can create in the "Belt and Road Initiative". In turn, the "Belt and Road Initiative" has also promoted upgrade of the Shanghai Shipping Center toward creating a high value-added, smart-network, low-carbon center.

3.3 *Shanghai's Global Economic Impact in the "Internet Plus" Era: Coordination with Shanghai FTZ Construction*

Shanghai Shipping Center's construction also benefits from Shanghai FTZ construction. Many supporting policies implemented in the FTZ enable Shanghai to be well prepared for financial and trade innovations, providing a good opportunity for the Shanghai Shipping Center to develop shipping services. Furthermore, Shanghai is able to effectively realize FTZ's financial and trade innovations by relying on the shipping industry and developing the shipping industrial chain. In 2012, Shanghai focused on enhancing shipping functions by implementing the following four measures: pilot application of futures bonded delivery business, tax rebate policy at port of departure, financial leasing business, and pilot application of bonded ship registration.

However, policies implemented in the FTZ may also affect the shipping center's construction. In accordance with the current policy issued on June 5, 2015 — *Ministry of Transport's Announcement on Policies for Pilot Programs of Maritime Transportation in National Free Trade Zones*, the FTZ set out new policy requirements for enterprises in the FTZ and the business operations they can be engaged in. However, based on assessment conducted by relevant parties, it was found that the implementation of these policies was not satisfactory, mainly because taxation and business environment are not aligned with international standards, resulting in extremely high operating costs, which international companies in Shanghai has to bear, and this led to a failure to attract international shipping companies and related enterprises.

To resolve these problems, Shanghai should gradually reduce the negative list for the shipping industry, and give more policy support in taxation and business environment. Shanghai should also develop its characteristics in terms of several aspects. Firstly, Shanghai should enable international companies to virtually settle themselves via "Internet Plus". In the information era, international companies have advanced technologies, service procedures, and management philosophies, which are brought in via the Internet to train local talents in Shanghai. This can prevent taxation and business environment problems caused by physical settlement, and reduce operating costs of multinational companies. Secondly, Shanghai can establish a platform connecting local logistics companies and international logistics companies, and expand domestic e-commerce transactions to the international arena to a greater extent. By implementing preferential tax policies in the FTZ, Shanghai can bring together international e-commerce transactions and spread them to various regions around the world via the Shanghai International Shipping Center platform. Thirdly, Shanghai can connect the world's shipping industrial associations through the Internet, so that shipping arbitration and legal services can be shared and exchanged through it, thereby promoting shipping service development. Of course, the three abovementioned measures also need appropriate new supporting policies based on the "Internet Plus" model rather than traditional FTZ policies. This also requires the government to make innovative policies and transform Shanghai into a low-carbon, smart-network international shipping center.

III. Core Measures Taken to Enhance Shanghai International Shipping Center's Agglomeration and Economic Impact

The "Internet Plus" era has led to enhanced requirements for international shipping centers including that of Shanghai. The emergence of new, high-end production factors bring with it, both challenges and opportunities. Thus, to build a world-class international shipping center and occupy a key node position in the shipping industrial chain, Shanghai needs to significantly change its economic impact mechanisms for domestic and international shipping industries and their industrial chains, surrounding areas, the country, and even the world. To ensure this, Shanghai has to break the original industrial chain structure and restrictions on areas subject to Shanghai's economic impact, and transform from a "production-type" international shipping center into a "service-oriented", "smart" and "low-carbon smart-network" international shipping center, based on the "Center for Scientific and Technological Innovation", "the Belt and Road Initiative", "Free Trade Zone" and other construction strategies. "Internet Plus" provides critical support to transform and upgrade Shanghai International Shipping Center, but it also provides opportunities and challenges that need to be treated with caution. Specific measures include:

1. *Strengthening Construction of "Center for Scientific and Technological Innovation"*

To build a "service-oriented" and "smart" international shipping center that serves the world, Shanghai first needs to become an important global innovation network hub, as well as an important source of major international scientific developments, original technologies, and high-tech industries. Specific measures are outlined here: (1) Strive for major national strategic programs such as civil aero-engine and gas turbine, Beidou navigation, high-end processor chips, integrated circuit manufacturing and supporting equipment materials, advanced sensors and Internet of Things, far-reaching marine engineering equipment with smart grid and new display systems, Big Data, and Cloud Computing. (2) Combine industries, universities and research institutions, and enhance industrialization of scientific research achievements. (3) Exert late-mover advantage and fully leverage international experience and information technologies. (4) Keep track of and invent latest shipping industry technologies, including barcode technology, database technology, electronic order system (EOS), electronic data interchange (EDI), quick response (QR), effective customer feedback (ECR), and enterprise resource planning (ERP), to build a logistics information port. (5) Start with the "base" and key parks, and establish demonstration areas and key industrial agglomerations to promote technological absorption and innovation such as Zhangjiang and Lingang Scientific and Technological Innovation Demonstration Areas (Research Group — The Development Research Center of the Shanghai Municipal People's Government, 2015).

2. *Upgrading Shanghai International Shipping Center's Infrastructure Facilities*

One of the shipping center's basic elements is port productivity, including wharf equipment, water depth of wharf apron, length and quantity, yard and storage capacity. In particular, P3 and other super-shipping alliances accelerate the trend for large-sized ships, and challenge the port's collection and distribution system's carrying capacity. This shall broaden Shanghai's production capacity as a "production-type" international shipping center. In addition, the first batch of pilot polices such as tax rebate policy at port of departure have been implemented. The container water–water transfer rate reached 45.4%, and goods throughput at Pudong International Airport is the third highest globally (Research Group — The Development Research Center of Shanghai Municipal People's Government, 2015).

The second element is the collection and distribution network, also known as inland transport; it is a link in the transportation process of the port's traded goods and a systematic concept of port clusters. The port's traded goods transport includes maritime transport, port handling, and collection and distribution network (Yu, 2009). Currently, internal economic impact promoted by allocation of shipping resources at Shanghai International Shipping Center is obviously restricted by the collection and distribution system. The main problem is that the collection and distribution system is not open enough, and that water, land, and air transportation services are closed in particular. In addition, from regional function and competition perspective, a reasonable pattern of labor division has not yet been formulated at ports located in the Yangtze River Delta region (Lin, 2010). Shipping logistics link needs to provide more efficient services through seamless connection of transportation networks, communications systems, and other scientific and technological elements (Han, 2006).

3. *Learning from "Shanghai FTZ" Construction*

Reforms and innovations at Shanghai FTZ directly provide good reference for Shanghai International Shipping Center's construction. In particular, there are currently eight institutional innovations — checklist management of customs law enforcement, fully-bonded supervision of offshore service outsourcing, bonded trading of commodity spot market, one-stop declaration and inspection, registration in one area and operation in four areas, facilitated customs clearance for artwork, application of classified administrative ruling nationwide, and commodity classification service system. These innovations have made important contributions for facilitation of customs clearance and expansion of Shanghai International Shipping Center's functions.[7] In future, it is necessary to explore how the FTZ can open up more to the outside world, develop innovative shipping policies, expand the center's functions, enhance service level and strengthen infrastructure construction, to facilitate Shanghai International Shipping Center's construction.

In addition, the FTZ strengthens the international shipping center's trade base, thereby elevating Shanghai's international trade status and boosting the international shipping center's construction (Zhang, 2014). With the help of the FTZ's construction, Shanghai is committed to conducting pilot application of functional international shipping services, focusing on port processing-based value-added and re-export trade, opening up more to both domestic and overseas markets, and improving shipping industry's global service capability. This will gradually elevate its position in the international shipping industrial chain using a model that meets innovative laws, and enhances Shanghai's ability to agglomerate and allocate resources and factors in Asia and even the world (Che *et al.*, 2013).

4. *Promoting Construction of a "Grand Shanghai"*

The rise of Yangtze River Delta urban agglomeration is a necessary condition for Shanghai International Shipping Center's construction, and an inherent advantage. The logic behind it is the win–win

[7] *Source*: Trade Regulation System Innovation 2.0 of Shanghai Free Trade Zone Launched: Classified Administrative Ruling Applicable Nationwide. Xinhuanet. Available at: http://news.xinhuanet.com/fortune/2015-06/24/c_1115713260.htm.

cooperation. Construction of a "Grand Shanghai" will make Shanghai an important agglomeration point in the international shipping industry, as vicious competition is affecting the shipping industry's global layout and overall international competitiveness. The objective of Shanghai International Shipping Center's construction is aligned with the *Opinions of State Council on Promoting Shanghai to Accelerate Development of Modern Service Industry and Advanced Manufacturing Industry and Construction of International Financial Center and International Shipping Center* published in 2009. This means "Shanghai should strive to build an international shipping hub port with Shanghai as the center, Jiangsu and Zhejiang as its wings, and Yangtze River Basin as the hinterland, in collaboration with reasonable labor division and close cooperation with other domestic ports." Specifically, it is necessary to build an integrated "community of interests" based golden waterways and ports, and integrate resources in the Yangtze River Delta port clusters through the Yangtze River golden waterway and coastal routes, thereby forming a port cooperative chain with Shanghai as the leader and with Nanjing, Wuhan, and Chongqing as the three major nodes.

5. *Laying out a "Global Talent Strategy"*

To upgrade the international shipping center, Shanghai's talent strategy has to be eased and resilient enough to attract and retain talented personnel. Firstly, Shanghai should develop attractive urban residence policies, and relax immigration policies to introduce high-end talents from the international shipping service industry, as well as offer preferential conditions for permanent residency. Secondly, Shanghai should establish a more flexible system of domestic and international shipping personnel's movement such as introducing local and international shipping professionals as consultants, technical consultants, support, and other short-term and flexible options (Zhen and Jin, 2010). Thirdly, Shanghai should accelerate cultivation of high-end shipping talents through a combination of industries, universities and research institutions, and allow students and teachers to communicate and collaborate with enterprises to enhance and strengthen their abilities in applying shipping knowledge, and create a good pool of shipping personnel for enterprises (Zhen, 2011). Regarding specific industries, Pudong New Area has played an active and demonstrative role in driving and promoting Shanghai International Shipping Center's construction. Pudong New Area has formulated and promulgated *Measures of Pudong New Area for Gathering Shipping Personnel*, *Opinions of Pudong New Area for Introducing Overseas High-end Talents*, and other specific policies, with the focus on supporting five types of enterprises and institutions. These include newly introduced key shipping service enterprises, large shipping-related advanced manufacturing and maintenance enterprises, high-growth shipping companies, high-end shipping service enterprises, and well-known domestic and foreign functional shipping institutions (Zhang, 2011).

References

Che Jun, Ji Lan, and Tang Lianbang. Discussion on the development orientation of Shanghai International Shipping Center. *Engineering Sciences*, 2013 (6).

Gao Jie, Zhen Hong, Li Jianli *et al.* Comprehensive evaluation of talent convergence level of Shanghai International Shipping Center. *Journal of Shanghai Maritime University*, 2009 (4).

Han Hanjun. Construction of Shanghai International Shipping Center: Foundation and guarantee of urban competitiveness, *Shanghai Journal of Economics*, 2006 (9).

Huang Yejing. Coordinated development of Shanghai center for scientific and technological innovation with "four centers". *Social Outlook*, 2005 (5).

Jiang Shaowen. Discussion on new ideas of Shanghai port strategic development. *China Logistics & Purchasing*, 2010 (20).

Jiang Yuantao. The Impact of electronic services on agglomeration of high-end shipping services. *Management and Administration*, 2011 (1).

Jin Jiachen and Zhen Hong. Connotation and basic framework of shipping industry chain. *Navigation of China*, 2013 (3).

Jin Zhendong. *Construction of and Evaluation Research on the Soft Strength Index System of International Shipping Center*. Dalian Maritime University, 2010.

Li Hehua and Tang Guochun. Discussion on logistics information integration in the Yangtze river delta region. *Modern Management Science*, 2006 (6).

Lin Feng. Building Shanghai International Shipping Center into a global shipping resources allocation center, *Social Science*, 2010 (6).

Lv Kangjuan and Zhang Rongrong. On the structure and characteristics of international shipping center based on complex network theory. *Journal of Systems & Management*, 2012 (1).

Martin, P. and Ottaviano, G. I. P. Growth and agglomeration. *International Economic Review*, 2001 (4): 947–968.

Peng Hui. Analysis of competitiveness of Shanghai International Shipping Center. *Market Weekly*, 2015 (2).

Qu Qunzhen and Wang Mingxin. Evaluation on talent cluster competitiveness in Shanghai International Shipping Center. *East China Economic Management*, 2012 (12).

Research Group of the Development Research Center of Shanghai Municipal People's Government: Study of basic ideas for Shanghai's "13th Five-Year Plan". *Scientific Development*, 2015 (3).

Xiao Lin, Zhou Guoping, and Qian Zhi *et al*. Study of key and difficult problems of Shanghai's economic and social development during the "13th Five-Year Plan" Period. *Scientific Development*, 2015 (1).

Xie Qi. Developing the modern shipping services industry and building Guangzhou International Shipping Center. *Guangdong Shipbuilding*, 2012 (4).

Yang Dagang, Wang Xuefeng, and Jin Lin. Quantitative comparison of synergic relationship between shipbuilding industrial cluster and International Shipping Center. *Navigation of China*, 2014 (2).

Yu Dongyun and Zheng Lifeng. Industrial agglomeration, innovative agglomeration and urban economic driver — Evidence from the Yangtze River Delta. *East China Economic Management*, 2013 (3).

Yu Xiaojing. Collecting and distributing system of international shipping center. *Shipping Management*, 2009 (7).

Zhang Jieshu and Zhou Dequan. On strong and weak points of international shipping center. *Oriental Morning Post*, September 18, 2012.

Zhang Li. Experience and revelation of London's development of international shipping center. *Port Economy*, 2008 (9).

Zhang Ying. "100 Talents Program" for Shanghai shipping gets shovel-ready. *International Finance News*, October 20, 2011, p. 2.

Zhang Yingjie. Study of the impact of Shanghai FTZ on the construction of Shanghai Shipping Center. *New Finance*, 2014 (2).

Zhao Xin and Shan Jun. Development Strategy of Shanghai Shipping Service Clusters, *Shipping Management*, 2010 (1).

Zhen Hong and Jin Jiachen. Shanghai is eager for high-end shipping talents. *Maritime China*, 2010 (5).

Zhen Hong. Development strategy of high-end talents for Shanghai's International Shipping. *Talent*, 2011 (2).

Zhuang Leng and Che Cihui. Take the lead in building the fourth-generation international shipping center. *Urban Insight*, 2010 (A01).

Chapter 8

Legal Protection and Public Security in a Core City in the "Internet Plus" Era

With historical progress and social development, a city is facing many more risks and public security issues while generating more wealth. Tianjin explosions in 2015 once again echoed public concern about urban public security. At present, China's social construction and social governance structure badly lags behind socio-economic development. Urban public security management system is also not aligned with the public's demand for security, based on socio-economic development. The foundation of public security is relatively weak, leading to an increasingly prominent contradiction between foundation and rapid economic development, thus seriously affecting and restricting comprehensive, coordinated and sustainable socio-economic development. Keeping such a complex background in mind, it is our top priority to solve major problems faced by public security management during China's social transformation, and to try to improve the country's ability to cope with public security issues.

Scholars have studied the impact of legal protection on urban public security from the following aspects: Firstly, new changes have been seen in China's major public events with regards to form, cause and formation mechanism, while irregularity, mutability, diffusivity, and uncertainty of these events have become increasingly obvious. Thus, legal concepts are used to treat the source of major public events, legal manner is used to guide handling of major public events, and legal methods are used to regulate normal management of major public events (Li and Zhong, 2014). Secondly, to mitigate new-generation migrant workers' behavior in expressing interests which are non-institutionalized and maintain a city's public security, it is necessary to increase number of people who represent interests of migrant workers at all levels of National People's Congress (NPC) and Chinese People's Political Consultative Conference (CPPCC). It is also imperative to legislatively grant appropriate power to trade unions, to empower them to play a proper role in creating checks and balances for enterprises (Zhang, 2014). Thirdly, in dealing with traffic accidents, it is important to pay attention to and improve rules of law, personnel training and invest in supporting infrastructure (Du, 2011). Some scholars however have put forward different ideas to address urban public security. Policy evaluation shows that judicial investment has no significant impact on crime rate, and that growing crime rate is largely caused by a variety of social and economic characteristics that have come together in the transformation period. Therefore, policy focus should shift to increasing welfare expenses, promoting education level, improving income distribution, and provide migrant residents local household registration (Chen, 2012).

Scholars have studied legal protection's impact on a core city's public security from a number of perspectives, laying an academic foundation for future research. However, above studies were mainly based on qualitative, descriptive and case analysis, and ignored modern research methods. Furthermore, some of the studies that applied data to study urban security management had some deficiencies. This section analyzes how legal protection impacts public security risks in China's core cities using sample data, and proposes specific, feasible and effective legal protection reform suggestions based on "Internet Plus" characteristics, which are of practical significance to the study of public security management in China's core cities.

I. New Challenges Faced by a Core City's Traditional Public Security Management in the "Internet Plus" Era

1. *Social Governance System Lags Behind Social Development*

Current public security system requires numerous management approaches, including comprehensive public policies related to public security issues, relevant management issues, and several topics related to public security. Therefore, public safety system should be self-adaptive, based on modern management concepts and organizational capabilities. However, during China's rapid social and economic transformation, government transformation is far slower than socio-economic transformation, and government's socio-economic governance structure lags behind rapid socio-economic development. Social construction and social management's development obviously lags behind, as evidenced by China's public investment's reversed priority, and the small proportion of state's public investment in people's basic livelihood. Due to slow improvement in people's livelihood, there is no bottom-line guarantee for basic living of Chinese people, thus widening gap between the rich and the poor, and causing various social contradictions that have many negative effects on social security. Therefore, social construction and social management's development apparently lags behind economic development, leading to increasingly prominent social contradictions.

2. *Traditional Urban Public Security Management System Lags Behind Social Development*

China's traditional urban public security management is obviously not on par with development of modern economy and society. China's handling of an urban public security issue generally implies establishment of a temporary leadership unit focusing on emergency action, while neglecting prevention, monitoring and evaluation, and lacking a comprehensive system and process. Urban public security management emphasizes the government's top-down control through public resources and public administrative power. According to Heinrich's Law, the best way to manage urban public risks is to focus on root causes of accidents, identify accident signs in time, and eliminate hidden dangers immediately (Cao Huimin, 2015). Therefore, we need to strengthen pre-control and systematic risk management. Urban public security governance emphasizes on cooperative governance between government and other social entities, relying on interactive participation of multiple social entities, and is focused on pre-control of potential public security risks, which can then be eliminated in the cradle itself.

3. *Rise of Network Data Technologies Poses New Challenges to Government's Traditional Public Security Governance Mechanism*

Recently, the rising networked society, in synergy with risk society and transforming society, has interactively amplified and complicated the risk of social changes in China (Zhang and Tong, 2015). Advancement of information technologies has reduced costs of communication, hence group size is no longer a major obstacle toward collective action (Lupia and Sin, 2003). With the Internet's widespread use, it is playing an increasingly prominent role in mobilizing collective protests, speeding up dissemination process and shortening protest cycle, thereby enhancing the extent of conflict (Garrett, 2006). Furthermore, the Internet also has a positive effect on urban public security. China's imperfect social security system and low official relief coverage shows that when ordinary people face any sudden disaster, they rarely if ever receive official and social relief. The Internet's emergence and popularity allows people to use it as a tool to call for assistance and mobilize relief; and another advantage is that network mobilization has lower intervention threshold and lower costs, as opposed to traditional media. The Internet's infinite scalability breaks constraints of traditional resource mobilization in terms of physically limited space, and achieves interaction between objects in a way that is difficult to measure.

II. Theoretical Mechanism Assumptions

1. *Legal Protection and Traffic Accidents in Core Cities in the "Internet Plus" Era*

According to revised Article 76 of the *Road Traffic Safety Law*, the principle of imputation of road traffic accident liabilities was amended to define the principle of fault presumption as basic principle of imputation, supplemented by the principle of fault liability. Both principles constituted a dual imputation principle system for road traffic accident liabilities in China. Different imputation principles consider different road traffic accident liabilities (Yan, 2008). The pressure to improve China's road traffic safety situation focuses mainly in regulation of motor vehicle drivers, and coefficients of legal dummy variables are significantly negative, showing that revision of the *Road Traffic Safety Law of the People's Republic of China* in 2007 has greatly reduced the road traffic mortality and injury rate per 100,000 persons (Ren and Peng, 2013). However, according to statistical data, it can be seen that average number of deaths caused by illegal actions such as speeding, failure to give way according to regulations, driving without driver's license or license plate, illegal overtaking, driving on the wrong side of the road and drunk driving, account for a high proportion of traffic accidents. Thus, these illegal actions are main factors leading to road traffic accidents (Dong, 2013). Figure 8.1 shows that there was a negative correlation between the number of traffic accident deaths and the level of public security expenditure in 16 central mega-cities from 1999 to 2013. Thus, the following assumption can be made based on the above analysis:

Assumption 1. Increased and enhanced legal protection measures can reduce traffic accident-related deaths in central mega-cities.

2. *Legal Protection and Fire Accidents in Core Cities in the "Internet Plus" Era*

Appropriate efforts can effectively reduce occurrence of fire accidents, including diligently following fire laws, regulations and standards, and

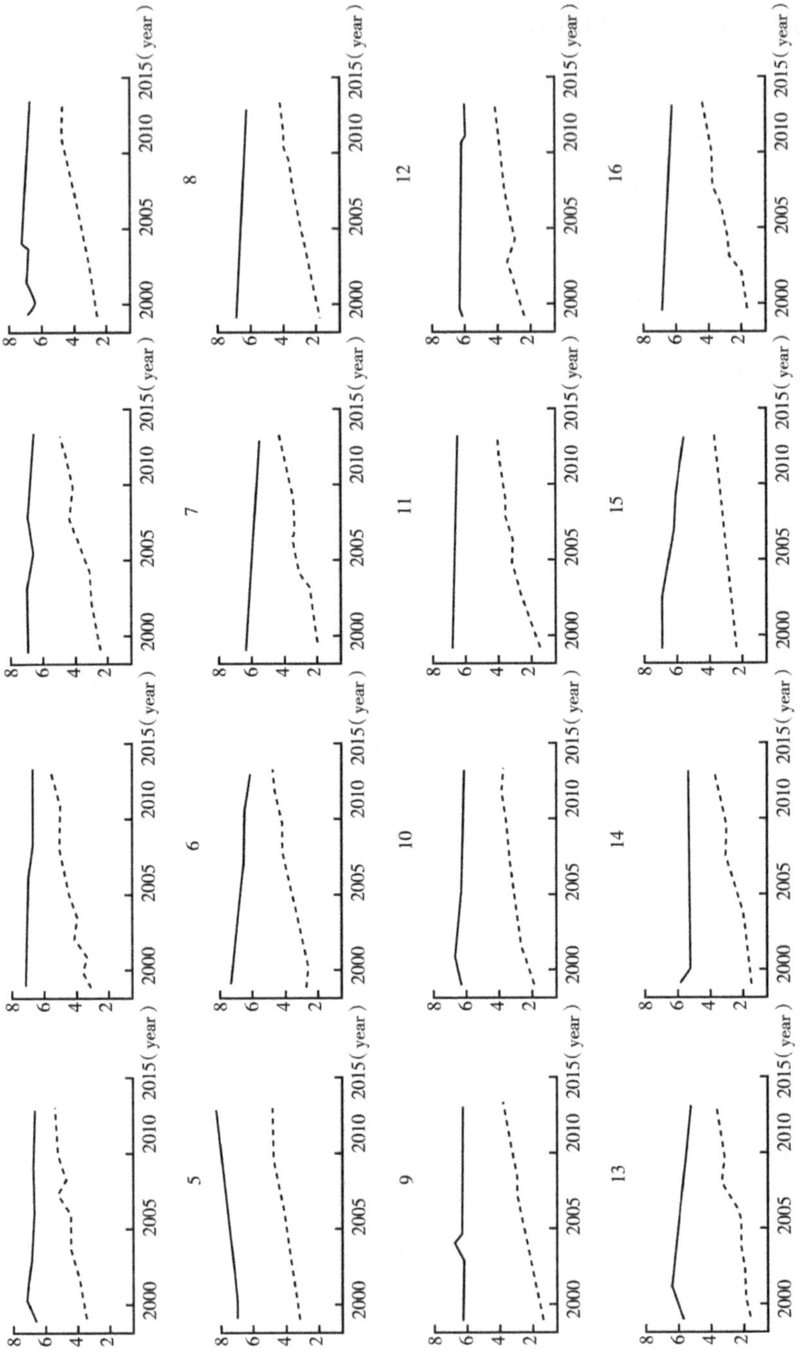

Figure 8.1 Relationship between Traffic Accident Deaths (Solid Lines) and Public Security Expenditure (Dotted Lines) in 16 Core Cities

ensuring design, construction, supervision, development, and other units can fulfill their respective fire prevention responsibilities. Some of the other efforts that make a viable difference include implementing a lifelong quality responsibility system for fires, design, construction, and audit and acceptance of construction projects, strengthening fire law enforcement, and investigating and dealing with fire standard violations (Li and Shang, 2012). However, as victims of fire accidents suffer personal and property damages resulting in civil liabilities, it is necessary to consider civil liabilities for fire accidents, study investigation of and compensation for civil liabilities for fire accidents from a legal standpoint, establish and improve an expert witness system for damages and fire insurance system, and optimize a fire accident civil compensation system. Increasing post-fire penalties and compensation pay-outs can effectively reduce fire accidents. Figure 8.2 shows that there was a negative correlation between number of fire accidents and level of public security expenditure in 16 central mega-cities from 1999 to 2013. As a result, following assumption can be made based on the above analysis:

Assumption 2. Increased and enhanced legal protection measures can reduce fire accidents in core cities.

3. *Legal Protection and Environmental Accidents in Core Cities in the "Internet Plus" Era*

Construction of ecological civilization requires not only renewed concepts and pursuit of values, but also strong and stable legal protection. To establish a legal protection system for ecological civilization, we should develop a complete legal framework system underpinned by the *Basic Law of Ecological Civilization Construction* or the *Basic Law of Environmental Protection*, with pollution prevention and control, resource protection, ecological protection, and resource and energy conservation laws as branches (Wang, 2014). However, sudden environmental accidents such as chemical leakage, oil spill, nuclear power plant explosion, and so on have become one of the main sources of hot news. These accidents raise great concern and directly affect safety of people at the places where they occur, with respect to personal health and property. Therefore, it is necessary to

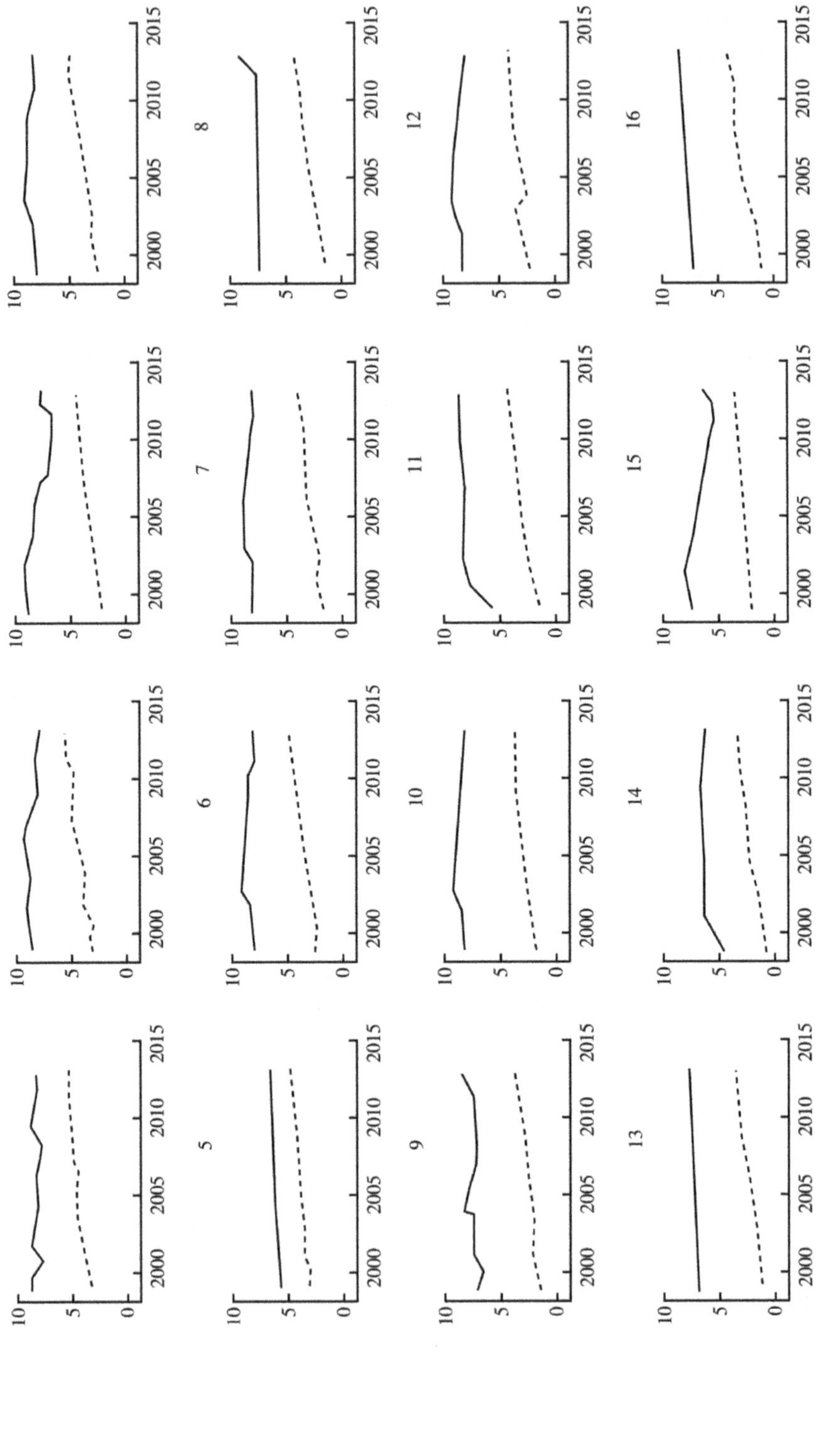

Figure 8.2 Relationship between Fire Accidents (Solid Lines) and Public Security Expenditure (Dotted Lines) in 16 Core Cities

establish a robust legal system for environmental accident emergencies to protect human and environmental safety. Based on information displayed in Figure 8.3, from 1999 to 2013, with constant increase in level of public security expenditure in 16 core cities, number of environmental pollution accidents increased first and then decreased, indicating that increase in level of public security expenditure was likely to inhibit or reduce environmental pollution accidents. As a result, the following assumption can be made based on above analysis:

Assumption 3. Increasingly enhanced legal protection measures can reduce environmental pollution accidents in core cities.

4. *Legal Protection and Crime Rates in Core Cities in the "Internet Plus" Era*

In the "Internet Plus" era, increasing crimes in networked society caused by popularity of the Internet is one of the important reasons why there is a constant rise in China's crime rates. Whenever Internet penetration rate increases by 1%, criminal offense rate increases by about 0.38% and property crime rate increases by about 0.48% (Chen *et al.*, 2014). In addition, there is a remarkable negative correlation between China's crime rates and public security expenditure and judicial efficiency (Xu, 2015). Moreover, Japan's crime prevention and control methods shows that it is not just a single department's responsibility, and that building a social security management mechanism with all elements linked to one another and a crime prevention and control system, is the basic institutional system required to prevent crimes and protect social stability (Zhang, 2015). Based on information displayed in Figure 8.4, from 1999 to 2013, number of crimes committed in 16 core cities either declined or increased, and rate of increase in the latter case was very slow. There was a growing trend in the number of practicing lawyers and level of public security expenditure in 16 core cities, indicating that increase in number of practicing lawyers and level of public security expenditure suppressed or reduced number of crimes committed in 16 core cities. Thus, following assumption can be made based on the above analysis:

Assumption 4. Increasingly enhanced legal guarantee measures can reduce crimes committed in central mega-cities.

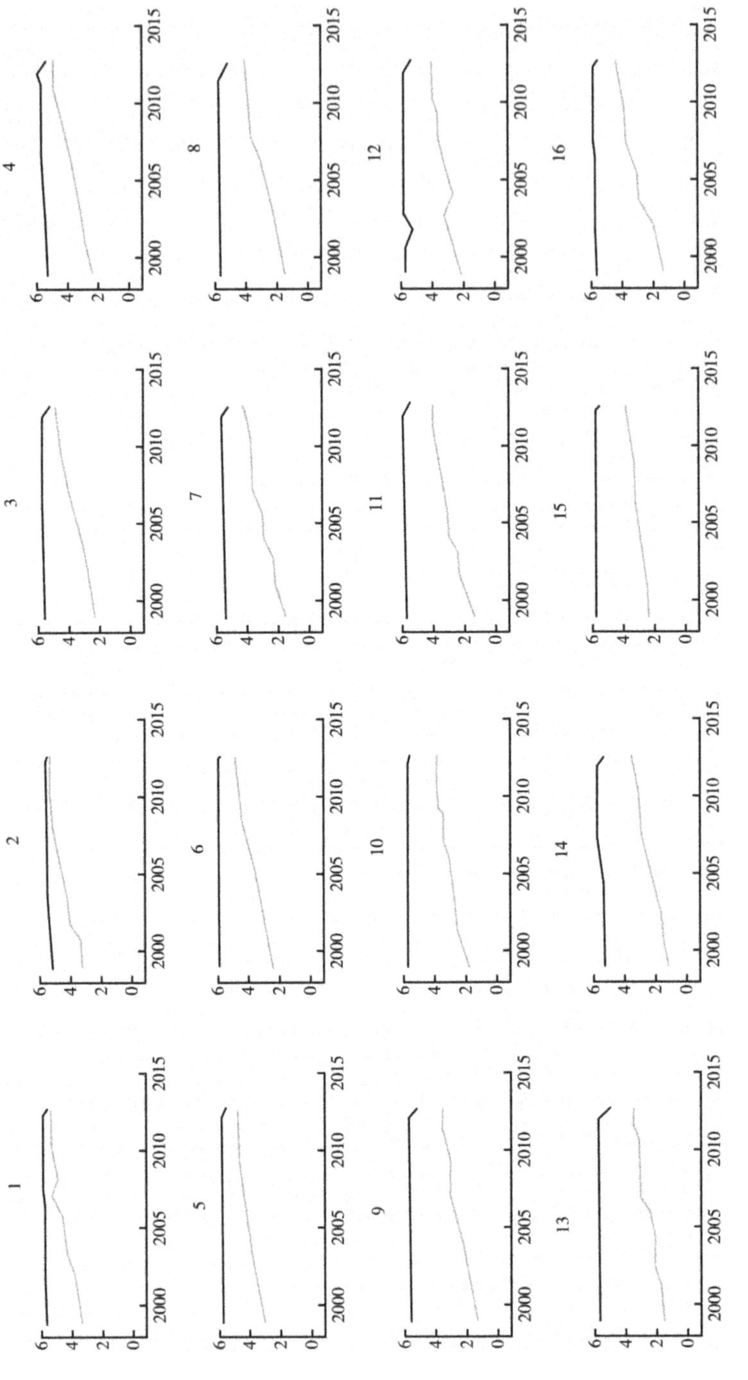

Figure 8.3 Relationship between Environmental Pollution Accidents (Black Lines) and Public Security Expenditure (Gray Lines) in 16 Core Cities

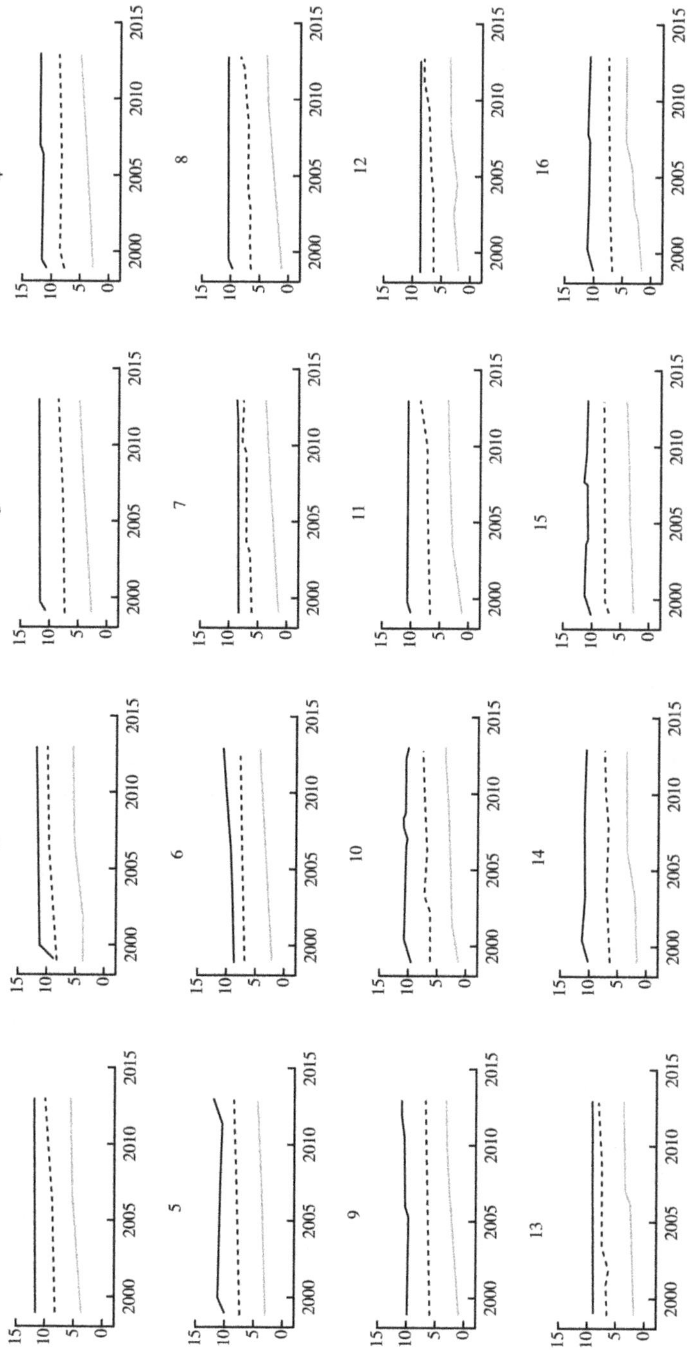

Figure 8.4 Relationship between Crimes (Solid Lines) and Practicing Lawyers (Dotted Lines) and Public Security Expenditure (Grey Lines) in 16 Core Cities

III. Measurement Modeling, Data Source and Research Method

1. *Measurement Modeling*

1.1 *Dynamic Panel Measurement Model Defining the Impact of Legal Protection on Traffic Accidents*

$$
\begin{aligned}
\ln TRA_{dt} = {} & \beta_0 + \beta_1 \ln TRA_{d,t-1} + \beta_2 \ln LAQ_{dt} + \beta_3 \ln POS_{dt} + \beta_4 LAW \\
& + \beta_5 \ln PGDP_{dt} + \beta_6 \ln(PGDP_{dt})^2 + \beta_7 \ln CAR_{dt} + \beta_8 GGDP_{dt} \\
& + \beta_9 \ln TRL_{dt} + \beta_{10} \ln URB_{dt} + \beta_{11} \ln DOQ_{dt} + \beta_{12} \ln PAC_{dt} \\
& + \beta_{13} \ln DEN_{dt} + \beta_{14} \ln EDU_{dt} + \lambda_d + \omega_t + \mu_{dt}.
\end{aligned}
$$

Explained variable: TRA_{dt} refers to the number of traffic accident deaths in city *d* within a period *t*. Main explanatory variables: LAQ_{dt} refers to the number of practicing lawyers in city *d* within a period *t*; POS_{dt} refers to the public security expenditure level in city *d* within a period *t*; *LAW* refers to the number of laws and regulations related to traffic safety (including national-level laws and regulations) in city *d* within a period *t*. Control variables: $TRA_{d,t-1}$ refers to the number of traffic accident deaths in city *d* within a period *t*–1; $PGDP_{dt}$ refers to per capita *GDP* in city *d* within a period *t*; $(PGDP_{dt})^2$ refers to the quadratic term of per capita *GDP* in city *d* within a period *t*; CAR_{dt} refers to the number of private motor vehicles in city *d* within a period *t*; $GGDP_{dt}$ refers to economic growth rate in city *d* within a period *t*; TRL_{dt} refers to highway miles in city *d* within a period *t*; URB_{dt} refers to urbanization level in city *d* within a period *t*; DOQ_{dt} refers to the number of practicing doctors in city *d* within a period *t*; PAC_{dt} refers to the number of households consuming alcohol in city *d* within a period *t*; DEN_{dt} refers to population density in city *d* within a period *t*; EDU_{dt} refers to the education level in city *d* within a period *t*. λ_d refers to the fixed effect of the city; ω_t refers to the period fixed effect; μ_{dt} is a random disturbance term.

1.2 *Dynamic Panel Measurement Model Defining the Impact of Legal Protection on Fire Accidents*

$$\begin{aligned}\ln FDA_{dt} = {} & \beta_0 + \beta_1 \ln FDA_{d,t-1} + \beta_2 \ln LAQ_{dt} + \beta_3 \ln POS_{dt} + \beta_4 LAW \\ & + \beta_5 \ln PGDP_{dt} + \beta_6 \ln(PGDP_{dt})^2 + \beta_7 GGDP_{dt} + \beta_8 \ln URB_{dt} \\ & + \beta_9 \ln DEN_{dt} + \beta_{10} \ln EDU_{dt} + \lambda_d + \omega_t + \mu_{dt}.\end{aligned}$$

Explained variable: FDA_{dt} refers to the number of fire accidents taking place in city d within a period t. Main explanatory variable: *LAW* refers to the number of laws and regulations related to fire safety (including national-level laws and regulations) in city d within a period t. Control variable: $FDA_{d,t-1}$ refers to the number of fire accidents in city d within a period t–1.

1.3 *Dynamic Panel Measurement Model Defining the Impact of Legal Protection on Crime Rates*

$$\begin{aligned}\ln CRM_{dt} = {} & \beta_0 + \beta_1 \ln CRM_{d,t-1} + \beta_2 \ln LAQ_{dt} + \beta_3 \ln POS_{dt} + \beta_4 LAW \\ & + \beta_5 \ln PGDP_{dt} + \beta_6 \ln(PGDP_{dt})^2 + \beta_7 \ln ROL_{dt} + \beta_8 GGDP_{dt} \\ & + \beta_9 \ln SIQ_{dt} + \beta_{10} \ln URB_{dt} + \beta_{11} \ln NHQ_{dt} + \beta_{12} \ln DEN_{dt} \\ & + \beta_{13} \ln EDU_{dt} + \lambda_d + \omega_t + \mu_{dt}.\end{aligned}$$

Explained variable: CRM_{dt} refers to crime rates in city d within a period t. Main explanatory variable: *LAW* refers to the number of laws and regulations related to criminal safety (including national-level laws and regulations) in city d within a period t. Control variables: $CRM_{d,t-1}$ refers to crime rates in city d within a period t–1; ROL_{dt} refers to the quantity of expropriated land in city d within a period t; SIQ_{dt} refers to the number of people covered by social security insurance in city d within a period t; NHQ_{dt} refers to the number of non-household population in city d within a period t.

1.4 *Dynamic Panel Measurement Model Defining the Impact of Legal Protection on Environmental Accidents*

$$\begin{aligned}\ln ENA_{dt} &= \beta_0 + \beta_1 \ln ENA_{d,t-1} + \beta_2 \ln LAQ_{dt} + \beta_3 \ln POS_{dt} + \beta_4 LAW \\ &+\beta_5 \ln PGDP_{dt} + \beta_6 \ln(PGDP_{dt})^2 + \beta_7 \ln CAR_{dt} + \beta_8 GGDP_{dt} \\ &+\beta_9 \ln URB_{dt} + \beta_{10} \ln INP_{dt} + \beta_{11} \ln DEN_{dt} + \lambda_d + \omega_t + \mu_{dt}.\end{aligned}$$

Explained variable: ENA_{dt} refers to the number of environmental pollution accidents taking place in city d within a period t. Main explanatory variable: *LAW* refers to the number of environment-related laws and regulations (including national-level laws and regulations) in city d within a period t. Control variables: $ENA_{d,t-1}$ refers to the number of environmental pollution accidents in city d within a period t–1; INP_{dt} refers to the value of industrial output in city d within a period t.

2. *Data Source*

According to the *Notice of the State Council on Adjusting the Standards for Categorizing City Sizes* issued by the State Council on November 20, 2014, a city having a permanent urban population of 5–10 million is classified as a mega-city, and a city having a permanent urban population of over 10 million is classified as a super city. To make the research more realistic, 16 central mega-cities were selected as sample cities, based on mega-cities and super cities classified by the State Council, including Shanghai, Hangzhou, Nanjing, Suzhou, Guangzhou, Shenzhen, Qingdao, Tianjin, and Beijing in the eastern region; Zhengzhou, Wuhan, and Changsha in the central region; Xi'an, Chongqing, and Chengdu in the western region; and Shenyang in the northeastern region; and 15 years' panel data from 1999 to 2013 were analyzed.

The data used in this section was derived from *China Statistical Yearbook*, relevant provinces' statistical yearbooks, relevant cities' statistical yearbooks, the China City Statistical Yearbook, the China Regional Statistical Yearbook, and relevant government websites.

IV. Testing of Assumptions

1. *Testing of Assumption 1*

Table 8.1 lists regression results of deaths by traffic accidents measured by the main explanatory variables. Models (1)–(3) use dynamic OLS, dynamic FE, and SYS-GMM models to test the number of traffic accident deaths affected by legal protection. The SYS-GMM model's test results may be more reliable as it is dynamic and uses instrumental variables, and was thus reported first. Although the SYS-GMM estimators are consistent, biased estimates might be generated in small samples if the instrumental variables in the regression of the system GMM are not predictive enough (Bun and Windmeijer, 2007). Thus, an intuitive method was developed to determine if a greater bias existed by comparing the lagged term of the GMM model's explanatory variable, with that of the OLS and FE models. The lagged term of the OLS model's explanatory variable was positively related to the unobservable regional effect, and therefore the OLS estimator was probably overestimated. Since the lagged term of the FE model's explanatory variable was negatively related to the random disturbance term, the FE estimator was probably underestimated. As a result, the GMM estimator of the explanatory variable's lagged term should be between the OLS and FE estimator. If the autoregressive coefficient obtained by the GMM model regression was less than that obtained by the OLS model regression but larger than that obtained by the FE model regression, the instrumental variables used in the system GMM model could be considered appropriate. In Table 8.1, the system GMM model's coefficient of lagged length of traffic accident deaths was 0.029, which was less than the OLS model's coefficient 0.084 and greater than the FE model's coefficient 0.009, indicating that the instrumental variables used in the system GMM model were appropriate.

After the other explanatory variables were controlled, the number of practicing lawyers, as a main indicator of the explanatory variables, had no significant coefficient of influence on the number of traffic accident deaths, while the coefficient of influence of public security expenditure level on the number of traffic accident deaths was significant at –0.074, indicating that increasing public security expenditure reduces traffic

Table 8.1 Regression Results of Legal Protection's Impact on Traffic Accidents

	Explained variable: Number of traffic accident deaths		
Explanatory variables	**(1) Dynamic OLS**	**(2) Dynamic FE**	**(3) SYS-GMM**
Number of practicing lawyers	−0.288 (0.085)	−0.007 (0.004)	0.018 (0.004)
Public security expenditure level	−0.132** (0.094)	−0.021** (0.011)	−0.074** (0.015)
Number of laws and regulations	−0.079*** (0.326)	−0.013* (0.004)	−0.029** (0.015)
Per capita GDP	0.150*** (0.0827)	0.033* (0.008)	0.028* (0.006)
Quadratic term of per capita GDP	−0.053* (0.040)	−0.001* (0.003)	−0.007* (0.006)
Quantity of private motor vehicles	0.215*** (0.062)	0.043*** (0.011)	0.048*** (0.011)
GDP growth	0.095** (0.009)	0.036*** (0.005)	0.066*** (0.009)
Highway miles	0.021*** (0.069)	−0.002** (0.001)	0.007** (0.001)
Urbanization level	0.011*** (0.003)	0.006 (0.015)	0.004 (0.015)
Number of practicing doctors	0.489 (0.138)	0.002 (0.001)	0.196 (0.001)
Quantity of urban household alcohol consumption	0.155*** (0.050)	0.002 (0.004)	0.052** (0.070)
Population density	0.042* (0.124)	0.003* (0.003)	0.018* (0.124)
Education level	−0.166 (0.055)	0.125*** (0.077)	0.142 (0.074)
Lagged length of traffic accident deaths	0.084*** (0.185)	0.009*** (0.018)	0.029*** (0.078)
Constant term	−4.92 (5.041)	−2.96 (2.071)	−1.74 (4.791)
R2	0.845	0.867	0.759
Sample size	240	240	240
AR(2) testing			0.475 (0.635)
Sargan testing			35.627 (0.051)

Note: *, ** and *** represent significance levels of 1%, 5% and 10%, respectively; the values in brackets are standard deviations; the values in brackets of the two types of testing are *P* values.

accident deaths. This is mainly because: (1) more number of practicing lawyers had no direct impact on traffic accidents, and hence the coefficient of influence was not significant; (2) increase in public security law expenditure level guaranteed more policemen and law enforcement equipment, and enhanced law enforcement motivation, thereby significantly reducing traffic accidents.

The coefficient of influence of the number of laws and regulations related to main explanatory variables on traffic accidents was significant at –0.029, indicating that relevant laws and regulations significantly reduce traffic accidents. As relevant laws and regulations were strictly implemented in transportation, promulgation and implementation of relevant laws and regulations played a significant role.

2. *Testing Assumption 2*

Based on Table 8.2, after the other explanatory variables were controlled, the number of practicing lawyers, as a main indicator of the explanatory variables, had no significant coefficient of influence on the number of fire accidents, while the coefficient of influence of public security expenditure level on the number of fire accidents was significant at –0.083, indicating that increase in public security expenditure level reduces fire accidents. The coefficient of influence of the number of laws and regulations related to the main explanatory variables on fire accidents was significant at –0.025, indicating that relevant laws and regulations significantly reduces fire accidents, the reason being that promulgation and implementation of relevant laws and regulations promoted fire departments to enforce laws more stringently, and ensured more compliance of fire laws and regulations by enterprises, and ensured they strictly followed operating procedures, thereby reducing fire accidents.

In addition, the impact of other control variables on fire accidents was in line with real situations, but the impact of per capita GDP on fire accidents as estimated by system GMM was not significant, probably because per capita GDP's impact was limited.

3. *Testing Assumption 3*

Based on Table 8.3, regression results of the two main explanatory variables as generated by system GMM were both not significant.

Table 8.2 Regression Results of Legal Protection's Impact on Fire Accidents

	Explained variable: Number of fire accidents		
Explanatory variables	**(1) Dynamic OLS**	**(2) Dynamic FE**	**(3) SYS-GMM**
Number of practicing lawyers	−0.064	0.012	0.038
	(0.035)	(0.005)	(0.019)
Public security expenditure level	−0.271***	−0.009*	−0.083*
	(0.173)	(0.001)	(0.006)
Number of laws and regulations	−0.029***	−0.018**	−0.025*
	(0.014)	(0.001)	(0.009)
Per capita GDP	0.092**	0.036*	0.057
	(0.077)	(0.013)	(0.008)
Quadratic term of per capita GDP	−0.008*	−0.002*	−0.003
	(0.019)	(0.003)	(0.001)
GDP growth	0.263*	0.029**	0.093**
	(0.394)	(0.007)	(0.031)
Urbanization level	0.029***	0.002**	0.011**
	(0.063)	(0.005)	(0.007)
Population density	0.016*	0.0014*	0.010*
	(0.009)	(0.001)	(0.003)
Education level	−0.074	0.024	0.021
	(0.038)	(0.017)	(0.005)
Lagged length of fire accidents	0.147***	0.045***	0.073***
	(0.093)	(0.005)	(0.019)
Constant term	−9.624	−1.901	−2.772
	(3.903)	(3.174)	(0.771)
R2	0.884	0.817	0.795
Sample size	240	240	240
AR(2) testing			0.371
			(0.719)
Sargan testing			40.821
			(0.067)

Note: *, ** and *** represent significance levels of 1%, 5% and 10%, respectively; the values in brackets are standard deviations; the values in brackets of the two types of testing are *P* values.

Table 8.3 Regression Results of Legal Protection's Impact on Environmental Accidents

	Explained variable: Number of environmental accidents		
Explanatory variables	**(1) Dynamic OLS**	**(2) Dynamic FE**	**(3) SYS-GMM**
Number of practicing lawyers	–0.017	0.002	–0.011
	(0.011)	(0.001)	(0.007)
Public security expenditure level	–0.025**	–0.0006*	–0.009
	(0.019)	(0.001)	(0.006)
Number of laws and regulations	–0.197***	–0.058***	–0.063*
	(0.071)	(0.032)	(0.025)
Per capita GDP	0.274***	0.031*	0.047*
	(1.737)	(0.052)	(0.011)
Quadratic term of per capita GDP	–0.008*	–0.002*	–0.003*
	(0.040)	(0.003)	(0.006)
No. of private motor vehicles	0.092***	0.055***	0.029
	(0.183)	(0.021)	(0.007)
GDP growth	0.157**	0.0773***	0.094**
	(0.581)	(0.011)	(0.017)
Value of industrial output	0.204***	–0.074**	0.069**
	(0.118)	(0.028)	(0.005)
Urbanization level	0.007***	0.003*	0.009
	(0.003)	(0.015)	(0.015)
Population density	0.077*	0.009*	0.041*
	(0.043)	(0.001)	(0.007)
Lagged length of environmental accidents	0.179***	0.083**	0.089**
	(0.115)	(0.049)	(0.021)
Constant term	19.63***	–5.92***	–8.35***
	(11.04)	(3.01)	(1.05)
R2	0.873	0.802	0.759
Sample size	240	240	240
AR(2) testing			0.192
			(0.327)
Sargan testing			13.848
			(0.239)

Note: *, ** and *** represent significance levels of 1%, 5% and 10%, respectively; the values in brackets are standard deviations.

The P-value generated from Sargan testing for over-identification was 0.239, indicating that the assumption that all instrumental variables were valid was not acceptable. There may be no endogenous problem; however, the use of instrumental variables disrupted the regression results, and therefore regression results from the dynamic FE model that didn't use instrumental variables were used. After the other explanatory variables were controlled, the number of practicing lawyers, as a main indicator of explanatory variables, had no significant coefficient of influence on the number of environmental accidents, while the coefficient of influence of public security expenditure level on the number of environmental accidents was significant at –0.006, indicating that increase in public security expenditure level reduces environmental accidents as the rise in public security expenditure level strengthens law enforcement inspection, thereby reducing environmental accidents, and also enhances *ex post* penalties and increases violation costs being borne by environment destroyers, thus having a deterrent effect on relevant parties involved in potential environmental accidents. The coefficient of influence of the number of laws and regulations related to main explanatory variables on environmental accidents was significant at –0.058, indicating that relevant laws and regulations significantly reduce environmental accidents.

4. *Testing Assumption 4*

Based on Table 8.4, after the other explanatory variables were controlled, the number of practicing lawyers as a main indicator of the explanatory variables, had a significant coefficient of influence on the number of crimes, indicating that increasing the number of lawyers reduced crimes, because lawyers brought people into court and resolved disputes through law, thereby reducing potential crime sources. The coefficient of influence of the public security expenditure level on the number of crimes was significant at –0.059, indicating that increasing public security expenditure level reduces crime, mainly because it suppresses criminal activities from different aspects. The coefficient of influence of the number of laws and regulations related to main explanatory variables on the number of crimes was significant at –0.007, indicating that relevant laws and

Table 8.4 Regression Results of Legal Protection's Impact on Crimes

	Explained variable: Number of crimes		
Explanatory variables	**(1) Dynamic OLS**	**(2) Dynamic FE**	**(3) SYS-GMM**
Number of practicing lawyers	–0.094*** (0.027)	–0.013** (0.026)	–0.037** (0.009)
Public security expenditure level	–0.263*** (0.163)	–0.047** (0.024)	–0.059*** (0.010)
Number of laws and regulations	–0.029** (0.012)	–0.006* (0.002)	–0.007* (0.011)
Per capita GDP	–0.098*** (0.015)	0.005* (0.003)	0.048** (0.024)
Quadratic term of per capita GDP	–0.023* (0.026)	–0.004* (0.004)	–0.009* (0.007)
Quantity of expropriated land	0.062** (0.216)	0.029* (0.020)	0.033* (0.009)
GDP growth	–0.071* (0.014)	0.009 (0.003)	–0.006 (0.001)
Number of people covered by social security insurance	–0.029** (0.831)	–0.015** (0.063)	–0.027** (0.072)
Urbanization level	0.064 (0.047)	0.037 (0.039)	0.029 (0.009)
Number of non-household population	0.362*** (0.314)	0.081* (0.039)	0.099** (0.048)
Population density	0.094* (0.197)	0.026* (0.010)	0.043* (0.051)
Education level	–0.027** (0.015)	0.003* (0.002)	0.016** (0.007)
Lagged length of crimes	0.052*** (0.017)	0.011*** (0.026)	0.045** (0.013)
Constant term	–9.68 (11.93)	–2.58 (2.112)	–4.91 (4.035)
R2	0.896	0.813	0.839
Sample size	240	240	240
AR(2) testing			0.394 (0.582)
Sargan testing			37.936 (0.047)

Note: *, ** and *** represent significance levels of 1%, 5% and 10%, respectively; the values in brackets are standard deviations; the values in brackets of the two types of testing are *P* values.

regulations play a small role in reducing crimes, probably because most criminals were less educated, with low legal awareness and did not have a strong law-abiding concept.

In addition, the impact of GDP growth and urbanization level on the incidence of crime was insignificant. While on the one hand, China's GDP growth brought about more economic activities leading to an increase in the incidence of crime, on the other hand, most of the lower and middle class people didn't benefit much from China's GDP growth, and therefore GDP growth could not effectively reduce crimes. Urbanization level improved people's overall living standards and quality, thereby reducing criminal activities, but it also increased population in cities, resulting in more crimes. The impact of other control variables on the number of crimes was in line with real situations.

V. Conclusions and Policy Suggestions

1. *Basic Conclusions*

This chapter explores the impact of legal protection on public security in central mega-cities in the "Internet Plus" era, and tests the following main conclusions through theoretical and statistical analysis. (1) Increased level of public security expenditure as well as laws and regulations reduce traffic accident deaths, and thus, increasing legal protection measures will reduce traffic accidents in China's central mega-cities. (2) Increased level of public security expenditure as well as laws and regulations significantly reduce fire accidents, and thus, increasing legal protection measures will reduce fire accidents in China's central mega-cities. (3) More lawyers, increased public security expenditure level, as well as laws and regulations play a certain role in reducing crimes, and thus, increasing legal protection measures will reduce crimes in China's central mega-cities. (4) Increased public security expenditure level as well as laws and regulations significantly reduce environmental pollution accidents, and thus, increasing legal protection measures will reduce environmental pollution accidents in China's central mega-cities and improve public security in these cities.

2. *Policy Suggestions*

2.1 *Legislation*

(i) In the Internet Plus era, the National People's Congress and local People's Congress, along with public security, firefighting, traffic police, environmental protection, and food regulation departments, should, based on open, transparent, shared and collaborative application of data, reconstruct the data management model, enhance relevance of legislation, and change the situation where traditional legislation lags behind social and economic development, by combining new features of public security events in the Internet Plus era.

(ii) The National People's Congress and local People's Congress should increase transparency in legislative activities by fully capitalizing on the Internet's characteristics such as soliciting public views via the Internet before legislation, and publishing the legislative process and result on the Internet, thereby enhancing the NPC's representation and credibility in the public space.

(iii) Due to the Internet's low cost and convenience, representatives of the National People's Congress and local People's Congress should set up Internet offices to accept and listen to industry opinions and those of the regional people that they represent, as well as publish their actions in NPC, thus enhancing their representation and credibility.

2.2 *Law Enforcement*

(i) Governments at all levels should, in combination with the new features and laws of social operation in the Big Data era, make use of Big Data to improve scientific and democratic decision-making process and refine their management level.

(ii) In view of the current state of fragmented and segmented functions in different emergency rescue systems, governments at all levels should actively explore how to reform the current urban public security emergency mechanism, and integrate response alarm dispatch systems such as 110, 119 and 120, as well as emergency rescue systems such as the mayor's hotline, flood control, earthquake control, and water, gas and other utilities, into a unified command and dispatch system using networking and Big Data technologies in the "Internet Plus" era, to provide the public with quick and comprehensive emergency rescue services (Yan, 2009).

(iii) Negative list management model is an important breakthrough in deepening the reform of China's market access system, and also one of the important actions in China's comprehensively deepening reforms. Therefore, governments at all levels should make full use of Big Data to carry out negative list management, shift the focus of law enforcement to supervision of macro-social and economic operations, and reduce intervention in micro-social and economic behaviors.

2.3 *Justice*

(i) In the "Internet Plus" era, the judicial department should analyze mass judicial trial data and summarize common problems in judicial trials using Internet-based information and Big Data technologies, thereby making scientific and accurate judicial reforms based on the data, exercise justice and improve credibility of the justice system.

(ii) Thanks to the Internet's convenience and quick information transmission capabilities, the judicial department should combine trial activities with the Internet and publish the trial process and result on the Internet, to enable the general public to understand the hearing process of each case quickly and easily, thereby building their trust in the judicial department.

2.4 *Legal Compliance of Governments and Officials*

(i) The National People's Congress should make full use of Big Data and Internet Plus information to strengthen government supervision at all levels, and should not tolerate any violation. Law enforcement officers who violate the law should be severely punished.

(ii) It is important to change traditional ways of social management and control, understand people's real needs through Big Data analysis, allow them to be more involved in social governance using modern information technology, and practice good governance to achieve maximum public interest.

References

Bun, M. J. G. and Windmeijer, F. The weak instrument problem of the system GMM estimator in "Dynamic Panel Data Models" (Mimeo, University of Bristol, 2010).

Cao Huimin. Study of urban public security governance strategy from the perspective of risk society. *Study and Practice*, 2015 (3).

Chen Lipeng, Xu Jianbin and Wei Juan. Impact of the Internet's popularity on China's criminal offence rate. *Criminal Science*, 2014 (5).

Chen Shuo. Judicial inputs and crime prevention in transitional China. *China Economic Quarterly*, 2012 (2).

Dong Yubo. Multiple linear regression models of road traffic accidents and their testing method. *Journal of People's Public Security University of China (Science and Technology)*, 2013 (2).

Du Mingxiao. On the improvement in public security's legal mechanism of a city. *Law Science Magazine*, 2011 (3).

Garrett, R. K. Protest in an information society: A review of literature on social movements and new ICTs. *Information, Communication and Society*, 2006 (2).

Li Hao and Zhong Jianming. Characteristics of major public events and legal treatment strategies. *Journal of Yunnan University Law Edition*, 2014 (2).

Li Jingming and Shang Hongsong. Analysis of fire accident and study of prevention measures, *Fire Science and Technology*, 2012 (2).

Lupia A. and Gisela S. *Which Public Goods are Endangered: How Evolving Communication Technologies Affect the Logic of Collective Action*, Public Choice, 2003.

Ren Ying and Peng Hongxing. Factors affecting China's traffic accident casualties: An empirical study. *Forecasting*, 2013 (3).

Wang Canfa. On the establishment of legal protection system for ecological civilization construction. *China Legal Science*, 2014 (3).

Xu Hongfa. Study of cause of crime in transitional China: From a perspective of crime economics. *Journal of People's Public Security University of China (Social Science Edition)*, 2015 (1).

Yan Zhong. Analysis of urban public security in the period of social transformation. *Sociological Studies*, 2009 (5).

Yang Lixin. Study of the principle of imputation of road traffic accident liabilities in China. *Legal Science*, 2008 (10).

Zhang Haibo and Tong Xing. Changes in China's emergency management structure and its theoretical generalization. *Social Sciences in China*, 2015 (3).

Zhang Jing. A study on Japan's social security management system and its crime prevention network. *Journal of Beijing Union University (Humanities and Social Sciences)*, 2015 (3).

Zhang Zhisheng. Analysis on the relationship between new generation migrant workers' non-institutionalized interest expression and city public safety. *Lanzhou Academic Journal*, 2014 (7).

Index

A
agglomeration, 56
agglomeration effect, 132
agglomeration function, 224

B
Belt and Road, 141
Big Data, 16

C
Center for Scientific and Technological Innovation, 218
China (Shanghai) Pilot Free Trade Zone, 149
collaborative innovation, 103
commodity pricing center, 147
compact city, 94
core city, 53
crisis of fragmented identities, 36
cross-border e-commerce, 183
cross-industry, 71

D
decentralization, 71
disruptive innovations, 31

E
e-commerce, 1, 173
EDI (electronic data interchange), 197
Era of Big Data, 15

F
financial center, 131

I
industrial chain, 229
industrialization, 107
Industrial Revolution, 4
Industry 4.0, 122
information economy, 16
information technology, 173

innovation, 9
intelligent manufacturing, 98
internationalization of the Renminbi, 153
international shipping center, 217
Internet Plus, 1
Internet Plus Finance, 145
Internet Plus Industry, 100
Internet Plus Manufacturing, 98

L

legal protection, 251

M

Made in China 2025, 122
manufacturing, 97
mechanisms, 132

N

network society, 40

O

online platforms, 191

P

public security, 247
public services, 33

S

service-oriented manufacturing, 98
Shanghai FTZ, 158
smart city, 12
smiling curve, 99
social governance, 33
social governance system, 249
social networking, 23
social relations, 34
social self-organization, 40–41
social structure, 38
socio-economic development, 247
superposition of multiple power legitimacies, 36

T

transformation and upgrade path, 127
transforming and upgrading, 98

Lightning Source UK Ltd.
Milton Keynes UK
UKHW021957220119
335998UK00002B/29/P

9 789813 272514

W. Weber (Ed.)

Familial Cancer Control

With 29 Figures and 29 Tables

Springer-Verlag
Berlin Heidelberg New York
London Paris Tokyo
Hong Kong Barcelona
Budapest

Priv.-Doz. Dr. WALTER WEBER

Swiss Cancer League
Monbijoustraße 61
3001 Bern, Switzerland

Library of Congress Cataloging-in-Publication Data
Familial cancer control / W. Weber (ed.).
(Monographs / European School of Oncology)
Includes bibliographical references and index.
ISBN-13: 978-3-642-77584-0 e-ISBN-13: 978-3-642-77582-6
DOI: 10.1007/ 978-3-642-77582-6
1. Cancer–Genetic aspects. 2. Cancer–Epidemiology. 3. Cancer–Etiology. 4. Cancer–Prevention. I. Weber, W. (Walter) II. Series. III. Series: Monographs (European School of Oncology) [DNLM: 1. Neoplasms–genetics. 2. Neoplasms–prevention & control. QZ 202 F198] RC267.4.F35 1992 616.99'–dc20 DNLM/DLC

Softcover reprint of the hardcover 1st edition 1992

Typesetting: Camera ready by editor

23/3145-5 4 3 2 1 0 – Printed on acid-free paper